About Island Press

Since 1984, the nonprofit Island Press has been stimulating, shaping, and communicating the ideas that are essential for solving environmental problems worldwide. With more than 800 titles in print
and some 40 new releases each year, we are the nation's leading
publisher on environmental issues. We identify innovative thinkers
and emerging trends in the environmental field. We work with world-
renowned experts and authors to develop cross-disciplinary
solutions to environmental challenges.

Island Press designs and implements coordinated book
publication campaigns in order to communicate our critical
messages in print, in person, and online using the latest technologies, programs, and the media. Our goal: to reach targeted
audiences—scientists, policymakers, environmental advocates,
the media, and concerned citizens—who can and will take action
to protect the plants and animals that enrich our world, the
ecosystems we need to survive, the water we drink, and the air
we breathe.

Island Press gratefully acknowledges the support of its work
by the Agua Fund, Inc., The Margaret A. Cargill Foundation, Betsy
and Jesse Fink Foundation, The William and Flora Hewlett
Foundation, The Kresge Foundation, The Forrest and Frances
Lattner Foundation, The Andrew W. Mellon Foundation, The Curtis
and Edith Munson Foundation, The Overbrook Foundation, The
David and Lucile Packard Foundation, The Summit Foundation,
Trust for Architectural Easements, The Winslow Foundation, and
other generous donors.

The opinions expressed in this book are those of the
author(s) and do not necessarily reflect the views of our donors.

City Rules

Emily Talen

City Rules:

How Regulations Affect Urban Form

Emily Talen

ISLANDPRESS

Washington | Covelo | London

ISLAND PRESS is a trademark of the Center for Resource Economics.

Library of Congress Cataloging-in-Publication Data

Talen, Emily, 1958-
  City rules : how regulations affect urban form / Emily Talen.
      p. cm.
  Includes bibliographical references and index.
  ISBN-13: 978-1-59726-691-8 (cloth : alk. paper)
  ISBN-10: 1-59726-691-4 (cloth : alk. paper)
  ISBN-13: 978-1-59726-692-5 (pbk. : alk. paper)
  ISBN-10: 1-59726-692-2 (pbk. : alk. paper) 1. City planning—United States. 2. City planning and redevelopment law—United States. 3. Zoning law—United States. I. Title.
  HT167.T34 2011
  307.1'2160973—dc23

                                                                2011026670

Printed using Stone Serif
Typesetting by Lyle Rosbotham

⊛ Printed on recycled, acid-free paper

Manufactured in the United States of America
10 9 8 7 6 5 4 3 2 1

Keywords: architecture; building codes; frontage; height restriction; land-use law; land-use regulation; lot size; New Urbanism; nuisance law; parking requirements; pedestrian realm; Phoenix, Arizona; planned unit development (PUD); Smart Codes; street design; town planning; traditional neighborhood development (TND); urban design; urban planning; urban policy; urban sprawl; zoning

To the beleaguered American city planner.

I hope this book will help you change the rules that—most likely against

your better judgment—you are every day required to enforce.

Contents

Foreword

Andres Duany

Emily Talen's book shows how the rules of city building—codes—have been used for good or ill. But let us be clear: codes are necessary.

Within the last half-century, some thirty million buildings have degraded cities and destroyed landscapes. We have tolerated this comprehensive disaster in exchange for the (perhaps) two thousand masterpieces that rampant architects have produced. This dismal win–loss ratio in architecture should be unacceptable to anyone who cares about America's cities and towns.

Planners have now been called upon to intervene and have discovered that codes are the most powerful tools available to affect reform. As this book uncovers, a century ago, city planners knew this power and exploited it fully, wisely embedding codes in the political and legal process. Under codes, the profit motive was capable of building the best places we still have.

Codes can assist in the restoration of this standard, as Talen argues. Those who are charged with designing, supervising, and building urbanism might tend to avoid education and exhortation, but they are accustomed to following rules. Bureaucracies have never been (and cannot be) dismantled. They will, however, willingly administer whatever codes are in hand. This has the potential to carry reform farther than education ever can.

Planners can reclaim codes and engage in the most rigorous and intellectually refined practice available to any architect. And, as this book makes clear, results are verifiable. By being projected into the world, codes engage a reality that can lead to resounding defeat of antiurbanistic practice. This is how planners can compensate for deficient professional training, where schools educate architects toward self-expression rather than toward context, toward theory rather than toward practice, toward the individual building rather than toward urbanism.

Designers should not resist this. They should prefer to work within known rules and for the common good rather than be subject to the whimsy of individual boards, politicians, naysayers, and bureaucrats.

The essential elements of urbanism must be coded—frontages, streets, the public realm. This is necessary because the default setting in contemporary design is mediocrity and kitsch. Those who object to codes imagine that they constrain architectural masterpieces (their own, usually). But masterpieces are few; the more likely outcome is kitsch. Codes can assure a minimum level of competence, even if in so doing they must constrain certain possibilities.

Codes allow the various professions that affect urbanism to act with unity of purpose. Without integrated codes, architects design buildings that ignore the streets of the civil engineer, and landscape architects ignore both the roads and the buildings. There is no cooperation toward the creation of a spatially defined public realm. The demands of parking, no less than the arbitrary singularity of architects, tend to create vague, sociofugal places. Add to this the idiosyncratic desires of fire marshals, civil engineers, poverty advocates, market experts, the accessibility police, materials suppliers, and liability attorneys. Without codes, there is nothing but the unassembled collection of urban potential.

Codes provide the means to distribute building design to others. Authentic urbanism requires the sequential intervention of the many. Those who want to design all the buildings in a place produce only architectural projects—monocultures of design—not urbanism. With codes, private buildings achieve a modicum of formal control; otherwise there would be no urban fabric. And by using codes, we protect the prerogative of civic buildings to express the aspirations of the institutions they accommodate, the aspirations of the wider community—and, as well, the inspiration of architects and designers. This is the dialectic of urbanism.

Unguided towns and cities tend not to vitality but to socioeconomic monocultures. The wealthy gather in their enclaves and the middle-class in their neighborhoods; the poor get the residue. Shops and restaurants cluster around certain price points, offices find their prestigious addresses and sweatshops their squalid ones. Artists pioneer gentrification en masse while vast tracts of once-mixed places self-segregate and decay. This process occurs ineluctably in traditional cities, no less than in new suburban sprawl. Codes can secure that measure of diversity without which good urbanism withers and dies.

Without codes urban municipalities tend to suffer from disinvestment because the market seeks stable investment environments. Codes level the playing field for the inevitable competition. Without codes, the competing private codes of the home-owners associations, the guidelines of office parks, and the rules of shopping centers create predictable outcomes that lure investment away from older cities and towns.

As codes provide predictability, they also protect the diversity of urbanism. Without them, wary neighbors tend to reject difference in proximity to their dwellings. Codes protect the character of a locale against the universalizing tendencies of modern real estate development. They apply general principles to specific places.

If applied intelligently, codes can assure that urban places are truly urban and that rural places remain truly rural, and that there is a specific transect in between. Otherwise, misconceived environmentalism tends toward the partial greening of all places. The result being neither one nor the other, but the monstrous garden city of sprawl. The location of the urban and the rural is of a fundamental importance that cannot be left to the vicissitudes of ownership. Codes require the preparation of maps that address the "where" no less than the "what."

Codes can insure that buildings incorporate a higher degree of environmental response than is otherwise called for by economic analysis. Buildings can be built to be both durable and mutable in proper measure. These are things that are crucial to the longevity required of urbanism.

Codes defy an architectural culture that incapacitates architects by presenting only the extremes of unfettered genius and servility to the zeitgeist. But there are positions between. We must reject the limits set by being subject to the realities of our time—we know that it is also possible to affect those realities. There is no need for relativism. There are urbanisms that allow for a self-defined pursuit of happiness (the stated right of Americans), and there are other urbanisms that tend to undermine that pursuit.

Acknowledgments

My deepest, warmest, sincerest thanks to the following people who supported me along the way in the writing of this book: Andres Duany, Lizz Plater-Zyberk, Sandy Sorlien, Paul Crabtree, Hazel Borys, Daniel Parolek, Galina Tachieva, Ellen Dunham-Jones, June Williamson, William Baer, Ann Diagle, Rob Steuteville, Besim Hakim, Kelly Turner, Julia Koschinsky, Howard Blackson, Michael Mehaffy, Tracy Geiger, Sungduck Lee, Marcia Nation, Nick Burkhart, Laurence Aurbach, Ian Rasmussen, Heather Boyer, Courtney Lix, Eran Ben-Joseph, Elif Tural, Eric Dumbaugh, Catherine Johnson, Asiya Natekal, Bruce Donnelly, Tyler Eltringham, Sue Mahalov, Marianne Martin, Bill Spikowski, David Brain, Dan Bartman, Doug Farr, Hank Dittmar, Jennifer Hurley, John Massengale, Doug Kelbaugh, Matt Lambert, Nathan Norris, Patrick Pinnell, Patrick Condon, Peter Swift, John Anderson, Rick Hall, Robert Alminana, Sara Hines, Daniel Slone, Stefanos Polyzoides, Steve Mouzon, Tom Low, Jason Brody, Zach Borders, Jim Kunstler, John Norquist, Phil Bess, Rachel Abrahams, and Annie Hale. And, of course, Luc Anselin.

Support for this research was generously provided by the National Endowment for the Arts, the National Science Foundation under grant no. DEB-0423704 CAP LTER, and the GeoDa Center and the Phoenix Urban Research Lab at Arizona State University.

1. Introduction

This is the story of how rules affect the physical character of cities. Using examples from around the United States, the book illustrates how rules, which collectively become codes,[1] affect urban pattern and form in explicit and direct ways. These effects are not well understood. The effects are known in general terms, on such things as density and land value, but the effect on physical form and character of place is often obscured. Just what kind of environment is our layered legal framework concocting?

Given their impact, the neglect of rules—the failure to understand their effect—is surprising. In the United States, most urban land has, at one time or another, either been prescribed by a legally enforceable rule or built in defiance of one. Yet there are few sources that document this effect. This is problematic since, increasingly in our legalistic environment, codes are the basis for public decision making in all matters pertaining to the built environment.

This book documents the rise and fall of rules—from hopeful means of urban redemption to legalistic burden. Most importantly, it dissects the best and worst urban places and seeks to determine whether they are the result of explicit rules. This requires making a judgment about what "best" and "worst" mean. Generally, my evaluation is based on the degree to which rules sustain good urbanism. I define "good urbanism" as compact urban form that encourages pedestrian activity and minimizes

---

1. The terms "rule," "regulation," "code," "ordinance," and "law" can be distinguished. Within the context of U.S. land development, rules and regulations make up a code, such as a zoning code. The term "ordinance" often refers specifically to municipal law, whereas "law" is more general and occurs at any scale of government.

environmental degradation; encourages social, economic, and land use diversity as opposed to homogeneity; connects uses and functions; has a quality public realm that provides opportunities for interaction and exchange; offers equitable access to goods, services, and facilities; and protects environmental and human health. Bad urbanism is the opposite: disconnected, automobile dependent, land consumptive, environmentally degrading, single-use, homogeneous, inequitable, and inaccessible, and with a low-quality, poorly designed public realm (see Talen 2011).

The connection between rules and good or bad urbanism is a matter of understanding both the effect and the neglect of rules. For example, the rules of Chandler, Arizona, created the landscape shown in figure 1.1—its municipal code states that there must be one parking space for every 250 square feet of commercial floor area. But there is also an absence of rules that might have been used to mitigate the negative effects (see box 1.1). Nothing in the rules prohibits parking from being the defining feature of the landscape.

Analyzing the effect of rules is a form of social history, and much is revealed: what do rules say about how American society values place, as well as neighbor-

Figure 1.1. Shopping mall in Chandler, Arizona, a product of what rules require and what they allow.
Source: USDA-FSA-APFO Aerial Photography Field Office, NAIP 2007.

Box 1.1. Rules that might have mitigated the negative effects of parking

- No parking between building and street
- Parking maximums
- Limits on size of surface parking lots
- More compact car spaces to save space
- Reduction of parking for mixed-use projects
- Shared parking credits (where there are distinctly different hours of operation)
- Substitution of on-street parking counts for required parking
- Walkways through parking lots
- Alley access that would make it easier to locate parking behind buildings
- Required bicycle parking

hood functionality, community organization, and social integration? Unraveling this is complicated by the fact that both the effect of rules as well as the motivations behind them, over the course of the twentieth century, became obscured. Rules are a reflection of values, but now, given the disconnect between rule and effect, it is hard to imagine that what people really want is sprawl, bad urban form, and monotony. This is certainly not what early city planners thought they were creating. As new code-reform efforts move forward, there needs to be a clear understanding and explanation of the underlying purposes and end goals. Any loss of connection between rule and purpose risks compromising the effect of the rule and obscuring more objectionable motivations.

Any hope of changing the rules that have disfigured the American landscape—sprawling and often disorienting, while at the same time, almost paradoxically, hypersegregated—requires a keen understanding of the source, historical evolution, and effect of these rules. Through their manipulation of pattern, use, and form, rules have a strong impact on quality of life, affecting everything from patterns of daily life to the demographic makeup of schools to who lives next to whom. Are good urban places the result of a conscious coding effort? What specific rules can we thank for the great places we have, or blame for the other, dispiriting ones? When we experience a great city, neighborhood, street, or place, how much of it can be attributed to rules? Understanding this connection can help us to avoid the types of rules that result in bad places, and embrace and build on those that create good ones.

Because I focus on the American experience, zoning dominates this story—it is the mother lode of city rules. Other kinds of rules, such as utility regulations, deed restrictions, neighborhood review panels, impact fees, and federal laws, can affect urban form, sometimes dramatically, but zoning has had the broadest effect. Planners, real estate developers, environmentalists, and citizens have a largely negative view of zoning, and in the decades since its adoption in the early twentieth century, zoning has taken on a significant amount of baggage. But there is nothing intrinsic about zoning that should elicit such a negative response: zoning is simply a set of rules tied to a specific location. Curiously, rules by any other name, such as deed restrictions, often escape a more negative judgment. Deed restrictions did significantly impact the public realm, but in many areas, their control of built form was subsumed by zoning and subdivision regulation in the early twentieth century (with the notable exception of Houston, which never embraced zoning but which continues to control urban form via restrictive deeds and covenants). Zoning has a colorful history, full of antics used in the unrelenting effort to avoid it (Flint 1977; Burgess 1994). Creative circumvention included, for example, the invention of new building types (e.g., the "apartment hotel") as a way of skirting zoning rules (Plunz 1993). In the 1950s zoning represented the view of the world at the time, as inequality, exclusion, and automobile dependence were rendered in built form. Zoning is what is behind the paving of paradise (Stone 2004), the inflation of housing costs (Glaeser and Gyourko 2002), and the constant drain on the implementation of smarter growth (Talen and Knaap 2003). Largely, this has to do with the gradual expansion of zoning's requirements. Figure 1.2 shows how zoning between 1948 and 2005 enforced the gradual expansion of lot size requirements in one American city. The change might seem modest for a single lot, but the cumulative effect of this rule change has been dramatic—spreading the city out, increasing car dependence and land consumption, and reducing both the possibility of walkable access and the viability of public transit. Many communities are now trying to reverse these expansion trends, making it, once again, legal to build compact urban form.

Despite the mythology of rugged individualism, rules have always been an integral part of the American experience, and in the early twentieth century, it seemed natural to have all kinds of rules guiding our behavior (box 1.2). Rules are essential to city building—even Adam Smith knew that.[2] The question is what *kinds* of cities do rules create? The answer is something of a mystery. Though rules often function as the default urban policy position—perceived as a way of getting something for

---

2. In *Wealth of Nations*, Adam Smith discussed such things as the need to require the building of party walls to prevent the spread of fire (p. 324).

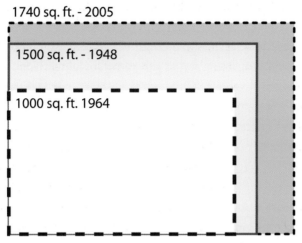

Minimum Site Area per Dwelling
Multi-family (R-4) zone - Tempe, Arizona

1740 sq. ft. - 2005

1500 sq. ft. - 1948

1000 sq. ft. 1964

Figure 1.2. Changes in multifamily residential zoning in the R-4 district (originally, the "B" district) in Tempe, Arizona.

nothing, without having to spend public dollars—it is a policy position we promote recklessly. Rules guide what gets built where, often without a clear objective. The character of place that results, de facto, is usually not preconceived, let alone desired. With no one and nothing in charge of maintaining an overall idea about what cities should be like, rules become the default overseers of urban form.

While there are many other forces to blame for the disfigured American urban landscape, city rules are not helping. Over the course of the last century, American urban development has been characterized by inner-city disinvestment, sprawl, segregation, and a general lack of quality when it comes to urbanism. Rules not only contribute to this, they actively block better ambitions. The places we love and flock to—such as Nantucket or Annapolis—can be difficult to create without a team of lawyers to change or circumvent the rules.

Without a clear connection between rule and objective—or better yet, between rule and physical outcome—city planners are left holding the bag on rules they probably care little about, trying to defend them in the face of a public that is at best apathetic about regulations. Planners can only dream of a world in which a clear connection between helping to create good cities is linked to the rules they are required to enforce. And rules, once put into law, are not easily gotten rid of. Plans

> **Box 1.2. "City Ordinances We Should Know and With Which We Should Comply"**
>
> Cruelty to animals; billboards; protection from fire; firearms; food and milk inspection; garbage; hack, express and automobile hire; ice; injury to property; licenses; medicine samples; milk and cream dealers; minors; numbering houses; quarantine regulations; shows, vulgar and immoral; slot machines; regulation of speed; spitting; street car fare; streets, alleys and sewers; setting out of trees; tuberculosis; cutting of weeds; weights and measures; building and factory inspection; smoke inspection; registry of births.
>
> *Pamphlet produced for Sioux City, Iowa, 1913.*
>
> *Source:* Van Buren (1915, 411).

and politicians can be ignored or voted out, but rules and laws last. Case in point: two years after New York became the first U.S. city to adopt a comprehensive zoning ordinance in 1916, the planning committee and its staff were fired. The basic outlines of the code endured.

Rules affect urban pattern and form in a myriad of large and small ways. A seemingly simple rule, such as the requirement that apartments must have a second means of egress, can affect building size and configuration, and, ultimately, how cities are experienced. A bay window may require approval from a public commission, with the result being that bay windows become a rarity. Maybe a certain density level triggers design review, resulting in lower densities. Rules about minimum distance between stairs may determine how many units front a street. Laws might be used to stimulate the consumption of certain materials, such as brick and steel, which in turn impacts the character of urban form. The number of parking spaces required for each housing unit can have a profound effect on building configuration. Chicago's antibetting law of 1905 had the effect of converting race tracks to housing (Hoyt 1933). Consider the federal tax code and its effect on urban form via rules about loan guarantee. Federally backed mortgages of single-family, detached housing have been one of the biggest generators of suburbia.

Many planners in the United States are now trying to turn the rules of city building around. The effort is monumental, and results have been gradual and mixed. Most urban advocates are convinced that different kinds of rules—more adaptive, more form-based—are needed to produce better places. By recounting the history of codes and putting the current popularity of code reform in a broad historical context, I hope to reveal what is new and what is unchanged about the attempt to implement vision and design through the application of rules.

There have been some important recent works on the history, meaning, and implications of urban codes. *Regulating Place* (2004), edited by Eran Ben-Joseph and Terry Szold, and *The Culture of Building* (1999) by Howard Davis do an excellent job of positioning building regulations and zoning in a broader context. One of the few attempts to link codes to the creation of actual places is *The Politics of Place: A History of Zoning in Chicago* (2006), by Joseph P. Schwieterman and Dana M. Caspall. Urban designers have long been interested in the "invisible hand" of planning law and its effect on place (Lai 1988; Punter 1999), exploring how policies shape cities in books like *Laws of the Landscape* (Nivola 1999). U.S. scholars have become particularly interested in understanding how planning regulations have become so universally despised. One reason is the way in which evolving public goals have been grafted onto old regulatory methods, creating strange hybrids when in fact new ways of thinking are needed. Eran Ben-Joseph (2005) makes this point in his book *The Code of the City*.

New Urbanists, a group of urban reformers who advocate walkable, diverse, compact urbanism of the kind that existed before cars took control of American cities, have been particularly vocal about the effect of rules on the built environment, drawing the attention of designers back to codes and how they affect urban pattern and form. Two publications have documented New Urbanist codes: Steve Tracy's *Smart Growth Zoning Codes: A Resource Guide* (2004), and the Congress for the New Urbanism's *Codifying New Urbanism: How to Reform Municipal Land Development Regulations* (2004). The state of form-based codes was reviewed in the book *Form-Based Codes* (Parolek, Parolek, and Crawford 2008).

City Rules differs from the foregoing texts by its focus on illuminating cause and effect—the impact of codes on place. This is unique in that it is not about general principles but about making clear that the world we have built and continue to build is strongly influenced by specific rules. This differs, for example, from the recent book *A Better Way to Zone: Ten Principles to Create More Livable Cities* (Elliott 2008), which explores how codes can be made more responsive, fair, efficient, and flexible, and can adhere to other generalized principles. This book's aim is to be more literal: what is the translation between rule and effect *on the ground*?

This connection is better understood by studying the motives and underlying intent of early rule makers—the city planners who convinced everyone in the first two decades of the twentieth century that rules were essential for good city building. What reasons were used to promote these rules, and how and why did they evolve the way they did? Surveying this history, it often seems as though the original intent of a rule made sense, and that the history of rules in the United States is the history of losing the connection between intention and outcome. As one example—junk shops, which could be noxious and unattractive, were considered a menace to tenement houses (i.e., apartment buildings) in the early twentieth century, so it made sense to create a rule to limit them. Later, this rule was extended to all kinds of shops, not just noxious ones, which undermined the notion of mixed use—now regarded as essential to good urbanism. In the end, the connection between rule and underlying reason seemed to have been lost. A few other examples of the ironies and contradictions of rules, to be further explored in this book, are listed in table 1.1.

Rules are a powerful way to enact change. Early city planners understood this acutely. They watched their ideas spread like a virus, as zoning, in particular, was being adopted by virtually every American city in the 1920s. Early city planners wanted a certain kind of city—ordered, efficient, beautiful, and socially just—and they wrote the rules that they thought would create it. There is a clear lesson to be drawn from this experience. If planners want to change these rules now to adapt to current conditions, they need to understand the effects that regulations have and could have on the pattern and form of cities. This book is intended to contribute to the understanding of the power of regulation and how it can make a real and substantial difference. In this it rekindles an old objective: that the writing of rules can help to achieve noble aspirations when it comes to city building.

Themes
Two broad and interrelated themes dominate this exploration:

- Over the course of the last century, a loss of understanding of the overall effect of rules, as well as what motivated their creation, has led to a substantial disconnect between rule and urban reality, which has undermined good urbanism.
- To recover this connection, we need to have a more explicit understanding of the effect of rules.

While there is great interest in the topic of place (Dovey 2009; Cresswell 2004; Lippard 1998), how place is specifically impacted by rules is not well studied. Related to this, planners—and in fact, American society generally—seem to have lost

Table 1.1. The ironies and contradictions of rules: A few examples

What the intent was:	What it became:
Zoning was to address public health, specifically, relief from tuberculosis	Zoning contributed to health problems by spreading people out, increasing their reliance on cars and a sedentary lifestyle
Zoning was seen as progressive because it protected the people who most needed protecting—the poor; reformers believed that "the greatest and most desirable effect" of zoning "has been a social one" (Hubbard and Hubbard 1929, 191)	Zoning segregated the wealthy away from poor people and did nothing to promote better urban form in poor areas
Zoning was to promote downtowns by limiting skyscrapers that block light and air	Zoning facilitated the low-density spread of cities, which hardly promoted the downtown core
In New York, zoning was to protect "the high-class private detached house district" at 5th Ave. and 74th St. (Hubbard and Hubbard 1929, 160)	High-rises now surround Central Park—the market would never have sustained private detached houses on 5th Ave.
Zoning and subdivision regulation was to produce "striking economies" and land-use efficiencies (Hubbard and Hubbard 1929, 190)	Rules promoted wastefulness and increased land consumption
Subdivison regulations sought to restrict dwellings on alleys	Now, dwellings on alleys are widely seen as a way to increase density and diversity
Deep lots were prohibited because they were believed to be "forerunners of slum growth" (Augur 1923, 16)	Now, deep lots are encouraged as a way of promoting accessory units and therefore increasing density and diversity
To promote health, rules promoted "open spaces on the front, rear and sides of buildings" (Baltimore BZA 1925, 29)	What is healthful is compact urban form, which promotes walking, bicycling, and transit use

sight of their principal ambitions when it comes to city rules. Rules used to *mean* something. Rules we now live with were formulated under an entirely different set of urban conditions—the conditions changed, but the rules did not. City rules went from being mostly revered to mostly despised. For urban reformers who want to tackle the problem of rules today, it is important to understand what changed and what needs to change.

The planners who first formulated the rules of city building in the early twentieth century—especially zoning and subdivision regulations—grappled with the connection between regulation and form. They often debated how rules would affect place and character. "The quality of life," proclaimed a 1931 report issued by the federal government, "is as dependent upon the way a subdivision is laid out . . . as upon any other factor" (Gries and Ford 1931, 12).

While there is no dispute that there is a lot more to good urbanism than rules, early regulations more effectively considered the link between rules and place. For example, the nation's first comprehensive zoning ordinance, adopted in 1916 in New York City, was trying to solve four very specific physical conditions that were compromising human health and quality of life: factories bringing pollution into retail and residential areas, skyscrapers blocking light, overly congested streets and sidewalks, and overcrowding in residential areas (Adams 1922). Planners were intently interested in physical planning and design, more than in bureaucratic application. Even Edward M. Bassett, lawyer and "Father of American Zoning," was mostly interested in "the physical development of the city," and he "felt more at home with architects and engineers than with his fellow-lawyers" (Makielski 1966, 10). Zoning seemed perfectly capable of attending to this interest in desired physical outcomes and effect on urban quality.

But these explicit connections between regulations and place quality have been lost. It is not uncommon for books on zoning to be much more concerned with process than outcome, to focus on the costs they exact, and to contain not one visual interpretation of zoning's on-the-ground effect. Babcock's classic book *The Zoning Game* (1966), insightful as it is, is devoid of any consideration of the effect of zoning on place, character, form, or how cities are actually experienced. This points to a detachment from social or moral purpose, such that critiques revolve around procedure rather than motivation: does zoning take away rights or bestow them? Does it give more power to developers or to neighborhood groups? (see Kayden 1993). These are important questions. But what are the city-building purposes of rules—ones that we won't be embarrassed to admit?

Commentaries on zoning as a legal process abound. The two main enabling acts (the 1926 Standard State Zoning Enabling Act and the 1928 Standard City Planning Enabling Act), as well as model land development codes and the procedures, policies, and programs involved in land-use regulation, have been analyzed in great detail (see, for example, American Planning Association 1996; Meck 2002). These have spawned a legal industry concerned with things like state review procedures, consistency and reform in land-use decision making, fair-share housing programs, judicial review of zoning, reviews of state and regional planning acts—in short, virtually everything *except* the impact of a rule on place. This is unfortunate because it is through form and pattern that zoning exerts control over things like social behavior, daily patterns of movement, and access to public goods. Rules impact how places perform—socially, environmentally, and economically.

Rules are decidedly not Daniel Burnham–style master plans, but their cumulative effect can be no less dramatic, working like an under-the-radar blueprint to coerce city form, one lot at a time. The difference is that top-down master plans are capable of producing an explicitly desired result. Layers of convoluted rules produce a city form that might never have been intended.

Rules now in force were formulated under an entirely different set of urban conditions—the conditions changed, but the rules didn't. Patterns of land use, expectations about the mix of housing types, reliance on public transit—all of these urban experiences were very different at the time city rules were first put into place. In fact the current principles of "good urbanism"—connectivity, pedestrian orientation, compactness, land-use diversity, enclosure, small blocks—were already there in the early twentieth century, and there was no need to code them. The tables in Morris Knowles's *Industrial Housing* (1920) or Harland Bartholomew's *Urban Land Uses* (1932) (summarized in tables 1.2 and 1.3) give a sense of what the urban reality was at the time.

The rules made sense at the time. In the initial decades of the twentieth century, urban living *was* dangerous, and rules were needed to tame it. In a single year, 1926, 200 children playing in the street were killed by cars on the island of Manhattan

Table 1.2. Dimensions of industrial housing, 1920

	U.S. Housing Corp.	Emergency Fleet Corp.
Single-family detached	57.6%	22.1%
Single-family semidetached	28.6%	37.5%
Row housing	13.3%	40.4%

Source: Knowles (1920, 45–46).

Table 1.3. Dimensions of American cities in the 1930s

	Mean average lot area, per family	Mean average density	Land-use ratios	Mean average ratio of stores
Single-family	6,679 sq. ft.	28.8 persons per acre		
Two-family	5,519 sq. ft.	68.7 persons per acre		
Multifamily	1,350 sq. ft.	105.9 persons per acre		
Residential			39.33%	
Parks, playgrounds, public use			13.94%	
Commercial, industrial, railroad			13.17%	
Streets			33.61%	
				2.29 stores per 100 persons

Source: Adams (1934, 65).

(Perry 1929; today, an average of ten pedestrians under the age of eighteen are killed annually by cars for all of New York City; New York City DOT 2008). Legitimate safety concerns were the reason reformers were arguing for more cul-de-sacs, longer blocks, and lower densities (see, for example, Woodbury 1929). In other words, the rationales for separating uses, which resulted in cities' spreading out, were justified. The problem is that the degree to which rules changed over the course of the twentieth century did not match the degree to which urbanism changed—especially its peripheral, low-density, uncentered spread away from the urban core. By midcentury, planners were coding for problems that no longer existed, or failing to code for problems that did.

Toward a New Appreciation of City Rules

It is widely recognized that fundamental change in our existing system of rules is becoming imperative. Can the link between rules, activism, and social justice, between the right to a good city and the power to create it through the force of law, be recaptured? Can rules once again be put to the task of creating what is believed to be good urban form? Is it possible to reignite a passion for city rules of the kind that existed when rule making first began? Can rules once again be directed toward improving quality of life and creating more civic beauty—rather than concerning themselves only with traffic flow, social separation, and consumption at the expense of civic identity?

To achieve such goals, the purpose and effects, both bad and good, of these rules need to be clear. The connection between the rules being applied and the cities that result—as physical places—needs to be better understood. That is the purpose of this book. Planners, architects, environmentalists, community activists—anyone who believes that the design of the built environment is central to urban life and community well-being—needs to understand how urban form is strongly affected by rules.

Method

This book focuses mostly on the American experience, although European rule-making history forms an important backdrop. The investigation here is limited to legally enforceable rules, mostly created by local governments—those that affect street pattern, land-use arrangement, and three-dimensional form. These rules—also called codes or regulations—operate with or without benefit of a plan. They are meant to guide urban development over the long term, lot by lot and street by street. This book incorporates a range of levels, from small-scale, incremental change at the parcel or individual building level to broader patterns of streets and land use. Mostly, this is an exploration of the effects of three kinds of rules: zoning, subdivision regulations, and, to a lesser extent, rules governing public facilities (e.g., rules and regulations from fire commissions, government agencies, transportation departments, school boards, parks authorities, and health departments). Zoning and, later, subdivision regulations have been the most explicit in their control of pattern, use, and form. At a larger scale, legislative acts, such as ones that establish an urban growth boundary, can produce a particular urban pattern, although this larger scale is not my primary concern.

Building or fire codes are included only if they impact the public realm—which is sometimes the case. Figure 1.3, for example, is a photograph of the Federal Title Building, 437 S. Hill Street, Los Angeles (now demolished). At the time of construction in the 1920s, Los Angeles required that a fire escape be placed on the front of the building. Using a four-foot recess on one side of the building, the architect found a clever way to keep the continuity of the facade intact.

Figure 1.3. Rules required a fire escape on the front of the Federal Title Building, 437 S. Hill Street, Los Angeles (now demolished).
Source: Historic American Buildings Survey, Library of Congress; Julius Shulman, Photographer, October 1980. From the "Built in America" website: http://memory.loc.gov/cgi -bin/query/D?hh:1:./temp/~ammem_Qswb::

This book is also more concerned with direct effects than indirect ones, although these can be difficult to distinguish. Although a rule may be direct—that is, intended to address something specific about urban pattern and form—there may nevertheless be plenty of unintended outcomes. Another complication is that sometimes what gets built is significantly less than what the rules allow. An example of this phenomenon is shown in figure 1.4, an area ruled by the RE-35 zone at the outskirts

Figure 1.4. The RE-35 zone on the outskirts of Phoenix, Arizona, an example of how, sometimes, what gets built is significantly less than what the rules allow.

of Phoenix, Arizona. The rules are shown in yellow; the dimensions of what was actually constructed are shown in white. The graphic shows that the houses have lower lot coverage, larger lot size, deeper setbacks, deeper lot depth, and lower height than the rules allow. In sum, a smaller house and a bigger lot. In some locations this is not a bad thing, but in other locations, it exacerbates sprawl.

Many other kinds of rules affect place indirectly—that is, in a way that is not about producing particular place characteristics but is a by-product of some other objective. The most substantial are (1) rules governing the process of building, (2) financing rules, and (3) rules concerning funding from government agencies.

The approval process is full of rules that indirectly affect place. For example, rules dictating the need for variances, conditional use permits, and planned unit developments (PUDs) all have an effect on cost and other dimensions of a project and thus ultimately affect built form. But the effect is indirect in that the primary intent of the rule is to guide process and procedure rather than a specific kind of pattern or form. Another example is financing rules, which can affect what kinds of buildings get built, their size, and their function—but their primary concern is finance, not form. They may prohibit the mixing of uses, or they may dictate the limits of mixing unit types, all of which can affect place. Rules might try to counteract the way developers behave, for example, by allowing higher density on larger sites in order to stimulate land assembly and motivate development in certain areas (Shoup 2008). Tax increment financing (TIF) districts, enterprise zones, and impact fees all exert control over where development takes place, and thus indirectly affect place.

During the review process for a development project, all kinds of organizations might weigh in, applying their own sets of rules. Standards for street width used by fire officials are common, as are the standards for parking and ramps imposed by the American Disabilities Act (ADA). There might be codes regulating particular components of the built environment, such as sidewalk ordinances that regulate sidewalk design (Loukaitou-Sideris, Blumenberg, and Ehrenfeucht 2004). If a community requires compliance with Crime Prevention through Urban Design (CPTED), these too act like rules, and the effect of "defensible space" concepts enforced through CPTED standards can be significant (Slone and Goldstein 2008). Development might need to acquire permits from such agencies as the U.S. Corps of Engineers, the U.S. Fish and Wildlife Service, the U.S. Forest Service, and the State Department of Transportation. Locally, a development might need to comply with a local tree code or the preservation of various natural features. Environmental protection ordinances have the potential to affect form significantly—although, as William Shutkin points out: "Environmental regulation is not, nor was it ever conceived to be, an instrument of place-making" (Shutkin 2004, 253). Some of the most significant environmental rules impacting physical urban form are rules protecting wetlands, which evolved out of the 1972 Clean Water Act. The U.S. Army Corps of Engineers administers the permits required for any development that impacts navigable waters (wetlands, streams, rivers, and lakes). The Clean Water Act and the Endangered Species Act protect species and their habitats, and the designation of protected areas and the buffers around them can seriously impact developable land—and thus the urban pattern. Sometimes the rules requiring protection of small patches of wetland can have significant consequences for built form; this has been much criticized by some developers, who argue that under current wetland rules, Boston would never have been built (Slone and Goldstein 2008).

Another area of regulation that significantly influences the built environment is affordable housing. Rules about financing, who is eligible to receive subsidy, and whether nonresidential uses can be included all affect what gets built, and where. An affordable housing project may be forced to locate in a specific place, or have a certain scale, or contain certain kinds of materials, all in compliance with rules. Often these rules have the perverse effect of dramatically increasing the cost of building affordable housing (Rosenthal 2009).

Design guidelines, architectural review boards, and historic preservation ordinances can impact urban form significantly, but they are not included here for the simple reason that guidelines and review processes tend to be advisory rather than regulatory. For the most part their "vagueness, obscurity, and lack of teeth" is exactly the basis on which they have been critiqued (Punter and Carmona 1997, 28). Historic district codes tend to focus on defining what is an inappropriate treatment of a historic building rather than implementation of a desired vision. The exception to this inexplicitness is when design guidelines have been transferred to code. This happened in San Francisco in the 1970s when some of the provisions of its urban design plan were translated into a new zoning ordinance in 1979 (Jacobs 1980). Predictably, some viewed it as too much constraint on architectural freedom, with its regulation of facade treatment details and its requirement that buildings be divided to look like townhouses.

While these indirect rules—that is, legislative acts, financing rules, procedures, design review—can affect urban pattern and form in significant ways, the interest here is squarely on those rules for which we can make a more direct connection between rule and outcome—zoning, subdivision regulation, and public facility standards.

Framework

This book looks at three dimensions of urbanism: pattern, use, and form. Each of these can be impacted by zoning, subdivision regulation, and public facility standards. The first category, pattern, is concerned with spatial structure in a two-dimensional sense—the pattern of lots, blocks, and streets. Pattern concerns arrangement and the question of *where*. The second, use, moves beyond the question of pattern toward the question of proximity, or to *what* use is located *where*. This implies a more socially controlled aspect, since much of the discussion of use involves rules that intend to exclude one group or function from another. The third category is concerned with urban form, which is about the three-dimensional form of built space rather than how that space is used or where it is located.

To the extent that city rules constitute the underlying political and economic forces that shape the built environment, this framework is aligned with the field of urban morphology, which is the study of physical urban form and the people and processes that shape it (Conzen 1969; Moudon 1994). As in urban morphology, the elements of town plan, building form, and land-use pattern are the main actors in this story. But my interest is in how they can be tied—as unambiguously as possible—to a specific rule. That the direction of causation goes both ways—social process (rule) affects built landscape, and built landscape gives rise to rules—the analysis is in the dialectical tradition of morphological study.

This analysis will be useful to planners who want to reform the existing system of rules into a system of rules that is more just and inspiring. Although the text includes historical and policy analysis, it is a practical book designed to help stakeholders identify the underlying causes of urban pattern, use, and form, and better affect the translation between written rule and place quality.

Chapter 2 gives a broad, historical overview of the evolution of city rules, focusing especially on the American experience, and on the linkages that can be made between rule and place. Chapters 3, 4, and 5 dissect the historical evolution of rules from three perspectives: rules primarily affecting pattern (3), use (4), and form (5)—although there are obvious interlinkages between all categories. Chapter 6 is devoted to rule reform. Calls for reform have coevolved with American rule making from the onset, and it is important to assess the current expansion of reform efforts within this context.

2. Regulating Place

This chapter provides an overview of the history of city-building rules, with a focus on the American experience. Understanding this history is essential for putting the contemporary situation in context. Who was behind the rules and what did people think of them? What motivations and urban conditions gave rise to their widespread use?

In the making of rules for city building, the United States was late in the game. In Europe, building ordinances and regulations influencing all manner of urban form were common in the seventeenth century and were standard fare by the nineteenth (Hall 2009), most often implemented for the protection of the very rich (Davies 1958). Though there were some restrictions on building materials in the North American colonies as early as the seventeenth century, and some colonial settlements before 1800 were regulated by the Laws of the Indies, the impact of rule making on city pattern and form before the twentieth century was sporadic. Examples include sanitation laws designed to protect public health and private investment, and housing codes, such as New York's Tenement House Act of 1867, which mostly perpetuated the status quo and only applied to one type of building. A few planned communities at the time had codes regulating form, but these were uncommon.

Regulations for safe building were at first all about the control of fire (Wermiel 2000). In fourteenth-century Munich, Germany, chimneys were required to be stone and roofs were to be tile so they were not flammable, and the "building police," as they were called, went around ensuring that the rules were followed (Logan 1972). From 1800 to 1916, fire departments in the United States maintained control of building rules, regulating such things as wall thickness and materials (Comer 1942).

Early U.S. nuisance laws regulated noxious trades and activities and sometimes banned them completely from the city. They were first instituted in colonial times and were the primary means of land-use control up until the twentieth century (Melosi 1999). Nuisance law was the basis of the 1692 regulation in the Commonwealth of Massachusetts designating that slaughterhouses be confined to specific parts of the town, and New York's 1703 law stipulating that certain types of industries like distilling liquor and making limestone could not take place within a half-mile of the city hall (New York Colony 1894). Nuisance laws were also the basis of zoning two centuries later. That nuisance laws could be used to institute some sort of grand plan for a better community is debatable: nuisance law had a "feudal appeal" that was regularly used to protect the well positioned (Power 1989, 11).

By the end of the nineteenth century, those involved in city building began to embrace regulations more widely, buoyed by new kinds of powerful political and social institutions. To some, this regulatory turn meant that cities could no longer adapt to change (Konvitz 1985), and the individual was rendered helpless. But to others, rules represented a powerful form of collective protection (Whitnall 1931). To the new profession called city planning, rules represented the triumph of community needs over market capitalism.

As America became more urbanized in the nineteenth century, building height regulations became more common, although controls aimed at street width and frontage were still rare. Heights were also controlled indirectly. For example, the tenements in Chicago were three stories tall (while those in New York were six stories tall) because above that height buildings were required to be fireproof (Williams 1919). In Rochester, New York, if commercial buildings were "sprinklered," they were allowed to be twice as large (Rochester 1931, 35).

Before zoning, deed restrictions controlled everything from setbacks to outbuildings in minute detail, as chronicled in C. P. Berry's 1915 *Digest of the Law of Restrictions on the Use of Real Property*. Often these were used to enforce a certain "quality" of residential character. For example, in the first decade of the twentieth century, building restrictions in a town in California allowed only private residences valued at at least $1,500 and set back from the street by twenty feet. These rules, intended to maintain low-density residential quality and to cater to a certain economic class, were challenged by some property owners but upheld by the California Supreme Court in 1911 (*Firth vs. Marovich*, 116 Pac. R. 729). This kind of rule making was more common in privately developed, newly planned communities. A list of the building regulations created by Frederick Law Olmsted and Associates for An-chorage, Kentucky, reveals the underlying purpose of rules such as those for mini-mum building costs and deep setbacks: keep the residential area socially homogeneous, free from intrusions, and obtainable only by white people of wealth. The rules they implemented permitted everything *except* what one would need on a daily basis. For example, the rules allowed zoos and circuses (albeit conditionally) but not small grocery stores. The strategy ensured a wealthy, bucolic environment. Today, Anchorage is one of the wealthiest communities in Kentucky (median household income in 2009 was over $150,000). Later in the 1920s, the firm claimed to have abolished some of its more exclusionary practices, such as the setting of minimum building cost and the prohibition of saloons and livery stables (Augur 1923).

Burgess's 1994 study of twentieth-century land controls showed how two sets of actors controlled urban pattern and form: property owners who subdivided land and placed restrictive covenants on the parcels, and public entities who controlled how the land was used. In her final analysis, she argued that it was the private restric-tions that exacted more control over the urban pattern. Similar studies have uncov-ered the effects on use, pattern, and form of zoning's alternatives: covenants, frontage-consent ordinances, and even fines (Ellickson 1973). Early planners, how-ever, felt that private restrictions' impermanence rendered them weak compared to zoning (Bassett 1922b).

No rule-making approach has had more impact than zoning. As transmitted to the United States, zoning was designed to remedy the negative externalities of the industrial city, stabilizing residential property values, maximizing profit for com-mercial areas, and keeping industrial areas efficient and functional. Practically speak-ing, however, zoning was really nothing more than building codes adapted to location. Many believed that building codes that were not place based were a serious problem: "building laws, apart from those applying to fire limits, treated all parts of the city alike whether inside or suburban, whether business centers or residential outskirts" (Bassett 1922a, 315). Thus zoning was defined as "planning in recognition of the differences in different parts of the city," whereby regulation would "adapt it-self to these differences." By analogy, wrote Williams in 1914, zoning was like cloth-ing that, "in order to fit equally well," was made "specially and differently" for "the short and the tall, the fat and the thin" (Williams 1914, 2). Under zoning, one area of the city was allowed to be denser, taller, and more diverse, while another area was required to be sparsely populated and more homogeneous. This is fundamentally different from a building code, which applies rules uniformly to all parts of a city.

The ancient Greeks and Romans had a version of this place-based rules approach we now call zoning. The Greeks zoned their cities to separate residential areas from civic and religious functions. Romans enacted laws to keep industry out of certain areas, residences in particular sections, main offices clustered together, and commercial uses "distributed where the traffic encourages them" (Cavaglieri 1949, 30; see also Ben-Joseph 2005). In the Middle Ages, noxious industries like leather tanning establishments were kept out of the city center, and in seventeenth-century London, shops were not allowed on main public squares nor on the streets leading to them. Napoleon imposed rules, contained in the fourteen articles of the Napoleonic decree of 1810, stipulating that unhealthy industries had to be kept out of towns (Hason 1977; Reynard 2002). Ancient Rome, seventeenth-century London, and nineteenth-century France all had regulations in which building laws varied by location—in other words, zoning. In some sense, early twentieth-century zoning only expanded on these earlier coding traditions.

This idea, where rules would vary by district, was an 1870s invention of a German engineer, Reinhard Baumeister. Germans called it zoning (or the zone system) because of the way cities were so clearly differentiated into zones of land value and intensity. This was in part a function of historical walls. The business center was typically encircled by a line where the old city walls had been, "within which the land was dearest." After the removal of the walls, the "dear land" was concentrated into a distinct zone.

Reinhard Baumeister and Franz Adickes were the first to formerly lay out the theory of zoning at a meeting of the German Architectural and Engineering Societies in 1874 (Williams 1922). Two years later, Baumeister spelled everything out in a book titled *Town Expansions Considered with Respect to Technology, Building Code and Economy* (1876). He traced the origins of zoning back to an 1810 decree of Napoleon I, which divided industry into three classes and established the boundaries of a "protected district." The creation of zones for different kinds of uses, therefore, was the first to appear. Next came bulk zoning, which laid out two sets of regulations, one for the city and one for the suburbs, and specified things like building height, setbacks, and the amount of lot area that could be built on. German cities adopted use and bulk zoning throughout the 1880s and 1890s.

The implementation of zoning in Germany was helped by the fact that it was not unusual for a municipal government to own one-half of its city's land area. This gave regulators significant power to shape their city. There was also a long tradition of rule making. Building regulations had been evolving in Europe since the medieval period, when the urban design schemes of benevolent rulers had been gradually transferred into rules grounded in notions of beauty, harmony, and order (Power 1989).

The German system gradually made its way to Britain. It was introduced there in 1909 in the first Town Planning Act. The overlap between zoning and the reigning Garden City movement was mostly conceptual; both rested on the idea that city size should be consciously controlled (Toll 1969). Garden City architect Raymond Unwin, writing in 1909, admired the German system of zoned-based regulation and lamented the fact that, in England, "any regulation which is deemed advisable in the most closely built up centre of the town applies equally to the most sparsely built areas on the outskirts" (1909, 402). Later on, British planners scoffed at the way American planners were using zoning, arguing that its "rigidity" and "much more de-tailed and intricate" approach, aimed at "reducing the possibilities of appeal to a minimum," was not the true intention of zoning (Mattocks 1935, 243).

By 1916, when comprehensive zoning was officially implemented in the United States (in New York City), Germany had more than thirty years of experience with the regulatory tool (Hirt 2007). American planners could learn a cautionary lesson from Berlin, where, in the absence of zoning, building regulations had allowed congestion to reach alarming levels. American planners wanted to protect their suburbs from congestion, claiming that, by limiting building bulk, zoning would allow "freedom of movement" (Adams 1931, 83). The fact that most zoning-related lawsuits took place in the suburbs is evidence that zoning was attempting to make the most change in suburban locations (Weaver and Babcock 1980). The use of zoning as a way of protecting the suburbs from too much density has remained a primary focus.

What unfolded after the 1916 adoption of the New York City zoning law was "the great American zoning parade" (Peets 1931, 225), or perhaps it was more ap-propriately labeled a storm (Kimball, cited in Simpson 1985, 126). Legal experts ques-tioned the application of German zoning to U.S. cities (Freund 1911), given political and cultural differences where "American Jacksonian democracy contrasted with Prussian authoritarian-type efficiency" (Mullin 1976/77, 12). The term "districting" was applied in the United States at first, but was later discarded in favor of "zoning" because of the confusion over political districting.

New York City's landmark zoning law changed city regulation dramatically. Par-tial zoning codes had existed earlier in Massachusetts, California, and Wisconsin. California was the first to establish separated and homogeneous residential zones, and Los Angeles was believed to have the nation's first zoning ordinance (Whitnall 1931), but New York's law consolidated multiple regulations—and multiple objectives—into one comprehensive set of city-building rules. Other cities were waiting in the wings; had New York not gone first, zoning rules would have been instituted elsewhere (Fischel 2004).

Much has been written about New York City's comprehensive zoning code of 1916 (see especially Ward and Zunz 1992; Bressi 1993), and some of that story is recounted here given its central importance in the lineage of city rules. The ordinance that started an avalanche was essentially written by two men, an architect (George Ford) and a statistician (Robert Whitten). Two other men, Edward M. Bassett and Frank B. Williams, both New York attorneys interested in city planning law, played key roles in advancing the idea publicly. Both were prolific writers. Williams wrote a major treatise called *The Law of City Planning and Zoning* in 1922, which filled 738 pages.

New York's 1916 code (see fig. 2.1) was defined at the time as a "reasonable plan for preventing over intensive development," containing only, proponents said, "a limited degree of segregation" (New York City Board of Estimate and Apportionment 1916, 144, 145). In fact it is sometimes difficult to view Edward M. Bassett's numerous, impassioned writings in the early 1900s as anything other than reasonable. The main problem, he said, was the way cities were developing: "a landowner could put up a building to any height, in any place, of any size, and use it to any purpose, regardless of how much it hurt his neighbors." According to Alfred Bettman, another leading zoning advocate, order was intended to prevent "a premature and avoidable spread-out of the city," and simultaneously help the business district develop "compactly and promptly" (Bettman 1925, 90). Zoning was the best tool, planners believed, to overcome the problem that Americans were "esthetically defective" and "blindly devoted to obsolete ideas" about property rights (Hall 1917, 1).

Who could argue against the view that the chaotic condition of American cities was a significant problem in need of a solution? Planners looked to zoning to create an urban form that could provide "visual assurances of maturity and success" (Scott 1969, 33). Lack of regulation was creating a dog-eat-dog world that "stimulated each owner to build in the most hurtful manner" (Bassett 1922a). Even two decades before the onslaught of post–World War II sprawl, chaotic conditions in the city, in turn a result of lack of regulation, were causing an exodus of the wealthy: "citizens whose financial ability and public enterprise made them most helpful

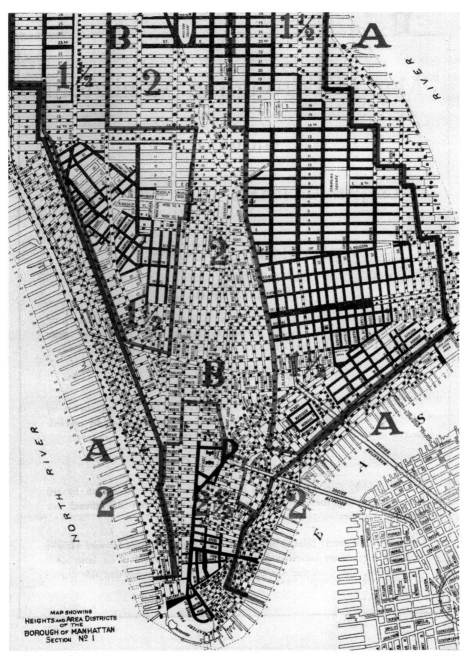

Figure 2.1. Height and area districts from New York City's original zoning map, 1916, the first comprehensive zoning ordinance in the United States.
Source: NYC (1916).

within the city limits were the very ones that would often be tempted to remove their families outside of the city" (Bassett 1922a, 315–16). Bassett was quite progressive in his arguments that the lack of regulation was creating disinvestment in central areas. In fact, zoning's supporters spoke in terms not unlike reformers of sprawl today, arguing that, without zoning, "waste on a large scale was inevitable," and that "chaotic conditions caused workers to travel daily too far from home" (Bassett 1922a, 317).

Zoning came on the heels of a wave of civic patriotism, as city planning texts like *Wacker's Manual* took stock of a "new impulse for civic good" and a rising tide of "devotion" to the city (Moody 1911, 1). There was intense public interest. In Baltimore in 1925, 250 people showed up at a single hearing, and one case having to do with a relatively minor change in use change garnered 500 letters and signatures (Baltimore BZA 1925). Even subdivision regulations, a key focus of the 1909 national real estate conference (the National Association of Real Estate Boards, or NAREB), were lauded on the basis of their ability to improve "civic conditions" and the achievement of "a more beautiful America" (cited in Davies 1958, 66).

There was a populist flare to zoning, a sense that neighborhoods should have the right to protect themselves against greed, pollution, and speculation, and that rules like zoning would provide those protections. Rules attended to the needs of the "community as a whole" and were even described in the early 1920s as "sustainable" (Baker 1927, 148). Zoning was thought to "stir the imagination of the community" and "invoke the public spirit" (Bartholomew, cited in Davies 1958, 146). It was meant to alleviate poverty; increase productivity, wages, and profits; and "improve" architecture (Adams 1935, 96; Hason 1977). It would stop the "indiscriminate scattering" of industry and business as well as stopping certain practices of "unthinking or selfish individuals" (Illinois Chapter of the AIA, 1919, 118). Zoning, in short, was a progressive cause. Its purpose was, according to Alfred Bettman, "always positive and constructive and not merely negative and preventive" (cited in Hubbard and Hubbard 1929, 164). It was to bring "order out of chaos" (Cheney 1920, 276) and would be capable of fostering "urban co-operation" (Baker 1927, 35). An editorial in 1912 in the *American City* magazine proclaimed: "wise regulations do not hamper civic activities; but, on the contrary, stimulate and encourage them" (American City 1912, 6).

In the latter part of the Progressive Era, around 1920, rules seemed an embodiment of a united civic interest. In this spirit, the "First Birthday" of Boston zoning in 1925 was a publicly celebrated event, its success attributed to "an unwonted de-

gree" of public endorsement (Herlihy 1925, 84). As each U.S. city passed a zoning ordinance, the town and the date of adoption were proudly listed in a special roster
published in the *American City* magazine, like an honor roll. Leading scholars at the
time wrote in high-minded terms that zoning would become an essential basis of
democracy (e.g., Hartman 1925). Even deed restrictions were valued in terms of how
they contributed to overall community welfare, not, as developer J. C. Nichols wrote
in 1929, in terms of "individual gains and losses" (Nichols 1929, 142). Everything the
city planner did required "a sense of what constitutes real and abiding values" and
"social aspiration," and zoning was part of that (Adams 1932, 103–4). Planners argued unequivocally that property value was not a proper motivation for zoning
(Adams, Lewis, and McCrosky 1929). Box 2.1 summarizes the 1920 perspective of
what zoning was expected to accomplish.

Because it was possible to connect zoning to these deeply held civic values, a
broad swath of society became involved. In New York City in 1916, schoolteachers,

---

Box 2.1. What zoning would accomplish: The 1920 view

Once adopted, we are convinced that a well worked out zone ordinance will:

Guarantee a definite and safe place for industrial investment

Protect home neighborhoods

Stimulate home ownership

Assure more contented labor conditions

Remove much of the suspicion and uncertainty from real estate

Stabilize property values

Afford greater security for mortgage loans and thus encourage building

Form a surer basis for investment

Provide the city for the first time with a firm foundation for the solution of the
problems of:

- Congestion
- Traffic
- Paving
- Sewers
- Public utilities
- Housing
- Schools
- Recreation

Source: Cheney (1920, 278).

children, ambassadors, and heads of major institutions like the New York Zoological Society and the Municipal Art Society weighed in on issues of value, beauty, and human scale and how zoning was intricately tied to those ideals (New York City Board of Estimate and Apportionment 1916, 82, 127). There was a strong belief in environmental determinism. Studies suggested that congested streets led to juvenile delinquency, and excessive stair climbing was bad for women (New York City Board of Estimate and Apportionment 1916). Prominent physicians spoke of zoning's contribution to solving everything from "eye trouble" to "nervousness" (New York City Board of Estimate and Apportionment 1916, 102), while children were enlisted as fieldworkers to find examples where zoning was most needed. Pro-zoning films with titles like *Growing Pains* were produced and widely distributed (Kimball 1923).

In fact zoning was initially cast as a means of keeping housing costs down for the working classes. The way European planners saw it, apartment buildings were inflating the cost of land, and density reductions via zoning would alleviate that pressure (Nettlefold 1914). Aspects of this logic transferred to the United States. Arguing for the "zone system" in 1912, a Philadelphia engineer wrote in the *American City* that zoning rested on the principle "that the economic progress of the nation and the integrity of its social fabric" should "transcend the prerogative of the individual" (American City 1912, 222). Even the most socially progressive housing advocates were in favor of zoning because they saw it as a way to improve the houses and neighborhoods of the poor. Thus the National Association of Real Estate Boards proclaimed in 1909 that "The subdivision that caters even to the modest working man must provide restrictions that will preserve that district along lines of home like beauty" (cited in Davies 1958, 66). "A zoning bill is a poor man's bill," argued the secretary of the American Civic Association in 1920 (Crawford 1920, 8). Bassett struck a progressive tone when he argued that, through zoning, land values could be equalized "instead of being absorbed by a few" (Bassett 1922, 322). Bassett, the main champion of zoning in the early twentieth century, argued that "police power," under which zoning is legalized, was the same thing as "community power" (Bassett 1922, 320). Recent analyses have sought to confirm the progressive strain in early zoning enthusiasm (Wolf 2008).

Early planners were at first highly attuned to the effects of zoning. After 1916, the federal Division of Building and Housing of the Department of Commerce started publishing its *Zoning Progress in the United States*. Said one reviewer at the time: "In no way can a zoning ordinance be better protected than by constant analysis and study" (Hubbard and Hubbard 1929, 175). And so ten years after the adoption of New York's zoning ordinance, planners observed that buildings around parks were too high, that industrial zones were in the wrong place, and that various other aspects of the ordinance were having unintended effects (Adams 1931). Zoning advocates used this knowledge to make their case. An illustrated literature developed to show the effects of "a garage next door to an apartment, an apartment in the midst of a residential block, or a junk yard adjoining a business house" (Baker 1927, 58).

This advocacy helped zoning expand rapidly. In just two years, from 1924 to 1926, the number of zoned cities in the United States increased from 62 to 456 (Baker 1927). By 1927, half of the urban population was living in zoned cities. Herbert Hoover, as secretary of commerce, crafted enabling legislation that pushed zoning even further, and by 1929 nearly eight hundred cities in the United States had zoning ordinances (Hubbard and Hubbard 1929).

Hoover was an engineer, and he promoted zoning as a tidy and technically efficient approach to city building. Hoover's 1926 publication, *A Zoning Primer*, likened the unzoned city to "an undisciplined daughter making fudge in the parlor" (Hoover 1926, 1). He was also a social conservative. Under his conservative guidance, zoning prioritized homeownership, tied its objectives to social morality, and practiced exclusionary tactics in which single-family, residential-only neighborhoods were legalized (e.g., the report issued by the President's Conference on Home Building and Home Ownership, *Planning for Residential Districts*, edited by Gries and Ford [1931]).

Unlike Hoover's more rigid approach to zoning, the original framers of American zoning tried to suggest a logical framework that relied on the idea of urban intensity. In modern parlance, these early rules were "transect" based (Duany and Talen 2002), which means that they recognized that each place has a particular character and quality that ranges from being more urban to less urban. Zoning, at least as initially conceived, was capable of responding to these contexts. The zoning ordinances of Frankfurt and Cologne, Germany, exemplified this straightforward, conceptually clear approach, shown in figures 2.2 and 2.3, table 2.1, and box 2.2.

Most cities in Germany followed this approach, although Berlin, which adopted zoning in 1892, was criticized for having a weak ordinance (Williams 1913). Williams wrote in his 1922 review of European zoning: "The purpose of the zoning rules, in Dusseldorf as elsewhere, is to produce structures which in bulk and type are, so far as possible, suited to the part of the city in which they are to be situated" (Williams 1922, 251). Different places in the city had a different feel, character, and intensity, and the rules were meant to enforce it. Thus the Saxon Building Law of 1900 set

residential area/quarter (Wohnviertel)

country home area/quarter (Landhausviertel)

mixed use area/quarter (Gemischtes Viertel)

factory area/quarter (Fabrikviertel)

central city/downtown (Innenstadt)

Figure 2.2. The conceptually simple zoning ordinance of Frankfurt, Germany, 1891.
Source: NYC (1916).

rules for setbacks, height, and lot coverage based on "the character of the place" (Williams 1922, 478). Mannheim's 1904 ordinance had three zones that varied rules by building intensity corresponding to central location: an inner zone where 60 per-

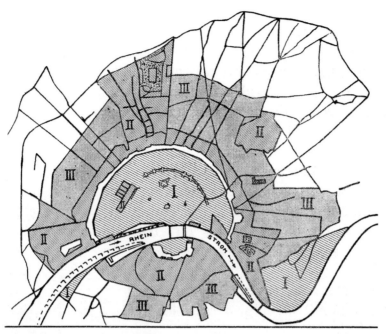

Figure 2.3. The zone system of Cologne, Germany, c. 1905.
Source: Triggs (1909). Key: I. The older part of the town, where the buildings are highest and very close together. II. On these parts still lower buildings only are allowed, and greater space is required between the buildings. III. Parts of the new town, where only lower buildings are permitted, with certain spaces between each.

cent of the lot could be built on, a surrounding zone with a 50 percent lot coverage limit, and a zone further out where buildings could not exceed 40 percent lot coverage (Logan 1972). Residential buildings were limited in these zones to five, four, and three stories, respectively. Other German cities, like Hannover, Frankfurt, and Munich, had similar types of spatially graded building ordinances.

American zoning ordinances, when they were first introduced in the 1920s, followed a similar kind of straightforward, simple logic. They were uncomplicated and easily read. Figures 2.4, 2.5, 2.6, and 2.7 show the original zoning ordinances for three cities: Rochester, New York; Minneapolis; and Memphis.

This brief overview of the history of American city rules forms the backdrop to the more detailed analysis presented in the next three chapters. Though interrelated, the three types of effects shown in chapters 3, 4, and 5—pattern, use, and form—have their own origination, evolution, and discernible imprint on the American landscape.

Table 2.1. Provisions of the 1891 Frankfurt Ordinance Concerning Building in

Quarters and zones	Yard space	Building heights	
		Main bldg.	Rear bldg.
Inner city	⅙ open	20 meters max.; equal street width plus 2 meters	
Factory quarter	⅓ open; 150 sq. met. per dwelling	Equal street width, min. of 10 meters	
Mixed quarter ───────── Transition zone	⅓ open; 30 sq. met. per dwelling	Same as for factory quarter; (if dwelling, max. of 18 met. and 4 storeys)	Equal court width, no max. (if dwelling, 3 storey max.)
Outer zone	⅓ open; 40 sq. met. per dwelling		2 storey max.
Residential quarter ───────── Transition zone	⅓ open; 60 sq. met. per dwelling	Equal street width, max. of 18 meters (if dwelling, 4 storeys max.)	Equal court width, max. of 14 meters (if dwelling, 3 storeys max.)
Outer zone	⅓ open; 100 sq. met. per dwelling		Equal court width, max. of 14 meters (if dwelling, 2 storey max.)

Abbreviations: ht., height; max. maximum; min., minimum; met., meters; bldg., building.
Source: New York City Board of Estimate and Apportionment (1913).

the Outer City

Courtyards	Side yards	Regulation of commercial bldgs.	
		Annoying	Obnoxious
	None	None	None
If dwelling, equal to ht. of bldg to front and rear, 8 met. minimum	None	None	None
Same as for factory quarter	None (on residential streets with front gardens, same as res. quarters)	None _____ None	None (in 1893 10 met. from lot line)
If dwelling, equal to ht. of main bldg to front & rear; 8 met. min.	3 meters each side	½ open; 20 meters all sides	Banned
	4 meters each side	⅔ open; 40 meters all sides	Banned

Box 2.2. Description of an early zoning ordinance from Frankfurt, Germany, c. 1884

The older inner city in the first zone or district. Here the highest buildings are allowed. They must not exceed the width of the street, plus about 10 feet (three meters). Or in any case however wide the street, about 66 feet (20 meters). This is to the cornice; the roof above this is restricted by an angle, and in no case may exceed about 30 feet (nine meters). The roof is more than mere roof; it is a roof story, in which there are rooms, which, however, may not always be used for residence. The number of stories is also restricted; in this zone it must not exceed five, and the roof story.

Here in the inner city, also, the greatest proportion of the lot may be covered with buildings, three-quarters for corner lots, five-sixths for others. Factories are allowed but are not numerous. Solid blocks are permitted. The city here presents the appearance of being fully built up to a fairly uniform height.

The outer city is divided into outer, an inner, and a country zone, in which the height of buildings allowed progressively increases. In each of these zones are residence, factory and mixed sections. In the residence sections, factories are so discouraged as to be practically forbidden. In the factory sections, situated along the railroads, the harbor, and out of the city in the direction so that prevailing winds will blow the smoke away from the city, residences are forbidden. In the factory sections, the restrictions on height and amount of lot covered do not become progressively greater. The mixed sections are near the factory sections, and there, too, under certain mild restrictions, many sorts of manufacturing are permitted.

In the residence section a space between neighboring houses of about 10 feet (three meters) in the inner zone and a third more in the outer zone is required. Groups of buildings are, however, allowed with a somewhat less proportionate amount of free space for the group as a whole.

Certain parts of the newly added territory of the city, beyond all the other zones, and forming a zone by itself, have been reserved for a villa section, in which only country houses are allowed.

In all these zones the amount of the lot that must be left free progresses, until, in the villa section, it is seven-tenths of the entire lot. Thus, also, the permissible height decreases to about 53 feet (16 meters) and the number of stories to two. This does not include the roof story and the actual roof, which together, in this zone, must not exceed about six feet (1.8 meters) in height. In no case, however, may the house exceed in height, except for the roof story and roof, the width of the street on which it stands.

Source: Logan (1972).

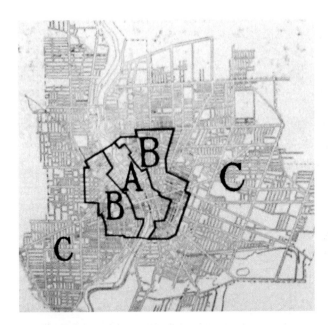

Figure 2.4. The uncomplicated, original zoning code of Rochester, New York, showing three "Height and Area" districts.
Source: Rochester, New York (1931).

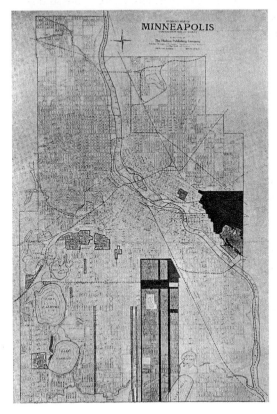

Figure 2.5. Zoning in Minneapolis, c. 1921. Original caption: "Districting in Minneapolis. Darker shading indicates industrial districts. Lighter shading indicates residential districts."
Source: New York City Board of Estimate and Apportionment (1916).

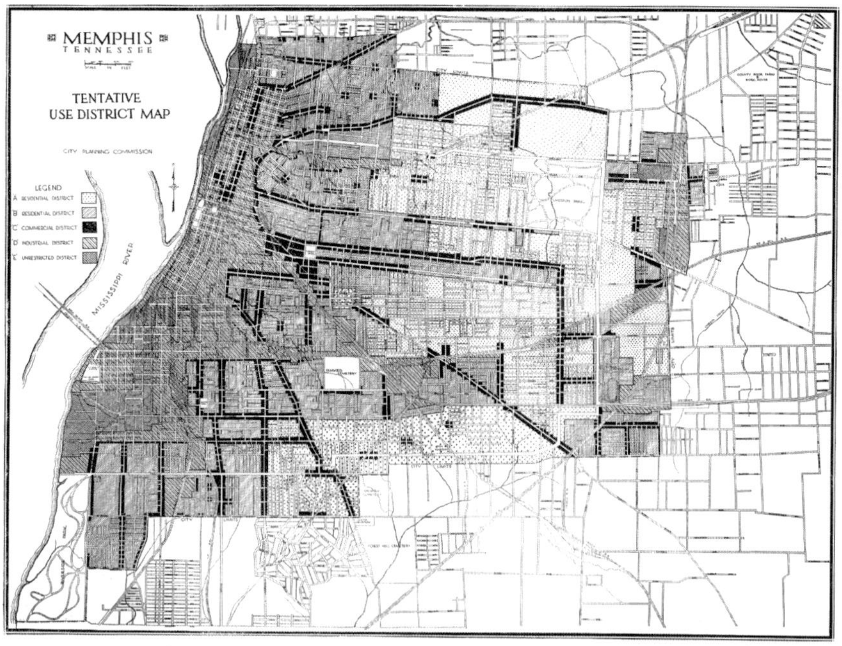

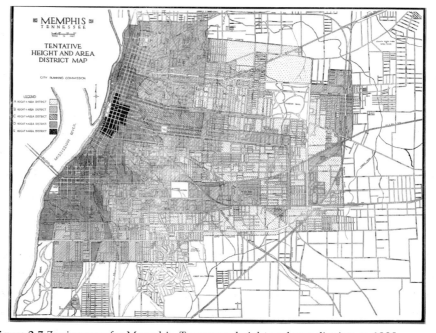

Figure 2.6 Early zoning ordinances had two maps, one for use districts and one for height and area districts. Zoning map for Memphis, Tennessee, tentative use districts, c. 1925.

Figure 2.7 Zoning map for Memphis, Tennessee, height and area districts, c. 1925.

3. Pattern

Urban pattern is affected by rules for land subdivision, street width and layout, and the spatial arrangement of zoning districts. The lineage of pattern regulation extends back at least four thousand years, when ancient India established rules for laying out towns, streets, and houses (Dutt 1925). As stated in the introduction, pattern concerns arrangement and the question of *where*. We know from the writings of Plato and Aristotle that there were laws governing streets and public squares (agora) in Greece in the fourth century BCE, and Roman laws included specifications for street layouts in military installments. In the first century, Vitruvius specified rules about siting new towns and laying out street directions to minimize wind. In the Renaissance period, surveyor-architect Daniel Stolpaert made use of a regulating plan in Amsterdam that dictated the locations of public buildings, streets, canals, and private residences. A corresponding ordinance established rules for building, including where the privies could be located, who paid for the streets, and rules about drainage. The ordinance was in effect for some four hundred years, and Lewis Mumford praised the plan and implementing ordinance for their "thoroughgoing attention to the conditions of health and social life" (Mumford 1961, 441).

Rules about how new towns were to be laid out affected the urban pattern on a mass scale. These include rules guiding the medieval *bastides* in Europe, colonial settlements, and the founding of Mormon towns, American railroad towns, and British new towns, all of which used rules to produce particular urban patterns (Reps 2002). In all cases, rules intended to standardize pattern created some variant of a grid (Stanislawski 1946). Replication of the same grid pattern was common: the same plat map was used thirty-three times in Illinois to spread towns across the state during the nineteenth century (Southworth and Ben-Joseph 2003). Earlier examples include William Penn's seventeenth-century rectangular street platting interspersed with public squares in Philadelphia, and the eighteenth-century city of Savannah, Georgia, founded by James Oglethorpe, which used deed restrictions to maintain an iconic pattern of public squares, streets, lots, and buildings. Sometimes the urban pattern was established by regulating cross street intervals. A nineteenth-century Liverpool ordinance required cross streets at least every 150 yards, which had a very standardizing effect (Robinson 1901).

Complete planned communities established pattern through a system of rules, dictating street layout, public space allocation, and building placement. Colonial Williamsburg, Virginia, is the product of a simple, prescriptive plan that operated like a code, regulating urban pattern and form (figs. 3.1 and 3.2). Planned communities like Shaker Heights, Ohio; Chatham Village, Pennsylvania; and Venice, Florida, all had rules guiding the urban pattern in precise terms. Factory towns like Kohler, Wisconsin, and Goodyear Heights, Ohio, used rules to create a pattern in which workers' homes were located within walking distance of a factory (Manning 1915).

Laws restricting where development could take place had an effect on urban pattern. One approach was to prevent new development from spreading into previously undeveloped areas. In sixteenth-century England under Elizabeth I, for example, new buildings had to be built on top of old foundations (Larkham 2001). The Prussian Building Land Act of 1875 prohibited construction on greenfields that lacked public utilities and infrastructure, which meant that German cities avoided the "squalid belts of privately-owned shanties" that surrounded French cities (Kostof 1992, 57). Germany enacted a law in the early twentieth century that forbade building on "virgin plots" and restricted development to lots that had been built on prior to 1887 (Arntz 2002). In England, environmental controls on land were, predictably, motivated by property owners seeking to protect their property value, a practice that evolved out of feudal systems of property relations (Baer 2007a, 2007b; Luithlen 1997).

Sometimes rules were aimed at ensuring a desired density or degree of compactness. Regulations in Italy from the mid-sixteenth century ordered that gaps between houses be filled in with buildings (Girouard 1985). In Plymouth Colony, dwellings could not be remote from a church. New Amsterdam had a rule that "in order to promote the population, settlement, beauty, strength and prosperity" of the city, houses could not be built near the walls and gates of the city until lots closer in had first been built upon (Laws of Connecticut 1672, 29).

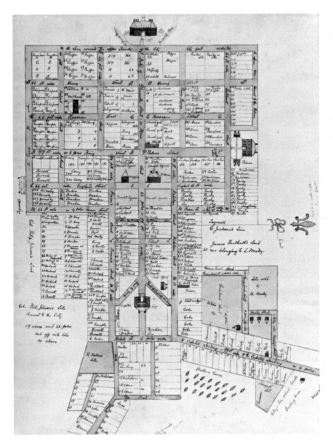

Figure 3.1. A simple code—streets, public building sites, and a six-foot front setback. Private collection of Mrs. Mary Ware Galt Kirby, Williamsburg, VA.
Source: Photo courtesy of Colonial Williamsburg Foundation.

Building codes can also affect pattern. A good example is the barring of wood frame construction in downtown areas. This occurred following Chicago's great fire of 1871, after which a fire prevention ordinance had the effect of creating a four- to five-story brick and stone downtown and, simultaneously, a new band of subdivision just outside the regulated area. Since workers could not afford masonry, the regulation created a belt of wooden, workingmen's cottages on the outskirts of the city (*Chicago Tribune*, 1872, cited in Hoyt 1933, 104).

A more direct use of rules to create urban pattern was the *Laws of the Indies*, a sixteenth-century ordinance imposed by the Spanish monarchy for laying out colonies. This code, which has been traced to the writings of the first century BCE Roman architect Vitruvius, dictated street arrangement, street width, public spaces

Figure 3.2. Williamsburg, Virginia, today.

(a central plaza), arcades, and the location of important buildings. It is possible to see traces of these laws in places like Los Angeles, Tucson, and Santa Fe, but very few towns followed the specifications closely (Reps 1965).

The next episode of rule-based urban patterning occurred in colonial New England. Some of the Thirteen Colonies had laws that mapped future street locations, and these were called "mapped street laws." These controls were later "forced out by adverse court decisions," only to be reinstated many years later through a different mechanism, the plat approval process of subdivision regulations (Van Nest Black 1935, 8, 9). In the early twentieth century, platting rules regarding size of blocks, lots, and streets were transformed into a new field called subdivision design (Diggs 1939, 29). The official city plat regulated public streets, private land, utility easements, and public lands, but more importantly, it was the basis for ownership titles, deeds, taxation, and insurance. Once recorded, the plat was very difficult to change.

Another main generator of the urban pattern in the United States was the Land Ordinance of 1785. Championed by Thomas Jefferson, the ordinance set the rules by which all publicly owned land west of the Appalachian Mountains would be subdivided. Right angles and numbering systems were not always consistent, but eventually most of the country was laid out in townships that were 6 miles square in square-mile sections. These were cut into fours, creating 160 acre quarter-sections that would be sold to each settler in "forties"—40 acre parcels. It was the same system the Romans had used two thousand years earlier (with differently sized units), and most of the cities and towns in the United States within the surveyed territory (Ohio and west), constituting some two thirds of the present United States, have the imprint of the original survey (Marschner 1958). In essence, it was the urban grid of Philadelphia imprinted on agricultural land. How cities were to be formed within this system must have "slipped the minds" of the grid designers (Stilgoe 1983, 256). In any event, cities—streets, blocks, lots, buildings—strongly conformed to the orthogonal pattern the Ordinance created. Chicago's 300 by 600 foot blocks fit the township divisions particularly well.

The effects of the Land Ordinance on Chicago's lot and block pattern are readily visible in figure 3.3: mostly square-mile sections (red square), except for the occa-

Figure 3.3. Northwestern section of Chicago, Illinois. The effects of the Land Ordinance are readily visible: mostly square-mile sections, except for the occasional platting flourish (Norwood).

sional platting flourish (Norwood), and the triangularization created by diagonal roads. The density in this section of Chicago is about 6.25 units per acre (gross).

Within a tract, there could be some variation in terms of how blocks were subdivided. Figure 3.4 shows some possible block arrangements for 40 acre tracts. According to Hoyt's analysis (1933, 431), "A" made sense (i.e., would yield the most aggregate value) where "each square foot is of equal importance"; "C," the most common arrangement, made sense for residential or apartment use; "D" made sense for commercial use since it has the most street frontage, but it is unrealistic because no subdivision would be composed entirely of commercial lots (Hoyt did not comment on the value of arrangements "B" and "E").

The Land Ordinance worked like a code, stamping, John Reps complained, "an identical brand of uniformity and mediocrity on American cities coast to coast" (Reps 1965, 314; see also Linklater 2002). Because of the Land Ordinance survey, a rectangular block plan was basically forced on subdividers. As Homer Hoyt described it in his book *One Hundred Years of Land Values in Chicago*, "except for the circular plan of Norwood, practically the only deviations from the rectangular lot and block plan of Chicago are caused by the radial and axial highways which cut across section lines at oblique angles and create many triangular and truncated lots along their route" (1933, 428).

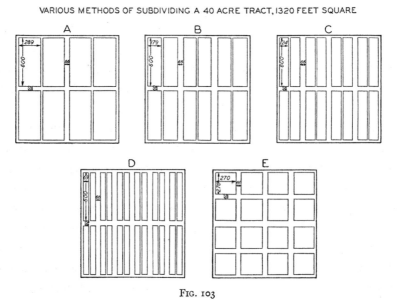

Figure 3.4. Block arrangements for 40 acre tracts, analyzed by Homer Hoyt.
Source: Hoyt (1933).

The delineation of lots and blocks in the platting process was permanent, and nearly impossible to change, unless the subdivider failed to sell the lots. New York City's 1811 Commissioners Plan, with its blocks of 200 by 600–800 feet covering Manhattan, is a classic example of the lasting imprint of land division. Platting—the further subdivision of land within the basic outlines laid down by the Land Ordinance—could be done quickly. A nineteenth-century history of Chicago described the process like this (Andreas, cited in Hoyt 1933, 30):

> The prairies of Illinois, the forests of Wisconsin, and the sand hills of Michigan presented a chain almost unbroken of supposititious villages and cities. The whole land seemed staked out and peopled on paper. . . . [Subdividers] would besiege the land offices and purchase town sites at a dollar and a quarter per acre, which in a few days appeared on paper, laid out in the most approved rectangular fashion, emblazoned in glaring colors, and exhibiting the public spirit of the proprietor in the multitude of their public squares, church lots and school lot reservations.

Earlier platting was much finer grained than today. Example dimensions from four cities are shown in figures 3.5–3.8. Approximate block sizes are 250 by 350 feet for Chicago, 200 by 630 feet for the longest blocks in Homedale, 600 feet square in Palmcroft, and 350 by 400 feet for Rome City, Indiana. Section by section, cities, towns, and neighborhoods were created from these rules of land subdivision. When plats were created one section at a time, this not only created a finer grain but permitted a more responsive patterning in which lower-density, more rural treatments with longer blocks were likely platted in locations farther away, while areas closer to the core were platted with much smaller blocks and a finer grain. Importantly, parcels faced the main streets, as shown on figure 3.7.

The application of rules about lot size is one of those aspects of urban regulation that seems to have started out innocuously, before it turned into a method of social segregation. Rules governing minimum lot size were included in a building ordinance in Philadelphia in 1892, which stipulated that an adequate amount of yard per family should be provided "in the part of the city devoted to the construction of dwelling houses" (Davies 1958). Soon after, minimum lot size rules increased because of rules about building lot coverage. A bigger building required the piecing together of lots, as in New York, where the standard lot size of 25 by 100 feet, coupled with the rule that towers could not exceed one fourth of the lot area, sparked lot mergers.

Often, concern for the development process seemed to overshadow attention to pattern (Knack, Meck, and Stollman 1996). In 1911, Charles Mulford Robinson and

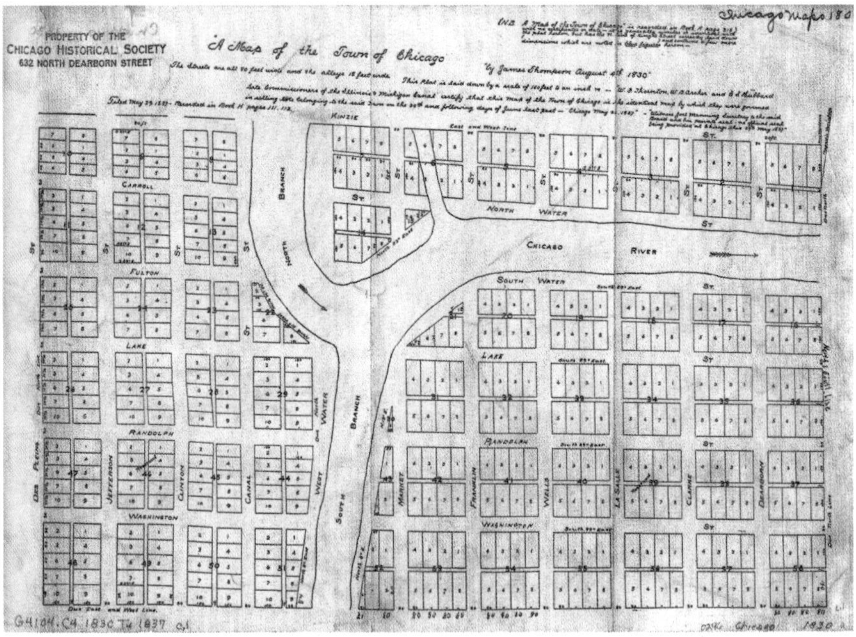

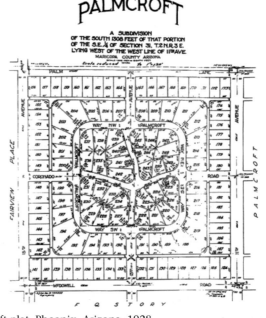

Figure 3.5. Thompson's Plat of 1830, Chicago, Illinois.
Source: Chicago Historical Society.

Figure 3.6. Palmcroft plat, Phoenix, Arizona, 1928.
Source: Encanto-Palmcroft Historic Preservation Association.

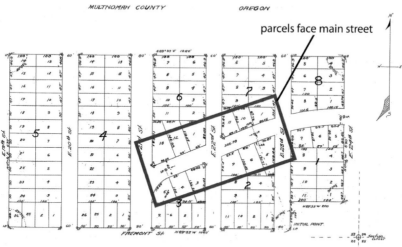

Figure 3.7. Homedale plat, Portland, Oregon.
Source: Alameda Old House History, alamedahistory.org.

Figure 3.8. A section of the plat of Rome City, Indiana.
Source: Indiana Historical Society.

others associated with the fledgling city planning movement were advocating for a Uniform City Planning Code that would focus primarily on street platting and the reservation of sites for future public use. The code was mostly dedicated to spelling out the process—rules for platting procedure rather than rules for platting pattern. They were strongly motivated by a desire to overcome what they saw as the uniformity of American cities and towns. They especially disdained the checkerboard planning that was the norm (Robinson 1916 discusses this at length), and they blamed Jefferson's 1785 Land Ordinance for imprinting a rectangular system of streets and blocks that compelled landowners to conform to it.

Planners in the 1920s were hoping that innovative subdivision layouts in places like Roland Park, Baltimore; Country Club District in Kansas City; Rancho Santa Fe in California; and other "parklike subdivisions" would trickle down into better sub-division design overall and move the country away from "stock type plats." This would include "streets adapted to topography" and "the fitting of block sizes to special needs" (Hubbard and Hubbard 1929, 155). To a twenty-first-century observer, the problem of poor adaptation seems like a minor point next to the problem of urban sprawl. Most early planners seemed blind to the larger problem that an ex-pansion of parklike subdivision platting would create. There are exceptions—some planners looked to subdivision regulations as a way of controlling urban growth. Cincinnati, for example, required utilities to be in place prior to plat approval and the sale of lots to prevent "costly problems of scattering development and suburban slums" (Hubbard and Hubbard 1929, 153). Mostly, subdivision standards were pro-posed in an attempt to maintain control over pattern and, it was believed, a higher-quality development. These involved rules about the platting of lots and blocks and the laying out of streets and open spaces (see box 3.1).

Subdivision regulations contained rules about street lengths and widths. These can have a significant social effect. Historians have shown how the patterns created from street rules meant that the city moved from "enclosed courts and alleys with shared space" to an open pattern where people and social worlds were highly inter-connected, leading, somewhat ironically, to greater public–private separation (Daun-ton 1983; Konvitz 1985). Rules for long, straight streets tend to prioritize traffic flow,

Box 3.1. Street regulations contained in subdivision regulations, 1929

Adjustment to adjoining street system	Provision of utilities
Street and subdivision names	Relation of streets to railroads
Street alignment	Building lines
Street planting	Treatment of dead-end streets
Street intersection and corner radii	Street grades
Alleys and easements	Street widths
Carrying of streets to boundary lines	

Source: Hubbard and Hubbard (1929, 147).

while rules based on pedestrian connectivity favor shorter streets. In the early twentieth century, planners advocated a rule of "1 to 25" for a width to length proportion,
some arguing that streets that are more grand (like boulevards) should not be longer
than three-quarters of a mile "as beyond this the eye is unable to distinguish the
focal point in which such streets should generally terminate" (Triggs 1909, 242).
Frederick Law Olmsted Sr. was similarly cognizant of the way in which streets, along
with alleys, blocks, and lots, could be used as "city-shaping devices" (Macdonald
2005, 296). By the 1920s, magazine articles with titles like "Tower Buildings and
Wider Streets: A Suggested Relief for Traffic Congestion" (Hood 1927) were beginning to signal the overthrow of rules aimed at place and design concerns in favor of
rules aimed at traffic flow and efficiency.

Subdivision regulations affected the size and dimensions of lots and blocks. These
seemed to be based on conflicting motivations. On the one hand, larger lots and
blocks had the effect of excluding those who could not afford larger lots, and planners were aware that rules about lot size and coverage promoted class segregation
"unnecessarily" (Lasker 1920, 279). On the other hand, having minimum standards
was believed to be a matter of social justice, resulting in higher standards for poor
neighborhoods. Milwaukee mayor Emil Seidel, the first socialist mayor of a major
American city, pitched the regulation of block sizes as a way of reducing costs and
helping the poor, writing in 1910 that "it is ridiculous to have streets every 300 or
400 feet. To build a city that way is economic waste." He wanted "fat" 50-foot lots
for "sunlight and fresh air from every direction" (cited in Davies 1958, 69). In con-
cert, members of the National Association of Real Estate Brokers (NAREB) were publicly urging that "no subdivision should be offered the poor people that lacks modern
improvements" (Davies 1958, 69).

And yet, most planners seemed oblivious to the issue that platting regulations
could be used to exclude certain segments of the population by making higher-
density, more affordable housing types infeasible. In fact, prohibiting higher density was exactly the point. Thomas Adams wrote that street design could make it
"impracticable" to erect apartments, and he saw that as a worthy objective (Adams
1932, 74). In the 1920s, planners emphasized that lots should not be too deep because that would encourage the construction of rear dwellings, "the forerunners of
slum growth" (Augur 1923, 16). These provisions were designed to make low-cost
housing better, not exclude it altogether. The control of platting was considered to
be "far more necessary for low-cost home neighborhoods . . . than for higher cost
homes on larger lots." Hubbard and Hubbard believed that the U.S. Shipping Board

and Housing Corporation towns of 1918–19 offered valuable "object lessons in lot planning" for just this reason—affordable housing on adequately sized lots (Hubbard and Hubbard 1929, 156).

It is also significant that the dimensions of what was considered a minimum standard changed dramatically. In 1912, the developer J. C. Nichols's "rules of thumb" for single-family homes was "25 × 100 feet . . . sometimes they are 30 feet" (Davies 1958, 70). Tracy Augur, a prominent planner during the 1920s, argued that single-family dwellings "very desirable in every way" could be built in attached rows without side yard requirements, and "even a twenty foot lot is by no means too narrow if equipped with the proper type of house" (Augur 1923, 18). The very upper limit of housing in New York's 1916 zoning code was the single-family detached house on a 40 or 50 foot lot. The "Zoning Engineer" of Des Moines, Iowa, called for a minimum lot area of 3,000 square feet per family for single-family residence districts (Taubert 1926). In Cleveland's 1922 ordinance, the most restrictive residential district required 5,000 square feet of lot area per family, and the least restrictive required only 312 square feet per family (Whitten and Walker 1921). This was not unusual—for multifamily districts, many cities had a restriction of 300 or 400 square feet of lot area per family (Taubert 1926). At one point Lawrence Veiller, a housing advocate, proposed that blocks ought to be only 25 to 30 feet deep "so as to get apartments only two doors deep between streets." Despite a "storm of disapproval" for this proposal, respected planning figures like Raymond Unwin and Thomas Adams thought Veiller's proposal had merit (Ford 1911, 213).

Early planners were aware that smaller lot dimensions could be a problem if too much housing was crammed onto one lot. Twenty-five-foot lots helped to create the miserable conditions of tenement housing in New York City and prompted the 1901 Tenement House Law requiring buildings with more light and air. Britain's Bye-law Street Ordinance of 1875 had been similarly motivated by the need for more light and air and required wider, straighter streets in an effort to open up neighborhoods that had small lots and high coverage. Earlier, London's 1593 "Act Against New Buildings" was intended to prevent overbuilding but ended up worsening living conditions for the poor by restricting housing supply (Layfield, cited in Weaver and Babcock 1980).

Rules about lot size and building coverage transformed gradually in response to market pressures. In Chicago, a 1910 ordinance required that windows be set back 3 feet from side lot lines, and this had the effect of making lots wider—increasing from 25 feet to 30 feet as the standard dimension. According to Hoyt (1933), the change was market driven: in conjunction with the 3 foot setback rule, a 25 foot lot had less than half the value of a 30 foot lot. Hoyt analyzed other arrangements to show how the basic 40 acre square was being subdivided according to market preference. By 1929, the most prevalent minimum lot width, as determined by a national survey, was 40 feet (Hubbard and Hubbard 1929). Rules changed to reflect the preference for larger lots, and lot size requirements in many places increased steadily after World War II (e.g., McDonald 2004).

As with lot size, rules for block sizes were significantly smaller in the early decades of the twentieth century. In 1929, the range was around 200–600 feet (e.g., Akron, OH, and Springfield, MA). Chicago set a maximum of 800 feet, while Richmond, Virginia, and Sacramento, California, had a maximum of 1,000 feet. Planners were aware that blocks that were too long would "interfere with proper circulation and access." They favored "six to eight hundred feet as a general maximum," explicitly stating that "minimum block lengths should not be specified" and that "pedestrian footways" should be provided wherever blocks were longer than 600 or 700 feet (Augur 1923, 24).

Early planners were hopeful that zoning could be effectively managed scientifically. Baltimore's Board of Zoning Appeals bragged in 1925 that their zoning ordinance "was a technically accurate piece of work based on mathematics" (Baltimore Board of Zoning Appeals 1925, 4). In part this was a defensive strategy. Planners continually warned that zoning rules would be thrown out unless they were based on a "comprehensive zone plan for the whole territory of the community, and not a mere attempt to pick out specific spots or portions and exclude special uses or developments therefrom" (Bettman 1926, 26).

The initial German conception of zoning was fairly sophisticated in terms of the prescribed pattern of urban functions. Baumeister's concept of districting was built on a well-developed spatial ideal of the city, which we would today call "sustainable": workers, housing, and services were to be in close proximity in all areas, and the organization of these functions was to vary by level of intensity, depending on location. Thus, on busier commercial streets, living quarters were above shops, while on quieter streets, live/work units (the "shop/house") were deemed more appropriate. In the United States, planners had initially followed suit, arguing that "small-lot districts" should be "closer to the center of activity of the community." Bassett wrote that "the logical places" for apartments were either in a buffer district between businesses and single-family houses, along main thoroughfares, or near a railroad station (Bassett 1925a).

German planners used zoning rules to maintain a pattern in which density resided at the urban center, leaving the periphery for lower-intensity, detached buildings in the form of either larger estates or worker's cottages. Williams described the underlying premise of the 1912 Dusseldorf ordinance in terms of its effect on pattern as follows: "the bulk of structures, in proportion to the area of their lots, decreases as the distance from the centers of business, congestion and high land value becomes greater" (1922, 251). Thus large-lot zoning had a role to play in early German zoning, but it wasn't about social exclusion. The pattern created was based on an intensity gradient, whereby buildings were regulated according to location. This had been the primary motivation for zoning in the first place—the problem of uniformly applied building regulations. The premise of zoning was that different types of places needed to have different types of rules (Logan 1972). New York's 1916 zoning code was structured similarly, where land use was regulated according to "intensity of building development." The intensity of each district depended upon "the character of occupation and use in that particular district" (New York City 1916, chap. 4, 25, 26).

The zoning pattern proposed by German planners, such as that shown in figure 3.9, seems a model of spatial logic. Near public parks and playing fields—urban open space—a row of "small-sized residential buildings" lies adjacent, but these are immediately surrounded by higher-intensity ("medium-sized") residential buildings. These are next to, and protected from, a row of commercial buildings fronting shopping streets. The tightly grained pattern reflected in these rules would mean that virtually everyone in the town would have good access to amenities.

Herbert Hoover's proposal in the 1930s to separate housing types into single-family, two-family, and multifamily unit types might have made sense had the higher-density housing been closer in and more accessible to urban amenities. The problem, however, was that Hoover's commission discussed separation apart from any kind of spatial pattern—in other words, apart from a *plan*. Although they did discuss the need for "access to local shopping centers in each residence neighborhood," and that "the ideal arrangement would permit a citizen to walk to his work," none of this was worked out in a codified, spatially explicit way. If it had been, they would have seen that there was a fundamental conflict being created with another common goal at the time: that "open spaces should increase proportionately" with population density (Gries and Ford 1931, 32).

At first, the pattern codified by early zoning ordinances was mostly a reflection of what had been developed through standardized platting procedures in conjunc-

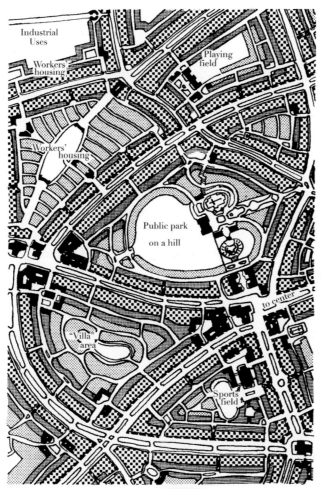

Figure 3.9. A 1904 proposed zoning scheme for a hypothetical town in Germany.
Source: Logan (1972).

▨▨▨	Commercial buildings
▦▦▦	Medium-sized residential buildings
▭▭▭	Small-sized residential buildings
- - -	Arcades
◣◢	Public buildings or other landmarks

tion with small-scale housing and commercial development. One town boasted: "The zoning problem in Middletown is greatly simplified by the fact that during its long slow growth the city has largely zoned itself according to logical principles of development" (Hinckley 1926, 56). But as zoning matured, the connection to "natural" urban development patterns was gradually lost (Goodrich 1939, 68). Of course, the whole reason for zoning in the first place was that people were unhappy with what had been evolving without rules. Many were especially unhappy with the un-

regulated mixing of uses, as there seemed to be nothing natural about it. Zoning bat-
tles often boiled down to a disconnect between the market-led progression of development that had been occurring (where, for example, stores were located in
residential neighborhoods), and the new patterns zoning rules were trying to impose. For a time, the disjuncture proved too great. In 1926, four out of five court decisions ruled against zoning (Bassett 1926b).

Rules were also aimed at correcting the effects of transportation systems. Initially
the view was that "a city's present transit system" would "lay down the lines of growth
and development for years to come" (Holliday 1922, 219), and rules were made ac-
cordingly. Edward Bassett, the lawyer who championed New York City's landmark
zoning ordinance in 1916, wanted zoning to be a countervailing force to the subway,
which he believed was unnecessarily concentrating population near subway entrances, increasing density in older "settled residential neighborhoods." Similarly, developer J. C. Nichols thought that shopping centers should be "built horizontally and
not vertically" (Nichols 1926, 19)—which may have made sense at a time when
sprawl, traffic congestion, and environmental degradation were of little concern.
Rather than sprawl, it was urban concentration that was seen as "appalling"—skyscrapers blocked light and air, noxious industrial uses polluted neighborhoods, values
skyrocketed, and the city became unbearable (Makielski 1966, 10). The view that the
remedy was to spread things out was backed by science: urban density was seen as a
major cause of tuberculosis and other health problems (Knopf 1909).

Until the late twentieth century, the decentralized pattern rules help create
seemed not to provoke much concern among practicing planners. New York's 1959
guide to rezoning listed the problems zoning needed to address: more parking, faster
traffic flow, and "a glimpse of the sky and a bit of open space" (Citizens' Housing and
Planning Council 1959, 1). This viewpoint was not confined to large cities. A 1956
informational pamphlet about zoning in Saginaw, Michigan, explained that
multiple-family dwellings required "large open spaces around buildings so that multiple dwellings will not crowd the land next to single or two-family dwellings" (Saginaw 1956, 4). The city of Phoenix, with a population of only 110,000 in 1950,
instituted a Planned Shopping Center zone that required a minimum of 5 acres, further promoting a spread-out, automobile-dependent city.

There was some awareness, however, that decentralization allowed by rules was
bad for business. The Urban Land Institute estimated in 1941 that Boston had lost
as much real estate value due to decentralization as London had during the Nazi
bombings (Urban Land Institute 1941). Lewis Mumford argued that the mechanisms

largely put into place with the help of planners—zoning, especially—had reduced the city's capacity to foster its primary function of human exchange—"the maximum interplay of capacities and functions" (Mumford 1949, 38). But some planners seemed to lose sight of the role rules played. One prominent planner, New York's director of the Department of City Planning, recommended in 1956 that zones requiring "plenty of open space around a house" should be located in areas "relatively close in, so that those who want this type of living will not necessarily have to travel several hours a day to and from work" (Williams 1956, 259). With these kinds of views, and despite more populist claims, it is sometimes hard to argue against the view that zoning sought "the greatest good for the fewest and richest in number," assuring more light and air for higher-income people no matter where they lived, and leaving the lower classes to live in homes adjacent to manufacturing and commercial uses (Power 1989, 7).

Effects

Today, communities seem to pay little attention to the random and disorganized patterns their rules are creating. Compared to the simplicity and clarity of earlier zoning codes, zoning ordinances now seem indecipherable. In order to satisfy an increasingly paranoiac need to control, sort, and exclude, rules became more and more complex over the course of the twentieth century. This has only further strained the link between code and on-the-ground effect.

This complexity is evident in many recent zoning codes, such as the one for Phoenix, Arizona, with its hundreds of amendments—246 of them since 1990 (table 3.1). The code is complex both in terms of the content, with its hundreds of amendments, and in the pattern of zones. In contrast to Frankfurt's original zoning map from the late nineteenth century (fig. 2.2), Phoenix's ordinance is a complex array of hundreds of different zoning categories (fig. 3.10). There are approximately 264 zones, the result of a variety of overlayed permutations—the "PCD planned community district" zone over the "R1-6" zone, for example.

It wasn't always this way. Figures 3.11 and 3.12 show how the number and pattern of zones changed for one section of downtown Phoenix between 1930 and 2004. The increase in the number and complexity of zones was due to a variety of ad hoc decisions. The area, a section of which is shown in figure 3.13, has developed into a hodge-podge collection of building types and uses, from corporate office towers to single-family homes—not a desirable pattern of mixed use.

Whether or not pattern is considered in some meaningful way is essential to the

Table 3.1. Phoenix, AZ, Zoning Ordinance: 246 Zoning Ordinance Amendments since November 1990

G-4559   Creates Sections 662 and 663 pertaining to Transit Oriented O.L. Districts

G-4566   Amends various sections pertaining to Commercial Development Standards

G-4596   Renumber Four Corners Overlay District from Section 656 to Section 660 to correct an error in Ord. No. G-4493

G-4602   Amends Section 662, Interim Transit-Oriented Zoning Overlay District (TOD-1); Section 663, Interim Transit-Oriented Overlat District (TOD-2); Added Section 647.A.2 hh. and ii

G-4603   Amends Ch. 8, Historic Preservation

G-4611   Amends Sections 202, 507 Tab A and 705, relating to dust proofing and signs

G-4629   Creates Section 664, pertaining to North Central Avenue Special Planning District (SPD) Overlay District

G-4650   Amends Section 655, Rio Salado Overlay District

G-4678   Relating to furniture auctions in C-2 District

G-4679   Relating to Residential density bonuses

G-4681   To increase the number of days to hear a zoning adjustment hearing; change appeal fees

G-4685   Relating to custom decorative wrought iron shops in C-3 District

G-4686   Relating to solid waste transfer stations

G-4690   Relating to access; circulation adjacent to park sites

G-4694   Amending Ord. No. G-4679; changing § 3 of said ordinance from 609.B.2 to 610.B.2

G-4702   Added "Airport Noise Impact Overlay (AIO) District"

G-4703   Fines for Zoning Ordinance Violations

G-4723   Prohibiting sexually oriented businesses in the Downtown Core and Warehouse Overlay Districts

G-4724   To increase the applicability for single-family design review standards

G-4739   To allow auto body and auto sales inventory storage lots in C-2 Zone, and subject to a special permit and to allow 8-foot block walls

G-4745   To clarify and/or add to the Transient-Oriented Development regarding high rise signage, 50% glass on ground floor, structural shading, build-to lines and parking

G-4748   Creates the East Buckeye Road Interim Overlay District

G-4759   Regarding temporary civic event parking in historic neighborhoods

G-4761   Allows sales and repair of musical instruments and sound systems

G-4769   Regarding off-street parking

G-4783   Establishes the Seventh Avenue Urban Main Street Overlay (SAUMSO) District

G-4784**   Relating to Airport Zoning; Zoning Commission; Airport Zoning Map (**The user's attention is directed to Ch. 4, Art. XIII, of the City of Phoenix Code of Ordinances)

G-4792   Amending Ordinance No. G-4783

G-4814   Added Squaw Peak Heights Special Planning District Overlay District

G-4815   Adds definition of lot area

G-4816   Added Church and school as permitted use in C-O, Commercial Office and R-O, Residential Office District

G-4817   Defines Non-Chartered Financial institutions and add as permitted use to C-1 District

G-4819   Interpretation, administration and enforcement of Special Planning Districts (Section 402); added Special Planning and Specific Plan Overlay Districts (Section 669)

G-4840   Definition of a "story"

G-4841   Created an Airport Overlay District for Deer Valley Airport

G-4857   Regarding use of tandem parking

G-4863   Off-Premises Signs

G-4864   Amending Commerce Park District

G-4867   Amending Deer Valley Airport Overlay District

G-4874   Increase boundaries of the Downtown Core District

G-4882   Modifying the development and design guidelines for structures within the Warehouse Overlay District

G-4887   Changes the method of classifying explosives

G-4937   Allowing recreational vehicle parking as an accessory use to a hospital

G-4938   Revising vesting language and simplify and update procedures for Planned Community Districts

G-5037   Revising development standards for places of worship

G-5050   R-4A—Simplifying building heights standards

G-5051   Eliminating the gap in allowable height

G-5084   Adding Biomedical and medical research offices and/or laboratories as a permitted use

G-5085   Deleting the requirement for rezoning to R-4 or R-5 upon completion of a project

G-5086   Deleting the requirement for rezoning to H-R or H-R1 upon completion of a project

G-5107   Amended Urban Residential, to remove applicability limitations and clarify other portions

G-5136   Pertaining to Landscaping, fences and walls, regarding the allowable height and location of fences and retaining walls

G-5137   Adding Planned Unit Development and amending the Fee Schedule

G-5138   Adding to Arts, Culture and Small Business Overlay District (ACOD) and amending the

Table 3.1. continued

Fee Schedule

G-5179   Amending *PHOENIX CITY CODE, Chapter 4 Aviation, Article XIII, Airport Zoning, replacing all existing text with the exception of the recently approved downtown zone (Section 4-240.F) and establish height limits for obstacles in the vicinity of Phoenix Sky Harbor International Airport that are not covered by the existing downtown zone.

G-5181   Amending Section 202; Adding the Hatcher Road Overlay (HRO) District

G-5217   Amending Section 649, Mixed Use Agricultural (MUA) District

G-5242   Amending C-2 Intermediate Commercial; C-3 General; A-1 Light Industrial Commercial

G-5243   Amending Definitions; Guidelines for Design Review; S-1 Suburban, Ranch or Farm Residence; RE-43 Residential Estate; RE-24 Residential Estates; Residence Districts; R-O Residential Office; C-O Commercial Office

G-5244   Amending Definitions; TOD-1; TOD-2

G-5267   Amending Off-Street Parking and Loading

G-5268   Amending Definitions; C-1 Neighborhood Retail and C-2 Intermediate Commercial

G-5290   Amending Definitions and Off-Street Loading Spaces

G-5329   Amending Various Portions of the Zoning Ordinance Regarding Wireless Communication Facilities and Satellite Earth Stations

G-5329   Satellite Earth Stations and Wireless Communication Facilities

G-5330   Regarding Master Planned Development Sign Plans

G-5351   Repealing the Squaw Peak Heights Special Planning District (SPD) Overlay District

G-5379   Ordinance Allowing All Designated City Staff to Enforce the Standards or Stipulations Imposed as a Part of the Various Development Plans or Subdivision Plats approved by the Development Services Department

G-5380   Amending Various Sections of the Zoning Ordinance to Delete Recovery Homes

G-5391   Amending the Zoning Fee Schedule

G-5440   Amending Ch. 2, to Define Bus Terminal and Bus Depot; Section 623 to add as Allowed Uses

G-5447   Regarding the Placement of Recycling Containers on Commercial and Multi-family Developments

G-5448   Commercial C-1 District—Neighborhood Retail—To Eliminate Restrictions on the Location of Gas Stations and Automobile Service Stations

G-5449   Amending TOD-1 and TOD-2 to Address the Minimum Depth Requirement of Arcades, Awnings, Trellises or Covered Walkways Attached to Primary Building

G-5453   Amending Chapter 2 (definitions) and Section 702 (Off-Street Parking and Loading) to Allow Parking Reductions for Adaptive Reuse Projects

G-5480   Amending Definitions, Design Review

Standards Committee; Architectural Appeals Board; Development Review Approval and Establishing the Downtown Code

G-5499   Regarding Design Guidelines, Definitions and Hearing Processes for Manufactured and Modular Homes

G-5534   Provides Standards For the Use of Electronic Message Displays on Ground and Wall Signs

TA 10-00   Takings appeal process, takings appeal officer

TA 10-90   Chapter 9, Nonconformities

TA 10-91   Design Review Standards Committee

TA 10-93   Creating a new Downtown Core (DC) District

TA 10-94   Outdoor barbecue and cookout areas

TA 10-95   Wall signs over 56 feet

TA 10-97   Street classification and propane containers

TA 10-98   Parking structures and surface parking

TA 11-00   Citizen notification procedure

TA 11-90   Chapter 10, Enforcement

TA 11-91   Open land uses prior to annexation

TA 11-92   Regulation of day care facilities

TA 11-93   Creating a new Warehouse Overlay (W) District

TA 11-94   Amend infrastructure financing specific plans

TA 11-96   Blood banks and blood plasma centers

TA 11-97   Dependent care facilities

TA 11-98   Parking requirements

TA 12-90   Development review

TA 12-91   Cellular phone monopoles and roof-mounted antennae

TA 12-93   Regulation of commercial thermal remediation facilities

TA 12-94   Design guidelines for communication towers

TA 12-97   Urban Residential District

TA 12-98   Neighborhood maintenance and enforcement

TA 13-90   Retaining walls and other technical issues of residential development

TA 13-90   Issues of residential development

TA 13-91   Section 633, High-Rise Incentive District

TA 13-92   Adoption of stipulations as part of the ordinance that changes zoning classifications

TA 13-93   Regulation of bed and breakfast establishments

TA 13-94   Thermal treatment of contaminated soil

TA 13-96   Wall signs over 56 feet

TA 13-97   Warehouse District Parking Overlay

TA 13-98   Single-family design standards

TA 14-90   Pocket shelters

TA 14-91   Preparation, distribution, and delivery of newspapers, periodicals, and other published materials

TA 14-92/15-92   Revision of the Sign Code

Table 3.1. continued

TA 15-91   Copy and reproduction centers in the C-O and R-5 districts

TA 15-92   Organization of Section 705, the Sign Code

TA 15-93   Fences/walls within hillside development areas

TA 15-94   Stadium and accessory uses in Downtown Core and Warehouse Overlay Districts

TA 15-96   Subdivision sales offices

TA 16-91   Governmental uses

TA 16-98   Standards for nonconforming uses

TA 17-91   Outdoor recreational uses as accessory to bars or restaurants

TA 17-92   Definition and regulation of adult novelty store

TA 17-93   Regulation of liquor-related uses

TA 17-B-93   Martial arts

TA 18-91   Public utility buildings and facilities

TA 18-92   Water conservation design review guidelines

TA 18-93   Regulation of compressed natural gas in the C-2 district

TA 1-91   Propane storage and sales

TA 1-92   Massage facilities as accessory to tanning salons

TA 1-93   Residential convenience markets in multiple-family districts

TA 1-94   Amending 308.B, composition and membership of Design Review Standards Committee

TA 1-95   Private prisons in Industrial, A-1 and A-2 districts

TA 1-96   Outdoor retail food sales in C-2

TA 1-97   Adult theaters

TA 1-98-6-8   Baseline Area Overlay District

TA 19-91   Group home regulations and the Fair Housing Amendments Act of 1988

TA 19-92   Deletion of section 307.A.7.c, the Transient and Inebriate Ordinance

TA 19-93   Calculation of area of high-rise wall signs

TA 19-98   Accommodating accessible parking spaces on existing parking lots

TA 20-91   Explosives and uses not permitted within the City limits

TA 20-93   Allowance of homeless shelters in the A-2, Heavy Industrial, District

TA 21-91   Spacing of adult businesses from the R1-14 district

TA 21-92   Amending section 620.A, purpose and intent of the R-O, Residential Office District

TA 22-91   Accessible parking standards

TA 22-92   Placement of billboards along freeway locations

TA 24-92   Boundaries of the Central City Village Core as described in the C-1, C-2 and C-3 zoning districts

TA 2-91   Signage for hospitals

TA 2-92   Massage therapists in conjunction with beauty salons

TA 2-94   Regulation of adult uses in C-2, C-3, A-1 and Downtown Core Zoning Districts

TA 2-96   Bus depots

TA 2-97   Wireless communication antennae, monopoles and related facilities

TA 2-98   Mixed Use Agricultural District

TA 2-99   New design standards for single- and multiple-family development

TA 3-00   Halfway houses, jails and prisons

TA 3-00   Transitional housing facilities

TA 3-00   Special permit uses: transitional housing facility

TA 3-00   Correctional transitional housing facilities and private prisons

TA 3-91   Accessible parking standards

TA 3-92   Clarification of historic preservation demolition appeals

TA 3-93   Dustproofing requirements for single-family and duplex uses

TA 3-94   Regulation of building height in A-1 and A-2

TA 3-95   Political signs

TA 3-96   Retaining walls

TA 3-97   Propane cylinder regulation

TA 4-00   Prohibited uses: commercial hazardous waste treatment, storage and disposal facilities

TA 4-00   Fee for request to waive prohibition against establishment of certain hazardous waste facilities

TA 4-90   Recycling facilities

TA 4-91   Specific plan amendments

TA 4-92   Obsolete sections of section 307

TA 4-93   Biomedical offices and accessory laboratories in the R-5 district

TA 4-95   Parking of commercial vehicles in Residential Districts

TA 4-96   Board of Adjustment appeals

TA 4-97   Drive-through facilities for restaurants

TA 4-99-4   Historic Canal-Side Restaurant Overlay District

TA 5-00   Special permit uses: limited outdoor uses in General Commerce Park District

TA 5-90   Special signage including animation for major community facilities

TA 5-91   Commercial loading of ammunition

TA 5-92   Design review standards

TA 5-93   Add "crematorium" to the permitted uses in the A-1 zoning district

TA 5-97   Demolition of Historic District properties

TA 5-98   Increased notice for specific plan public hearings

TA 5-99   Design Guidelines for single-family residential

TA 6-91   Section 608, Residence districts

TA 6-92   Technical issues of section 705, the Sign Code

Table 3.1. continued

TA 6-95	Capitol Mall Overlay District
TA 6-96	Newspaper distribution centers
TA 6-97	Development regulations along canal banks
TA 7-90	Organizational structure
TA 7-91	Commercial schools in C-O districts
TA 7-92	Radio and television broadcasting stations in the Commercial Office (C-O) District
TA 7-93	Limitations on the height of accessory structures in required residential rear yards
TA 7-94	Definition of "shade structure"
TA 7-96	Establishment of new Golf Course (GC) District
TA 7-97	City-wide design review guidelines
TA 7-98	Regulation of wireless communication antennae when attached to public utility poles or lattice-type tower structures
TA 8-90	Temporary signs/banners
TA 8-91	Interim regulations to replace the Transient and Inebriate Ordinance
TA 8-92	Interim stabilization regulation of hotels and motels
TA 8-93	Environmental remediation facility
TA 8-94	Regulation of satellite antennae in commercial installations
TA 8-96	Secondhand/used merchandise, sales
TA 8-97	Guesthouses
TA 9-00	Mobile vendors
TA 9-90	Chapter 1, Purpose and Applicability
TA 9-91	Temporary signs
TA 9-92	Interim stabilization regulation of sale of secondhand goods
TA 9-93	Restriction of residential development in commercial districts
TA 9-93B	Restriction of residential development in commercial districts
TA 9-94	Thermal treatment of contaminated soil
TA 9-96	Design guidelines for Historic Districts
TA 9-97	Design review guidelines
TA 9-98	Temporary uses

Source: City of Phoenix, Arizona.

critique of American zoning. Changes to zoning ordinances over the course of the twentieth century constitute a gradual wearing down of the connection between place, character, and rule, to the point where zoning schemes became a seemingly random, ad hoc distribution of zones. There seems to be no meaningful set of principles guiding the pattern being created. A significant problem was that the relationship between where people lived and the things they needed to go about their daily lives was being undermined by city rules that were oblivious to these required patterns. This negligence coincided with a newfound reverence for supermobility: anyone could get anywhere with a car, so what did pattern matter? The problem was realized early on. Frederick Ackerman complained that zoning categories did not "stand in rational, functional relationships to each other," that zoning maps had become a "hopelessly confused pattern" with a "constantly increasing number of use categories" (Ackerman 1935, 21).

Absent a meaningful plan, the spatial logic of city building—that rules about *what* should depend on *where*—evolved into either an attempt to overzone for commercial development, or an ad hoc quest to separate uses. Though the pattern zoning rules established affected many dimensions of urban life—access, connection, proximity, and so on—these effects were gradually lost sight of. Regulations were applied as if floating in space somewhere, with little thought about their overall arrangement or

Figure 3.10. The zoning map of Phoenix: 264 zoning categories.
Source: City of Phoenix.

pattern, how one zone fits with another, how they collectively create patterns, and how, in aggregate, they can produce congested cores or peripheral wastelands.

Two examples from Phoenix show the absence of a connection between zoning category and spatial location. Figure 3.14 shows single-family zones, outlined in yellow, adjacent to an eight-lane freeway. A more appropriate spatial pattern would put

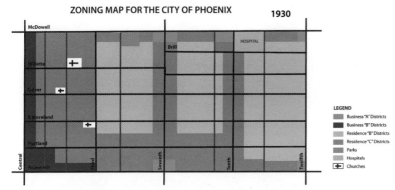

Figure 3.11. From logic to chaos: zoning in 1930 versus 2004 (shown in fig. 3.12) for a section of the downtown area of Phoenix.
Source: City of Phoenix.

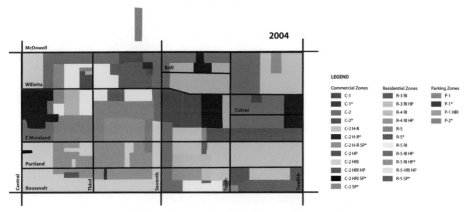

Figure 3.12. Zoning in 2004 for a section of the downtown area of Phoenix.
Source: City of Phoenix.

open space or more resilient uses adjacent to freeways—not single-family housing. The other example, figure 3.15, shows that, in the very core of downtown Phoenix, a stadium, a convention center, and lots of vacant land take up prime locations. There are no rules preventing these vacancies, despite the social and economic importance of centrally located land. In other places and times, from ancient Greece to the American colonies, rules would be enacted to require that land be put to good use in these kinds of central locations.

Zoning was initially conceived as a way of limiting congestion in the suburbs or around transit stops, but, in the face of sprawl and decentralization, this objective no longer makes sense. Absent a clear tie to urban realities, many rules seem to have nothing supporting them but inertia. Over time, such rules became dogma. Donald

Figure 3.13. A section of the area shown in figures 3.11 and 3.12 today: a hodge-podge of uses and building types.

Figure 3.14. Single-family zoning adjacent to freeways in Phoenix, Arizona.

Figure 3.15. The downtown of Phoenix, Arizona, showing vacant land and sprawl right into the core.

Shoup (2005) showed how outdated rules for parking were still in place due to just this kind of inertia. And with this blind attachment, there is little recourse for development that satisfies the intent of the law but fails the letter of it (Davis 1999).

It is difficult to change this inertia. Phoenix created the "residential infill" overlay zone in downtown areas, shown in figure 3.16, to try to stimulate infill development in more central locations (which makes sense from a spatial pattern point of view), but the requirements of the zone seem more suburban than urban. One problem is that the R-I (residential infill) district overlays the R-3, R-4, R-4A, and R-5 residential zones. The district is meant "to encourage new multifamily development within the central portion of Phoenix" because the city wants to encourage development "for people to live and work downtown," resulting in "greater use . . . of existing under-utilized public facilities and services." This is laudable, but the minimum lot area requirements of the R-I zone, even though intended as urban infill in a downtown area, are not particularly urban, despite their location. Subdivided lots must be at least 6,000 square feet and at least 60 by 94 feet. Units in R-3 RI must have 2,000 square feet of lot area per dwelling. Units in R-4 RI must have 1,250. Permitted uses do not go beyond what the residential zones allow.

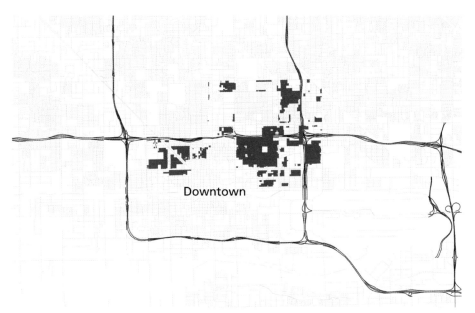

Downtown

Figure 3.16. Residential infill zones in Phoenix, Arizona.

Sometimes the problem with pattern is the placement of single-family zones adjacent to commercial uses—especially where these commercial uses have no particular neighborhood orientation. For example, figures 3.17, 3.18, and 3.19 show the pattern of zones and the corresponding situation on the ground. Bunny's (fig. 3.18), a car dealership, is located in a C-3 commercial zone (fig. 3.17). Directly across the street is a single-family house (fig. 3.19) in a "residential infill" zone. The existing rules reinforce this kind of pattern, where the rules allow single-family housing adjacent to a car dealership. There are no rules preventing these kinds of inappropriate adjacencies, where residences are juxtaposed with uses that have almost no neighborhood-serving utility.

Figures 3.20 and 3.21 show a similar situation, in which the juxtaposition of zones creates an unfortunate pattern. Shown is residential zoning adjacent to commercial zoning. With no attention to the regulation of form (as discussed in chap. 5), the adjacency of commercial and residential zones has no positive effect. R-5 RI is an overlay of the multifamily and residential infill zones.

Some rules prohibit multifamily housing in commercial zones in places where it might make sense to combine uses, if designed appropriately. Most often, however, rules provide no support for integrating use, and abrupt patterns emerge. Figure 3.22 shows this situation in Urbana, Illinois. While the B-3 commercial zone, outlined in

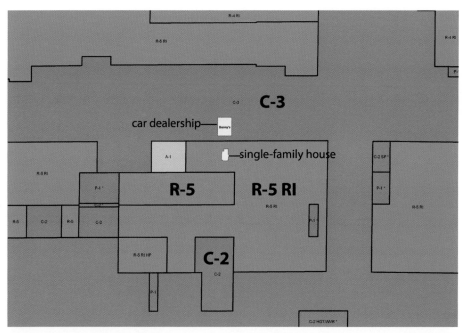

Figure 3.17. Zoning designations on the south side of Phoenix, Arizona: a single-family house (R-5 RI zone) adjacent to a car dealership (C-3 zone).

Figure 3.18. Car dealership in Phoenix in the C-3 zone, as shown in figure 3.17.

Figure 3.19. A single-family house adjacent to the car dealership (fig. 3.18), per zoning shown in figure 3.17.

red, allows multifamily dwellings with a special use permit, it is hard to get a special use permit for two reasons: neighborhood opposition, and because the city wants to maximize revenues from commercial use. Still, the resulting pattern in the area shows an array of unpatterned uses—single-family housing adjacent to large-format commercial structures, multifamily housing isolated by open space, with no thought given to the logic of the spatial patterns created. Perhaps this is a legacy of Thomas Adams, who had recommended that "residential areas should be surrounded by open areas so as to give them a certain degree of isolation from other neighborhoods" (Adams 1932, 74).

The Federal Housing Administration (FHA) has provided further impetus for a sprawling development pattern. Its standards for land subdivision had a significant impact on spreading things out and decentralizing, all of which was geared toward "uniformity of technique" (Federal Housing Administration [FHA] 1935). In the 1930s, the FHA advocated zoning whereby each land use would be "protected from the other by a logical sequence," rules that required "only one dwelling on each lot," as well as restrictive covenants that controlled "racial character" (Clark 1938, 112). Subsequent attempts to produce places of diversity and compactness have had to contend with this legacy of American rule making.

The progression of zoning in downtown Phoenix: 1930, 1978, and 2008, shown

Figure 3.20. Zoning in south-central Phoenix, residential infill adjacent to commercial.

Figure 3.21. Aerial view of figure 3.20.

in figures 3.23, 3.24, and 3.25, documents the dissolution of meaningful spatial pattern. Zoning in 1930 reflected an urban pattern in which residential zoning was both closely integrated and became progressively denser as one moved closer to com-

Figure 3.22. B-3 zoning in Urbana, Illinois, which allows multifamily dwellings, with a special use permit.

mercial streets. Neighborhood commercial zones were located at intersections, while the more intensive general commercial zones lined downtown streets. In an attempt to reinstate more life in the downtown, a large "downtown core" zone was overlayed in 2004 with a number of specialized "Character Area" districts with their own sets of requirements and bonus possibilities. Unfortunately, these rules did little to help produce a more viable, concentrated, walkable downtown core.

A similar loss of pattern in central Phoenix can be seen by looking at residential

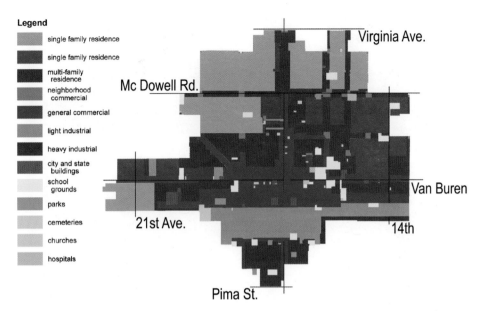

Legend

- single family residence
- single family residence
- multi-family residence
- neighborhood commercial
- general commercial
- light industrial
- heavy industrial
- city and state buildings
- school grounds
- parks
- cemeteries
- churches
- hospitals

Virginia Ave.

Mc Dowell Rd.

Van Buren

21st Ave.

14th

Pima St.

Figure 3.23. Central Phoenix zoning, 1930.

zoning only (figs. 3.26 and 3.27). Between 1930 and 2008, residential zoning in downtown Phoenix lost its tighter grain—zones became larger, and the pattern of residential zones no longer seemed to follow any particular spatial relationship. Many residential areas took on various commercial zoning designations (areas in gray).

Rules can play a strong role in maximizing access. Smaller blocks, higher densities, and a tighter, closer-knit pattern maximize the number of people with access to amenities—a basic feature of good urbanism. Large lot and block sizes have the effect of blocking this access. This is why the notion of providing bonus densities for developers who provide amenities like plazas, playgrounds, and day care makes sense—but only if the added density is close to these amenities.

If city rules had a spatial logic to them, the rules would prioritize adjacency for people most in need. One example is people who don't have outdoor living space—that is, people who live in apartments. But the relationship between proximity and need is often in reverse. For example, figure 3.28 shows an area zoned single-family residential surrounding two beautiful parks in Phoenix. Rules limit building intensity around this park by setting maximum allowable densities, maximum building coverages, and maximum building heights. Figure 3.29 shows the on-the-ground effect in another area of Phoenix. In the subdivision shown, the rules allow only low-density single-family housing near public open space. Combined with the sprawling

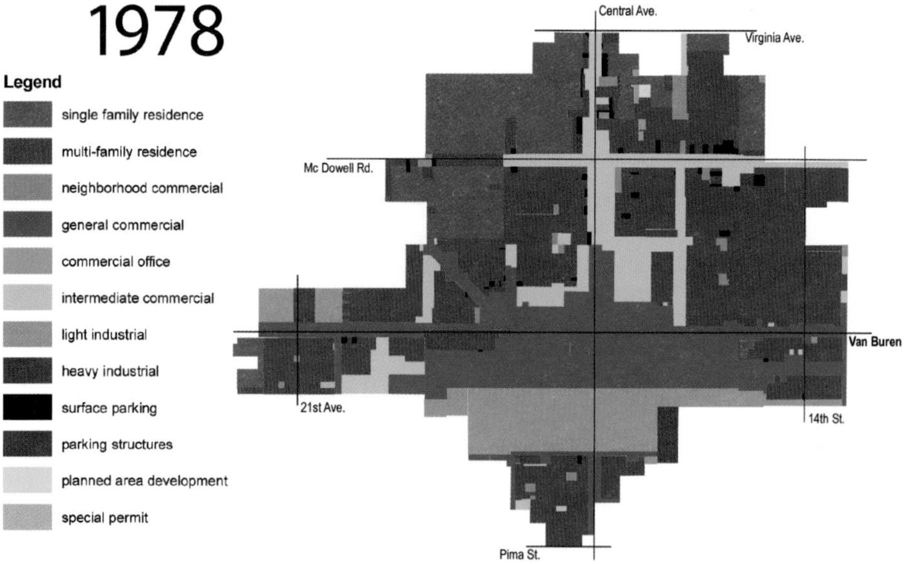

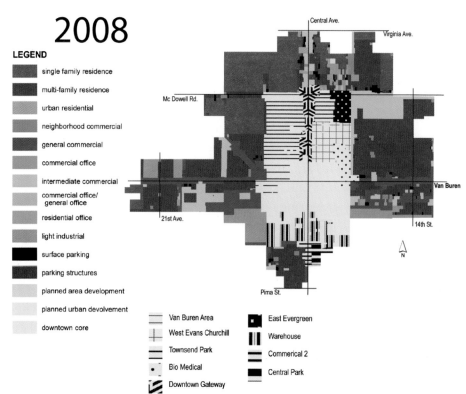

Figure 3.24. Central Phoenix zoning, 1978.

Figure 3.25. Central Phoenix zoning, 2008.

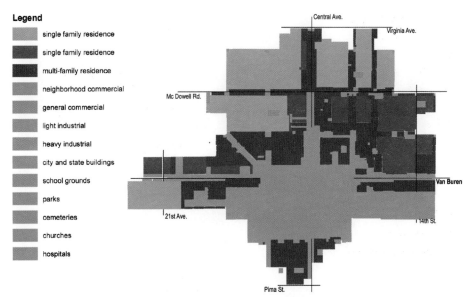

Figure 3.26. Central Phoenix residential zoning, 1930.

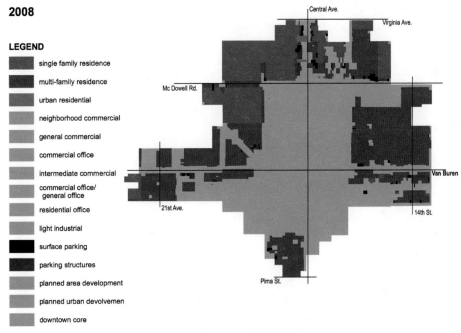

Figure 3.27. Central Phoenix residential zoning, 2008.

Figure 3.28. Existing pattern of zones around two parks in north central Phoenix, Arizona.

Figure 3.29. A subdivision in Phoenix, Arizona, showing single-family housing and parking lots around parks, blocking access.

Figure 3.30. Proposed pattern of zones around two parks in north central Phoenix, Arizona.

school and parking lots on the other side, the arrangement guarantees limits on the ability of apartment dwellers to access the public open space.

A better spatial logic, such as that shown in figure 3.30, would put apartment dwellers closer to the park. Not only would this give more people better access to an important public amenity, it would have the added benefit of potentially increasing park usage. Jane Jacobs, among others, argued that what matters most about parks is what surrounds them. Rather than blindly assuming that more parks are always better, Jacobs implored planners to consider first whether there was sufficient density and diversity surrounding parks, and access to them, which would dictate whether they would be sufficiently used. Diverse surroundings are key, she argued, because they generate mutual support and "complex pools of use" that inhabit parks at different times of the day and therefore increase safety by way of natural surveillance (Jacobs 1961). The rules guiding development around amenities like parks are a key component of instilling an optimal spatial pattern.

Often the haphazard pattern of single-family zoning is a mystery. Figure 3.31 shows the random pattern of minimum lot sizes for residential zones in the northern part of Phoenix, from low to high density. The arrangement doesn't follow a clear spatial logic in which the densest places would be closer to services or public

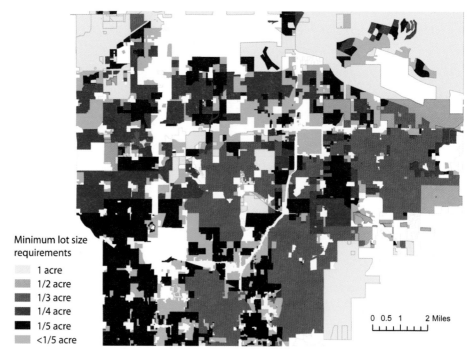

Minimum lot size requirements

- 1 acre
- 1/2 acre
- 1/3 acre
- 1/4 acre
- 1/5 acre
- <1/5 acre

0 0.5 1   2 Miles

Figure 3.31. Haphazard pattern of lot size requirements for residential zones in a northern section of Phoenix, Arizona.

facilities. Instead, the rules for minimum lot size seem to create a pattern in which fairly large lot sizes are adjacent to smaller ones in every part of the city. Figure 3.32 shows a random spatial pattern for multifamily, single-family, and commercial zones. The pattern doesn't appear to make any particular sense: any zone is adjacent to any other zone.

A better spatial logic might place wider, larger lot sizes on wider, busier thoroughfares, with narrower lots on narrower streets. This is because bigger and wider lots often accommodate more intensive and robust uses, while smaller and narrower spaces are more appropriate for less intense uses. This was the case in New York and many other cities that developed before we became auto dependent: wider lots faced wider avenues, while narrower lots faced the narrow, numbered streets between them. The rules guiding street width, building height, and use were interrelated, and this was the basis of the pattern created.

One variation of this is the need to get as much activity as possible close to intersections and main streets. In some cases, intersections and corners might be exactly the places where fine-grained diversity—small lots and blocks—is most needed.

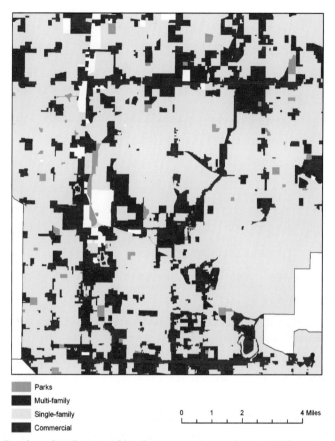

Parks
Multi-family
Single-family   0   1   2   4 Miles
Commercial

Figure 3.32. Random distribution of land-use zones in north central Phoenix, Arizona.

Very large parcels near intersections might block fine-grained diversity where it is most needed. If cities are about maximizing exchange and interplay, as Lewis Mumford wrote, then rules guiding development around intersections should help maximize that.

Unfortunately, in Phoenix there seems to be no pattern to large or small lot sizes relative to major streets. Figure 3.33 shows large lot sizes in yellow and small lot sizes in dark gray, along with major streets shown in red.

Patterns of lot sizes in American downtowns are often the result of lot mergers and splits that occurred subsequent to initial platting. In the suburbs, uniform patterns were created across entire states because of land development codes, or boiler-plate subdivision regulations lifted verbatim from model ordinances. The dimensions involved in the suburbs are usually significantly greater than for downtowns. For ex-

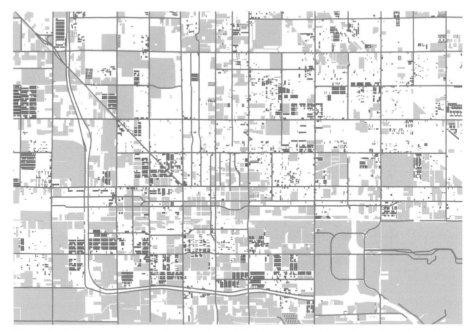

Figure 3.33. Random pattern of large and small lots in central and northern Phoenix, Arizona.

ample, the section of Gilbert, Arizona, shown in figure 3.34 has blocks that are 1,200 feet long on one side, which is below the maximum requirement on block design established by Gilbert's land development code (box 3.2). To show the contrast in dimensions, figure 3.35 shows blocks in Oklahoma City that are 300 by 400 feet, still the maximum allowed today, laid out in accordance with the U.S. Land Ordinance.

The code used in Gilbert, shown in box 3.2, is evidence that the dimensions, which allow long, straight streets, prioritize car traffic rather than pedestrian movement. Contrary to the needs of pedestrian access, the emphasis of these streets is on avoiding "ingress or egress," which limits connectivity. The main arterial in Gilbert, shown in figure 3.34, has commercial uses on the corners, but the rest of the street has no function other than to move traffic. Note how most parcels do not face the main street.

Two sets of rules ensure low-density sprawl: rules against land-use diversity, and rules against density. City rules sustain single-use subdivisions (some call them "monocultures") like the development near Las Vegas, shown in figure 3.36.

These homogeneous, disconnected, car-dependent patterns can first and foremost be blamed on land-use requirements. In these vast residential neighborhoods, stores and mixed-use buildings are not allowed. The ubiquitous American subdivi-

Figure 3.34. A section of Gilbert, Arizona, today. Long straight streets prioritize traffic flow over pedestrian movement.

Box 3.2. Block requirements in Gilbert, Arizona
9.22 Block design.
A. *Block length.* No block shall be longer than one thousand five hundred (1,500) feet. Where a subdivision adjoins a major thoroughfare, the greater dimensions of the blocks shall front or back upon such major thoroughfare to avoid unnecessary ingress or egress. When blocks are over one thousand (1,000) feet in length, a crosswalk easement not less than eight (8) feet wide shall be required if necessary to provide proper access to schools, playgrounds and other facilities.
Source: Gilbert, Arizona (2011, 13).

sion is therefore not just single family, it's also single use. There is little variation in unit type, and uniformity is virtually required.

Rules governing density may be more varied, but again, the pattern created is ad hoc. Density differences are not organized into any kind of logical progression—for example, where denser housing would be located closer to a main street. An example is shown for areas near Olmsted's 1914 planned community in Anchorage, Kentucky, outside of Louisville. Figures 3.37 and 3.38 show disconnected commercial uses surrounded by parking, and residential areas that allow increasingly denser, but disconnected, housing subdivisions. The rules for the zones shown in figures 3.37 and 3.38 can be contrasted with Olmsted's original rules, listed together in table 3.2.

Figure 3.35. Downtown Oklahoma City, showing short block sizes that prioritize pedestrian access.

Figure 3.36. Housing development in Las Vegas, Nevada, a monoculture.

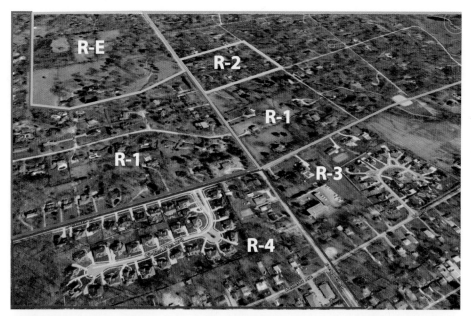

Figure 3.37. Housing developments, each zoned differently, near Anchorage, Kentucky.

Figure 3.38. Zoning for an isolated commercial parcel near Anchorage, Kentucky.

Table 3.2. Comparison of Olmsted's rules and the current zoning restrictions in Anchorage, Kentucky

	Front setback	Height	Min. lot size	Off-street parking
Olmsted, 1905	100 ft.	2 stories plus attic	None Specified	None Specified
R-E	90 ft.	2.5 stories; 35 ft. max.	105,000 sq. ft.	1 per dwelling
R-1	75 ft.	2.5 stories; 35 ft. max.	40,000 sq. ft.	1 per dwelling
R-2	30 ft.	2.5 stories; 35 ft. max.	20,000 sq. ft.	1 per dwelling
C-N	None	2.5 stories; 35 ft. max.	None	1 space per 200 sq. ft. retail; 1 space per 100 sq. ft. for a restaurant
C-1	None	2.5 stories; 35 ft. max.	None	

Sources: Augur (1923, 51–52) and City of Anchorage, Kentucky (2011).

Olmsted did not specify minimum lot size, but the effect, with large setback requirements and controls on use, was the same.

Many other requirements reinforce uniformity and sprawl: First, minimum lot size requirements, applied via subdivision regulations or zoning, and maximum permitted densities, applied through the zoning ordinance. In some cases, there may be a conflict between the two. One important point about minimum lot size requirements, especially in the case of residential zoning, is that their intent is to create *private* open space rather than public open space.

When minimum unit size is required, it means that a smaller, more affordable unit is impossible. An accessory unit of, for example, 500 square feet cannot be accommodated. Rules in support of compact development would put a maximum—not a minimum—limit on lot size and unit size. Instead, a pattern of low density results from many rules, including maximum units per acre, minimum lot size per unit, minimum street frontage per unit (thus making units behind the main structure infeasible), front-yard setbacks that eliminate the possibility of additional units on a lot, side yards that eliminate the possibility of rowhouses and duplexes, and the requirement that each unit must have a separate driveway. Two manifestations of the lot size rule are shown in figures 3.39 and 3.40. Each image shows lots within the same land area: a quarter-mile square. Figure 3.39 shows 25 foot wide lots in San

Figure 3.39. In San Francisco, California, 25 foot wide lots for a quarter-mile square yield 480 single-family dwellings.

Francisco. Figure 3.40 shows 75 foot wide lots in Cave Creek, Arizona. The difference in land-use efficiency is enormous. The 25 foot wide lots yield 480 single-family dwellings. Cave Creek yields about 70 dwellings. Incidentally, in 2010 the average home price in this area of San Francisco was $750,000. The average home price in this part of Cave Creek was $450,000.

Figures 3.41 and 3.42 show more examples of the effect of lot-size rules. In the oldest cities, lots could be very narrow, such as the 16 foot lots permitted in Washington, D.C. (fig. 3.41). Cleveland, Ohio, permitted 25 foot wide by 110 foot long lots in its older sections, along with a street right-of-way of 55 feet (fig. 3.42). By 1929, 40 foot lots were common.

Sometimes sprawl is the result of weak rules. Figure 3.43 is an area that was laid

Figure 3.40. In Cave Creek, Arizona, 75 foot wide lots for a quarter-mile square yield 70 single-family dwellings.

out according to subdivision regulations for Gilbert, Arizona. In the absence of re-quirements for shorter block lengths, better connectivity, and a host of other details necessary for creating pedestrian realms, the street pattern is disconnected and the pedestrian experience is compromised. Specifically, the pattern created is the result of several problems:

- Weak limits on block length. There is only a stipulation that no block shall be longer than 1,500 feet, and cul-de-sacs can be up to 600 feet long. The result is a development composed of winding streets and cul-de-sacs that only increase the amount of impervious surface.
- Weak connectivity requirements. In terms of connection, the regulations state that streets in a new subdivision "shall make provision for continuation of the principal

Figure 3.41. In older cities, lots were permitted to be very narrow, such as these 16 foot lots in Washington, D.C.

Figure 3.42. Cleveland, Ohio, permitted lots 25 feet wide by 110 feet long in its older sections.

Figure 3.43. A section of Gilbert, Arizona. In the absence of requirements for shorter block lengths and better connectivity, pedestrian access is compromised.

existing streets in adjoining areas" or, if adjoining land is not subdivided, then provision should be made for "their proper projection." Under "landscape and open space criteria," the following rule applies: "Opportunities for nonmotorized access (e.g., horse, pedestrian, and bicycle) between adjacent land uses should be provided wherever appropriate." In other words, connectivity is ignored. What rules *could* require, for example, are through-block connections, coordinated bike routes, pedestrian crossings, and allowances for future street extensions.

- Weak attention to the pedestrian realm. Rather than ignoring the needs of pedestrians, subdivision rules *could* require: limitations on curb cuts (perhaps 20 feet maximum; or one per lot; or one per 100 foot frontage); requirements for transit shelters; allowance of shared driveways; requirement that garages be set back further than a house; requirement that parcels not turn their side to a main street; requirement that there be a tighter grain (smaller lot and block sizes) closer in to amenities and main streets.

Also working to spread development out are rules related to landscape buffering and water filtration. Unsightly retention ponds are the result of on-site stormwater management requirements, such as the rules for Gibraltar, Michigan, listed in box 3.3.

Box 3.3. An excerpt from the performance standards contained in the Gibraltar, Michigan, zoning ordinance

An adequate storm drainage system, which includes necessary storm sewers and retention/detention ponds shall be required in all subdivisions and may be required in other areas of development. Detailed plans for storm drainage systems shall be submitted to the city engineer for approval. Detention or retention ponds shall not be placed within a residential lot. Detention and retention ponds shall be placed in outlots, so dedicated with appropriate easements for drainage purposes. Such detention or retention ponds shall be set back from any road right-of-way a distance equal to the front yard setback requirements for the subdivision and from all other boundaries of the outlot a sufficient distance to meet side yard setback requirements. Applicant shall grant an easement to the city should it be necessary for the city to take over maintenance of the detention and retention ponds.

Source: From Sec. 44-227, "Requirement of storm drainage system including detention and retention ponds."

Instead of filtering water through parks and other types of open spaces, unusable retention ponds disrupt connectivity and waste open space, resulting in development like that shown in figure 3.44. In places where a more dense form of urbanism would be beneficial, green buffers and "visible" stormwater management may be counterproductive.

Section 800 of the 2006 Prince William County Subdivision Ordinance, "Buffer Areas, Landscaping, and Tree Cover Requirements," is shown in tables 3.3, 3.4, and 3.5. These rules require that every use be buffered from every other use—a recipe for sprawl. Figure 3.45 shows the effect on the ground for a single-family housing development. Figure 3.46 shows how the rule contributes to separation between multifamily apartment complexes and other housing. The rules create more distance between land uses, thus spreading development out. The idea of buffering one use from another follows in the tradition of treating multifamily housing as a potential nuisance to be kept separate from single-family homes (see Larco 2009).

This chapter has surveyed the pattern effects of rules. Looking over the historical record, there has been a gradual wearing down of the spatial logic rules once applied, where ideas about how one land use or building type relates to another, or how intensity levels should be arranged, were translated to codes. With the loss of these connections, American cities are now saddled with rules that work against the formation of compact, diverse, walkable urban places.

Figure 3.44. Buffering and retention pond around a subdivision in Gibraltar, Michigan. Unusable retention ponds disrupt connectivity and waste open space.

Table 3.3 . Buffer requirements in Prince William County, Virginia

Proposed use/development	Minimum buffer area required											
	Adjoining existing use/development											
	1	2	3	4	5	6	7	8	9	10	11	12
RESIDENTIAL												
1. Single-Family Detached		A	B	B	B	D	B	C	B	C	C	C
2. Single-Family Weak-Link (used only for previously approved weak-link developments that are still valid)	A		A	B	B	D	B	C	B	C	C	C
3. Single-Family Attached	B	A		B	B	D	B	C	B	C	C	C
4. Multifamily	B	B	B		B	D	A	C	B	C	C	C
PUBLIC/SEMIPUBLIC												
5. Institutional (e.g., schools, church, library)	B	B	B	B		D	A	A	A	B	C	C
6. Public Recreational Use	D	D	D	D	D		D	D	D	D	D	D
7. Care Facilities (e.g., nursing home)	B	B	B	A	A	D		D	A	B	C	C
8. Public Facilities (e.g., pump station, treatment plant)	C	C	C	C	A	D	D		D	D	D	D
9. Office	B	B	B	B	A	D	A	D		D	B	B
10. Commercial/retail	C	C	C	C	B	D	B	D	D		A	B
INDUSTRIAL												
11. Light	C	C	C	C	C	D	C	D	B	A		A
12. Heavy	C	C	C	C	C	D	C	D	B	B	A	

Abbreviations: A,B,C, buffer in accordance with "Buffer area width and plant requirements"; D, determined on a case-by-case basis, depending on activity.

Table 3.4. Buffer area width and plant requirements in Prince William County, Virginia.

	Buffer area width and plant requirements	
Type	Width feet	No. of plant units per 100 feet of R/W or property line
A	15	50
B	30	100
C	50	200
D	Case by case—min. 15 ft.	Based on approved width

Table 3.5. Plant unit equivalents in Prince William County, Virginia.

Plant type*	Plant units*
1 large deciduous tree	10
1 evergreen tree (any category)	5
1 deciduous understory tree (medium, small, or compact categories)	5
1 shrub	2

*Minimum plant size in accordance with Section 804.01 G

Figure 3.45. Every use buffered from every other use: the effect of buffering requirements in Prince William County, Virginia.

Figure 3.46. Buffering requirements contribute to the separation of housing types in Prince William County, Virginia.

4. Use

How land is used moves beyond the question of pattern toward the question of proximity, or to *what* use is located *where*. The pattern rules discussed in the previous chapter focused on the laying out of lots, blocks, streets, and the broader spatial patterns dictated by zoning, which of course touch on use. But this chapter narrows in on the regulation of use alone and how this has affected the quality and character of place. The constant obsession with controlling use in American regulation, and what the effects of that have been, warrants special attention.

Rules about use were initially about keeping nuisances and noxious functions away from people and important civic functions (Melosi 1999). Cities drew up lists of unwanted uses and required them to obtain special approvals. In Baltimore in 1912 and Seattle in 1913, the rule was that the building inspector would not issue a building permit for potentially objectionable uses—ranging from "sanatoriums" to "lumber yards" to "candle factories"—without the approval of the mayor (New York City Board of Estimate and Apportionment 1916, 66).

There have been times when rules about use were proactive—that is, they compelled property owners to use their land in a certain way. In the American colonies, for example, landowners might have been required by law to add improvements. In Plymouth Colony, failure to improve land and help maintain the "strength of society" would result in the government seizing control of property (cited in Hart 1996, 1260). By the 1830s, communities had the legal right to seize private property for the purpose of creating public spaces (Baker 1927).

Rules about where dwellings could be built could be similarly proactive.

A seventeenth-century law in Massachusetts Bay Colony required that dwellings be built within a half-mile of the meeting house. These proactive rules connect to earlier town planning requirements, such as the *Laws of the Indies*, which required all towns to contain a public square, or the rules of ancient Greece that required all towns to have an agora.

The regulation of use through zoning in the early twentieth century was a dramatic change in the history of city rules—much more comprehensive and detailed than anything seen before. The change was not taken lightly. Arguments over zoning in the early twentieth century were generally about use, not area, height, or bulk, and this was reflected in zoning litigation (Goodrich 1939). One irony of the obsession with controlling use is that uses tend to segregate even without zoning, as Siegan's study of Houston (1972), and Cappel's study of New Haven (1991) have shown. Historian Sam Bass Warner observed that builders were self-regulating even before there were any rules for them to worry about. They sought uniformity and built according to what was already in the neighborhood (Warner 1969). According to Fischel (2004), the social sorting that occurred before zoning, largely by virtue of the electric streetcar, was an important precondition to zoning's later acceptance.

In the United States, zoning rules were dedicated to constraining land-use diversity. The effort was rationalized on the basis of health and safety. The NYC Commission on Building Districts reported: "It is more difficult to keep a mixed district containing stores and dwellings clean and sanitary than a residential district" (New York City Board of Estimate and Apportionment 1916, 120). They had a point. Stores increased fire risk for residences, especially if a store with gas stoves was in the same building as an apartment. But the overzealousness of rules devoted to separation has been one of the most dramatically negative consequences of all rules ever applied to cities. Ideas were taken too far. Zoning advocates claimed, for example, that mixed uses promoted juvenile delinquency because busy streets with pushcarts and sidewalk obstructions thwarted the child's ability to play (New York City Board of Estimate and Apportionment 1916).

Some of the most influential early framers of zoning are on record supporting land-use control for the purpose of class segregation. Robert Whitten, who co-wrote New York City's 1916 zoning ordinance, believed that "bankers and the leading business men should live in one part of town, storekeepers, clerks and technicians in another, and working people in yet others where they would enjoy the association with neighbors more or less of their own kind" (Survey 1922, 114). Atlanta's zoning plan, crafted with Whitten's help, took the idea further and divided the city into three residential districts: white, colored, and undetermined. Use segregation was thus based on stereotyping and classifying both functions and people. The report that led up to the New York City 1916 zoning ordinance discussed types of people (and the kind of areas they required) at length, arguing, for example, that office workers, as opposed to factory workers, were "not prone to interfere with the orderly and regular use of streets" (New York City Board of Estimate and Apportionment 1916, 116).

On the other hand, there is evidence that use segregation was more nuanced than we might expect, at least initially. Olmsted warned in 1910 that the "districting system" was "no child's play to apply it intelligently" (Olmsted Jr. 1910, 16). The attorney for New York's 5th Avenue retailers—the ones who pushed for zoning because they wanted factories and factory workers out of their retail areas—argued for what we would now call a "sustainability" angle—that workers ought to be located in factory areas so that they would be "within walking distance," and that a better connection between where people lived and where people worked was both "logical" and "unquestionably possible" (New York City Board of Estimate and Apportionment 1916, 118). Some enlightened planners recognized the problem of racial and class segregation caused by zoning and voiced their concern in the early 1920s in *The Survey*, a progressive political magazine.

The American experience with zoning for land-use separation was entirely unlike the German experience. European controls did not involve separation by use, consistent with their conceptualization of zoning as more of a policy document than an extension of nuisance law (Punter 2000). This is why a complex thinker like Patrick Geddes could be enthusiastic about the possibilities of zoning based on the German experience. In reference to Frankfurt's system he wrote: "Place, work and folk—environment, function and organism—are thus no longer viewed apart, but as the elements of a single process—that of healthy life for the community and individual" (Geddes 1915, 198). Baumeister, the German engineer who invented zoning, had proposed "functional differentiation" in the 1880s, but it was more about controlling intensity of use than keeping functions separate. Even where there was separation of factories into distinct districts, the compact form of the European city put uses in close proximity. Land uses in Europe had been mixed like that for centuries; therefore, unlike housing reform or monumental city design, functional separation had no constituency (Logan 1972, 114). In the United States, a "throw-away" spirit made land use highly changeable, where residential use gave way to commercial use, and commercial use gave way to industrial use in the span of a few years (Mullin

1976/77, 8). It is not surprising that this instability created strong public support for rules that controlled use.

In this chapter, the historical progression of use-related rules is divided into two categories: rules that separate people, and rules that separate functions. These are highly interrelated phenomena: the separation of functions further complicates the separation of people, and the separation of people complicates the ability to provide a diverse set of functions within one neighborhood.

Rules That Separate People

There has been a long history to the use of zoning to keep "lower class" people out (Fischler 1998; Jackson 1985; Pendall 2000; Stockman 1992). Rules accomplish the separation of people primarily by (1) not allowing attached housing—apartments, duplexes, and the like in single family home areas; (2) not allowing housing of a particular size; and (3) not allowing lots of a particular dimension. Setback and frontage requirements can have a similar effect. Before zoning, building codes and restrictive covenants could be used to achieve social separation. Apartments could be excluded by height limits, or by simply requiring concrete or steel construction in buildings higher than one story. Wide side yard requirements could be imposed on narrow inner-city lots; for example, Philadelphia's 1895 building code required multifamily dwellings to have 8 foot side yards even on 25 foot lots (Baar 1992).

The effect of zoning in particular on separation and exclusion is well studied. There have been analyses of the motivations behind the Euclid decision (Lees 1994; Rabin 1989), the exclusion of multifamily housing (Baar 1992), the exclusion of blacks and Jews (Lands 2004; Larsen 2002), and even the exclusion of people who required housesharing arrangements or accessory units to earn a living (Netter and Price 1983). Some claim that zoning was essentially an attempt to redistribute wealth away from low-income renters and toward existing property owners (Clingermayer 2004).

In some places, the use of rules for racial separation was central to the concept of zoning (Flint 1977). It started in the 1880s with California's laws against laundries, which were intended to exclude the Chinese. Modesto, California, was the first to create a laundry-free district, in 1885. Then, shortly after 1900, many cities in the South passed racial zoning where each block was allocated to one or the other racial category, depending on the majority of occupants. Members of the other group were not allowed, by law, to move in (Williams 1956; see also Silver 1991). The U.S. Supreme Court declared racial zoning unconstitutional in 1917 (*Buchanan v. Warley,*

245 U.S. 60), but there were always ways around it. In places like Atlanta and St. Louis, strict zoning requirements ensured that blacks would not be able to meet the standards for new construction (Flint 1977). Glynn County, Georgia, did not allow alleys adjacent to lots greater than 120 feet in depth because they didn't want rear dwellings—populated with poor blacks, presumably—fronting them. As Babcock argued, zoning was popular because suburbanites were "concerned not with *what* but with *whom*" [emphasis added] (1966, 31). This use of rules for social effect—for example by setting minimum lot sizes and setbacks that have the effect of excluding smaller, more affordable homes—is in full force today.

Sometimes early developers of planning regulations seemed naive about how these rules could be used to manipulate social outcomes. Thomas Adams, writing in 1922, said that "it would not be proper even if desirable to restrict the value of houses erected in a particular district," but then went on to argue in favor of rules governing lot size, height, and use (Adams 1922, 161). Through their proselytizing of zoning especially, planners let loose a tool that provided a way for people to act on fear and maximize protection in unnecessary and socially damaging ways. Unfortunately, the more people learned, the more they demanded it. In 1917, 16 percent of zoning changes in New York were for tighter restrictions on who, or what, could occupy the land; just five years later, it was 77 percent (Baker 1927).

The 1909 Los Angeles zoning ordinance was awkward, to say the least. There was one giant residential zone, along with twenty-seven industrial districts and about a hundred "residence exception" districts in which industry was allowed in scattered sites (one or two lots) throughout the residential zone (Williams 1919).

Use rules that began in the late nineteenth century were a new phenomenon. Socially mixed settlements were the norm until then, a result of economic necessity: nobles needed to be near their serfs in the medieval city, while workers and owners needed to be close to factories in the early industrial city. People lived where they worked, not where their social class was geographically confined. In many European cities, rich and poor were separated only through vertical zoning within apartment buildings, but out on the street, classes shared the public realm. But as industrialization progressed in the nineteenth century, class began to trump ethnic affiliation as the main driver of social geography. Olivier Zunz's (1982) study of Detroit showed how a "silent social revolution" in the first decades of the twentieth century created urban worlds defined more and more by class and industrial production and consumption rather than by strong ethnic bonding or proximity to workplace. New transportation technologies had a lot to do with this, as they made spatial sorting that much easier. The replacement of neighborhoods formerly composed of multiple classes with neighborhoods sorted by class and race was something zoning helped solidify, making segregation seem logical, orderly, and necessary for the modern city.

The three primary mechanisms for codifying separation of people were subdivision regulations (platting control), zoning, and deed restrictions. Government wasn't the only entity enacting these rules. In *The Rise of the Community Builders: The American Real Estate Industry and Urban Land Planning*, Weiss (1987) showed how community builders helped put in place the deed restrictions, zoning, subdivision regulations, and other land development controls that engendered the segregated pattern of postwar suburbanization. Rules were good for business: they allowed greater ease of large-scale production building and efficient separation by price point, and they helped tap a market of home buyers motivated by exclusion. Federal rules had a similar, separating effect. The Home Owners Loan Corporation (HOLC) and the Federal Housing Authority (FHA) used an underwriting manual that called for investigating whether a neighborhood had a mix of "incompatible" social and racial groups (Schill and Wachter 1995). Highway construction financed by the federal government served to further isolate and separate neighborhoods, just as the lack of funding for public transportation ensured that the poor would be immobile. The zoning of single-use residential areas exacerbated these conditions.

Rules became devoted to maintaining homogeneity. Sometimes the approach was blunt, such as the simple rule that only single-family housing of a certain size was allowed, but subtler approaches could have similar effects. For example, there were rules requiring excessive infrastructure, which had the effect of gold-plating residential subdivisions. What seems shocking to us now is how taken for granted the objective of separation was, even among progressives like Theodora Kimball and Henry Hubbard, who lauded a Dayton, Ohio, rule that "the subdivider should restrict by covenant in the deed part [or] all of his plat against industrial or business use, or against multiple-family houses either permanently or until the section be zoned, such restrictions to be filed and recorded with the plat" (Hubbard and Hubbard 1929, 158). The three pronged approach—platting, zoning, deed restrictions—was sold as being "productive of orderliness in community living" and would work well for both the developer and the community since "his interests are inextricably bound up in the long run with the best interests of the community" (159).

In Germany, arguments in favor of zoning that appeared in the 1860s and 1870s were rooted in a defense of single-family housing, but much more attention was paid to the effect on social mixing. In fact, German planners actively looked for ways that the built environment could provide "opportunities for mixing classes of population," as early as the 1860s (Logan 1972, 57). The outlying residential districts established in late nineteenth-century German cities allowed both larger "country houses" and smaller working-class cottages with attached workshops. The smaller houses were allowed to be close together and front the lot line. The point was to establish a character of lower-intensity detached buildings, not to preclude a certain class of people. When, in the mid-nineteenth century apartment buildings started to take over in the outlying districts of Berlin and rules that allowed only "villa" construction were imposed, nineteenth-century planners like Baumeister and later Hegemann objected on the grounds that such areas were being reserved for the wealthy, not for lower-priced, low-density housing for the working classes (Logan 1972). An 1892 ordinance governing suburban development rectified this problem and allowed both larger country estates and smaller work cottages alongside each other in peripheral areas. In addition, Baumeister's 1884 ordinance for Frankfurt used lot requirements (150 square meters per dwelling) to discourage the building of residences in factory zones, which could not be excluded on the basis of use (Logan 1972).

In contrast, in the United States, planners used zoning to exclude and separate, although they instinctively knew the practice would be challenged. Alfred Bettman admitted in 1926 that "the single-family district from which the apartment house or multiple-family structure is excluded is the feature about whose validity the most anxiety has been felt" (Bettman 1926, 25). Still, the apartment building was believed to be a "children-devouring, family-destroying" parasite of modern cities (Crawford 1920, 1, 7). Multifamily dwelling units were to be excluded from single-family residential areas based on "noise, street danger, litter, dust, contagion, light and air, and fire risk." Thorough exposure of these risks was considered to be "the right way to prepare zoning cases" (Bassett 1923, 17).

In the United States, the separation of people via rules occurred gradually. Residential mixing was at first allowed under 1920s-era rules. The first zoning ordinance in New York included a residential-only zone that allowed both single-family homes and apartment buildings. Many cities had residential zones that mixed single-family homes and duplexes. Bassett thought it "hazardous" to separate out single-family detached residences as a separate use, on the grounds that he didn't think the courts would allow it (1922a, 323). He proposed just four use categories: heavy industry, light industry, business, and residence. Thomas Adams also thought it was "doubtful" that residential-only zones would ever be constitutional (Adams 1922, 174).

Caution about separating use changed when the U.S. Supreme Court sanctioned single-family-only residential districts in the 1926 Euclid decision (*Village of Euclid, Ohio v. Ambler Realty Co.*, 272 U.S. 365). When a 1928 report showed that there was plenty of land available for any given use, "the authorities refused to break up single-family districts for row houses, for which land was found to be available elsewhere" (National Capital Park and Planning Commission, Annual Report, 1928; cited in Hubbard 1937, 185).

Restrictive covenants attached to subdivisions also contributed to social exclusion (Fogelson 2005). It was the approach offered by J. C. Nichols, developer of the Country Club District outside of Kansas City, who attached controls to deed restrictions. Perpetuation of neighborhood character was to be maintained by controlling "the use of property, the design and color of the building, setbacks, side building lines, frontages" and the like (Nichols 1929, 142). Size, height, and area requirements in zoning and subdivision regulations could have the same effect. Open space requirements could mean that the building of apartments, though allowed, became impractical. Or the exclusion of apartments could be based on maximum rather than minimum lot size—Newark, New Jersey's 1919 ordinance used maximum lot area requirements so that it became "uneconomic" to put multifamily housing in single-family districts (Newark, New Jersey, 1919).

Many felt that land devoted to single-family housing was being threatened. Walter S. Schmidt, president of the National Association of Real Estate Boards, wrote: "in the average American city many times as much property as can ever be used has been allocated for apartments, business, manufacturing, and industrial purposes, crowding out and destroying home neighborhoods" (cited in Davies 1958, 184). This was statistically accurate. In Chicago's 1923 zoning ordinance, for example, land area devoted to single-family dwellings was set to decrease by 8.8%. Multifamily dwelling, commercial, and manufacturing areas increased under the zone plan, 8.3, 9.1, and 11.2 percent, respectively (Young 1937).

Social progressives were at first skeptical of zoning. The charge against it was led by Lawrence Veiller, founder of the National Housing Association, an organization "to improve housing conditions both urban and suburban, in every practicable way" (Veiller 1910, 5). He thought that the idea of separating uses—"factories in one section, dwellings in another, commercial buildings in another and tenement houses in another"—was not only undemocratic but also fostered "class-consciousness." He must have been conscious of the decentralization and separation that were emphasized at the First National Planning Conference in 1909, where Robert Anderson Pope argued for "wider dispersal of the laboring class" (Sies and Silver 1996, 462).

Veiller later refused to sign New York's 1916 zoning report, despite being on the committee that produced it, because he believed that it prioritized financial interests over social goals (Lubove 1962).

These concerns were eventually overcome, and zoning came to be seen as a powerful tool for social reform. It was pitched as a progressive, reformist solution to the harmful effects cities were having on working people. Testaments about zoning's progressiveness were widespread and were mostly based on the optimistic idea that regulating out multiple-family dwellings meant that poor people, too, would get to live in single-family housing with its light, air, and other benefits. Figure 4.1 from the 1916 NYC Building Commission study had the caption: "The attractive cottages with a vacant lot between, gave the semi-residence interloper a chance to steal his lights, and air and view and to ruin the other properties." When located adjacent to single-family houses, apartments were viewed as parasites, benefiting from the yards of their neighbors but offering none of their own amenity in return. "The apartment took, took, took. It never gave," in the words of New York City's zoning committee secretary (Swan 1920, 46).

The reduction of densities via zoning was seen as a method of housing *reform*, not exclusion. In the years leading up to New York City's comprehensive zoning in 1916, that was exactly the argument being made (e.g., Haldeman 1912; Logan 1976; Olmsted Jr. 1910). Edward M. Bassett argued that "fine new apartments" were for "white-

Figure 4.1. Apartment houses next to single-family homes were labeled "interlopers." *Source:* New York City Board of Estimate and Apportionment (1916).

collar people," and he interpreted arguments in favor of apartments as attempts to "belittle" the single-family house. The single-family ("E") zones he promoted in Baltimore in 1922 were, he argued, "rapidly building up with the homes of the best sort of citizens who are not wealthy" (Bassett 1922a, 6). The point was to promote ownership, and that objective was synonymous with single-family housing. Charles H. Cheney wrote in 1920: "the poor man with a family is as much entitled to an opportunity to live in a home neighborhood restricted from flats, apartments, business and other undesirable buildings as is the wealthy man, who builds his home in a privately restricted tract." The opponents of zoning, he believed, were "never the poor man, but rather the real estate speculator" (Cheney 1920, 275, 276).

The underlying economic rationale was that cheap housing for industrial laborers would be impossible without limits on speculation, and limits on speculation could only be stopped by limiting density. This way of thinking came from Germany, where zoning was motivated by a desire to keep land prices lower by limiting density: higher density meant higher land prices. But, as Logan (1976) points out, this was nearly the opposite approach taken by Henry George and proponents of land value taxation.[1] They believed that restrictions on density would mean higher, not lower, housing costs, and thus, George's followers believed, the solution was to tax land and stimulate housing supply. For progressives in the Georgist camp, zoning was resorted to only when the first choice, taxation reform, proved politically difficult. This turned out to be exactly the case. In the early 1900s, the focus of attention was the Lower East side of Manhattan, and extreme overcrowding there had been met with proposals for taxing land rather than buildings, which, it was believed, would encourage building in the outlying parts of the city and release land for development that was currently being held for speculation (Marsh 1909; see also Williamson 1916). But the untaxing of buildings never occurred. Zoning, as it turned out, proved to be a much more realistic proposition.

Many urban planners saw single-family detached housing *in relation to* apartments, not as a replacement of them. Jane Addams, founder of Hull House in Chicago, called the focus on single-family houses a "fetish" (1902; cited in Baar 1992, 42). At the 1918 National Conference on City Planning, the argument was made that "those whose needs demand an apartment should not be compelled to live in the congested sections of the city in order to secure that advantage" (1918, 35–37,

---

1. Henry George (1839–1897) promoted the idea of a single tax on land. In his book *Progress and Poverty* (1879) he made the argument that the economic rent of land, because its value is created by society and not individual effort, should be shared equally.

cited in Baar 1992, 44). The New York Commission on Building Districts realistically asserted that "many families prefer Manhattan apartments for social reasons or because of proximity in time and space to clubs, hotels and theatres, or because of nearness to place of business or work" (New York City Board of Estimate and Apportionment 1916, chap. 4, 26). There was also an understanding that all attached housing was not equal. The photograph shown in figure 4.2 was published in the *American Architect* magazine around the same time zoning was first being proposed—1912. It was used to argue that apartments could be a valued urban form—if architects were permitted the freedom to design them well. The caption read: "One to five room apartments erected by a Berlin building society. This picture taken in a

Figure 4.2. This courtyard in Berlin, published in the *American Architect*, 1912, was used to argue that apartments could be a valued urban form—if architects were permitted the freedom to design them well.

court shows the lighting and ventilation values and the work the architect had a chance to do." Two decades later, a study commissioned by the Regional Plan of New York and Its Environs, called *Buildings: Their Uses and the Spaces about Them*, featured Philadelphia row housing, shown in figure 4.3, with the caption: "Usually two stories high and two rooms deep, these houses enjoy plenty of sunlight and fresh air" (Adams 1931, 224).

Whatever claims were being made about the value of single-family housing, they were not backed up with actions or policies that would ensure equal access. It is easy, then, to interpret the otherwise progressive claims about light, air, and play space as rhetoric. According to Power, Bassett's advocacy for better housing for the poor "was all puff." Bassett was really only interested in "the professional and managerial class into which he had climbed," and zoning "only served as an excuse for failure to provide constructive solutions such as public housing" (Power 1989, 10).

It is harder to pin this hypocrisy on the housing advocate Lawrence Veiller. According to Veiller, the problem with multifamily units was that they tended to "interfere" with "proper social conditions and the development of true civic spirit"(Veiller 1914, 11). There is no denying that single-family homes afforded substantial benefits, such as dramatically increasing play space for children. Theodora Kimball Hubbard argued that prohibiting apartments and shops and requiring ample

Figure 4.3. Philadelphia row housing shown in this photo had the caption: "Usually two stories high and two rooms deep, these houses enjoy plenty of sunlight and fresh air."
Source: Adams (1931, 224).

yards was about providing "conditions favorable to home life and the rearing of children" (Hubbard and Hubbard 1929, 164). When families were squeezed into accessory units along rear alleys—what we might now advocate as granny flats—it was not a matter of promoting healthy infill development or income-generating opportunities, it was a matter of families living in hovels and sharing space with cesspools, stables, and holes filled with garbage. This reality was powerful when coupled with the common belief that bad housing was causing bad behavior. Decrepit housing was "the cancer that sends its poison to the finger tips of the social body" (Bacon 1911, 10), or, as Thomas Adams in *Buildings: Their Uses and the Spaces about Them* put it, "dark rooms with a mean outlook create dark-minded citizens with a mean outlook" (Adams 1931, 208). Chicago School sociologists provided theoretical and scientific backing for this perspective. Writing in the journal *City Planning*, Nels Anderson of the University of Chicago noted that, "If an area of single homes can keep out apartments it is better able to retain face-to-face community relationships. The apartment breaks down neighborhood spirit and is not congenial to family life" (Anderson 1925, 159).

But it is also clear that the early proponents of zoning never envisioned the downside to promoting single-family housing—especially the possibility of homogeneous sprawl. They saw the zoned city as an interconnected city. Bassett explained his vision—and zoning's role in it—in terms not unlike those used by planners today. He held up the Flatbush area of Brooklyn as a model, claiming that "nowhere in the United States can the effect of zoning be exemplified better than in Flatbush" (1925a, 60). It was an "inter-dependent community of buildings and uses" consisting of "home districts where children can grow up," "apartment houses for young married people [and] for old people after they have brought up their families." Integrating houses and apartments in the way—where one zone was seen in relation to another—meant that "the apartment dwellers are better off than in solid apartment house areas because the tenants have more light and air and can walk out on pleasant streets" and "the private home owners have the benefit of more stores, better local facilities and lower prices due to the presence of the apartment house customers" (Bassett 1925a, 61). This would occur not by putting an apartment building next to a single-family house, but through the spatially integrated arrangement of small, homogeneous zones.

Rules That Separate Functions

The use of rules to separate functions has predominantly been a matter of separating residential use from commercial and industrial use. The separation of functions was originally seen as something humane and progressive, backed by two strong reform movements: public health and housing (Logan 1976). Again separation was conceived as a way of protecting the poor. Planners argued that the "first function" of zoning was to "protect those who cannot protect themselves" (National Conference on City Planning 1921, 32). The reasoning would sometimes draw upon anti-apartment sentiment. There was concern, for example, that a factory in a residential area would lead to conversion of single-family residences to multifamily, and the resulting lowered rents and lowered maintenance would lead to slums (Flint 1977).

Separation by function mirrored separation by class, and already by 1900, U.S. cities were exhibiting a segregated land-use pattern where commercial and office space dominated the center, and residential uses were increasingly pushed to the periphery (Jackson 1985). In central locations, separation was uneven. While residential districts had been established to keep out glue factories, slaughterhouses, and any other number of noxious uses, some residential areas were zoned to allow industrial use, especially where the poor and minorities lived. The consequences of this type of zoning were often tragic, as poor, often black neighborhoods suffered the effects of pollution (see especially Flint 1977). On the south side of Chicago in the 1920s, parks and playgrounds in manufacturing areas were illegal, but homes were not, a terrible outcome for blacks forced to live in manufacturing districts. Similar effects occurred when land was rezoned opportunistically. In Chicago, a large tract of farmland next to a residential neighborhood was zoned for industrial use in 1942 so that Ford Motor Company could build an airplane engine plant. Following the plant's closure after the War, successful redevelopment of the site, which was converted to Ford City Mall, has been a constant challenge.

Just as with housing, American planners approached separation of functions in a way that Germans never did (Scott 1969; see also Logan 1976). Perhaps the failure of planners to better understand the consequences of functional separation—or, in the case of residences next to polluting industries, dysfunctional proximity—was the result of a break in communication with German planners. Mullin (1976/77) has pointed out that World War I changed the way Americans viewed Germany and essentially halted the U.S. study of German material in architecture and planning journals after 1910. Ironically, modernist principles regarding functional separation were launched by the Congrès internationaux d'architecture modern (CIAM) at its 1929 congress in Frankfurt, site of one of the world's first zoning ordinances several decades earlier. The conference promulgated modernist ideas about functional separation, which later made their way to the United States when German planners were forced into exile.

The amount of land zoned for commercial use, and sometimes apartments, was exorbitant. In Chicago, Homer Hoyt estimated that the amount of area zoned in 1923 for business was enough to satisfy the needs of three times the present population. In Santa Barbara, California, 91 percent of the city was zoned for apartments and businesses, and only 9 percent for single-family homes. Portland, Oregon, was derided in the 1930s for having too much zoning for apartments (40 percent of its incorporated area). The population that could be accommodated under Los Angeles's zoning code was calculated at twenty million in the 1920s, based solely on the number of apartment districts (Hubbard and Hubbard 1929, 187). It was also estimated that, in 1941, commercial zoning in Los Angeles would be sufficient to service a population of fifty-two million (Urban Land Institute 1941). Figure 4.4 was used to argue

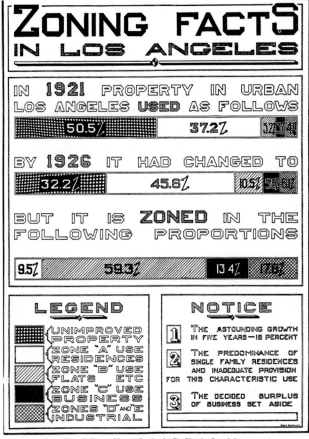

Courtesy of Gordon Whitnall, Director-Manager, Los Angeles City Planning Commission

Figure 4.4. This graph of land uses in Los Angeles was used as evidence that zoning did not prioritize single-family housing.

Source: Hubbard and Hubbard (1929), p. 164.

that zoning did not prioritize single-family housing nearly enough. In any case, if there was pressure to rezone land for a higher use, this was easily granted, "as the five thousand amendments to the zoning law testify," noted Hoyt (1933, 440).

Planners kept insisting that zoning be part of a comprehensive plan in part to avoid overzoning for one use. The theory was, as Bassett argued in 1922, that "one cannot know how to zone any spot in a city until he knows how to zone the entire city because the use of any one locality has some relation to all others" (Bassett 1922a, 329). But the zoning scheme of most cities left the impression that planners had no idea what they were doing. One perverse consequence was that overzoning for commercial "accelerated outward pushes" (i.e., it was a generator of sprawl) (Hason 1977, 41). A related problem was that cities did not include enough land zoned for single-family housing in more close-in locations, and this was causing people to relocate to the suburbs (Flint 1977). This was not what planners had wanted. The most prominent planners in the field, people like Thomas Adams and Harland Bartholomew, wanted zoning to restrict heights, restrict apartments, and restrict areas zoned for business; in other words, make building envelopes smaller and less intense—not chase people out of the city (Adams and Bartholomew 1935). What was emerging already in the 1920s was a disconnect between regulation and intended outcome.

Three characteristics of zoning prior to World War II made the practice of regulating by use fundamentally different from today. First, regulations were much simpler in terms of the number of zones used. Many zoning codes were less than eight pages long. Chicago, the second-largest city in 1923, adopted a twenty-page ordinance in that year. This was the result of having fewer designations (although, as previously noted, use could also be controlled by limiting building envelope). Chicago's ordinance had four classes of use districts—residential, apartment, commercial, and manufacturing—and five "volume" districts. Seattle's 1923 zoning ordinance had just two residence, two commercial, and two industrial districts. The town of Euclid's 1922 zoning ordinance had only six use districts, four area districts, and three height districts. In many cities there were just three use zones—residential (unless a separate "apartment district" was also used), commercial, and industrial. New York City's 1916 zoning ordinance, which essentially codified existing land uses, had three use districts: residential, business, and unrestricted. Today, New York City still has three basic districts (residential, commercial and manufacturing), but these have been further divided into numerous subzones, special purpose districts, and detailed "use groups."

A zoning review in 1939 claimed that the number of zoning categories cities were using was decreasing, to about eight: four residential, two business, and two industrial (Goodrich 1939, 65–66). This trend was not only soon reversed, but use overtook height and area requirements as the most important dimension of zoning regulation. After the 1920s, rules about use were the main criterion of zone definition, and height and area rules were absorbed into use requirements.

A second difference is that earlier zoning maps allowed a much finer grain of mixing. This was not "spot zoning," but had the effect of mixing uses in a given spatial area. Zones were to be small and spatially arranged to allow local businesses to be adjacent to residential zones and, in some cases, apartment zones to be near single-family zones. Zones could consist of a single block or part of one (Haldeman 1912).

Lawrence Veiller had been an advocate of small geographic boundaries for districts, in the range of a single side of a single block, because "anything larger than this is bound to cause trouble . . . with the units thus limited to one side of a block, it is possible to give to each part of a city the special treatment that it needs" (Veiller 1914, 14).

Although planners believed that "business streets" were not places for children to be raised (Bassett 1925a, 61), as long as there were "single family dwelling districts" nearby, planners believed that proximity was a good thing. The annual report of the Baltimore Board of Zoning Appeal shows how zoning advocates were perfectly happy with businesses dispersed every few blocks; what they didn't want were stores between every other house. The 1916 New York Building Commission report included a graphic showing the "orderly arrangement of business districts," shown in figure 4.5. In the first decades of the twentieth century, the amount of land zoned for business in proximity to residential was high. Adams (1932) reported that 7,000 square feet of business area was needed for every 100 persons in self-contained cities, and 4,500 in small communities.

Commentary leading up to the adoption of New York's 1916 ordinance included pleas to "separate the stores from the residence districts, and yet not to put them too far away, but always have them within reach" (New York City Board of Estimate and Apportionment 1916, 137). Typically, there would be business zoning along a commercial street corridor, with apartments in the next block and then single-family housing in the blocks after. In many places, this pattern was preconditioned by the electric streetcar, and zoning simply reflected the kind of use pattern the streetcar lines had established: apartments and businesses close to the streetcar lines, single-family housing only a few blocks away (von Hoffman 1996). Motorized buses liberated industry and apartment dwellers to some degree (Fischel 2004), but initially,

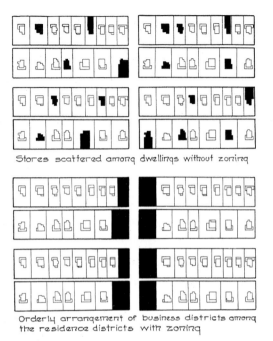

Stores scattered among dwellings without zoning

Orderly arrangement of business districts among the residence districts with zoning

Figure 4.5. Proposal for orderly business districts.
Source: Baltimore Board of Zoning Appeals (1925).

finely grained zoning maps supported the close proximity of many kinds of uses. Charles H. Cheney described the approach of how fine-grained proximities of use zones kept things in balance:

There is a common misconception of zoning which we have to contend with in all cities at first, and that is that the districts for one or another type of dwellings are great zones or belts in which we shut out all convenient adjoining locations for apartments, stores, or industries. As a matter of fact, in the Portland, Alameda and other recent zoning ordinances of the West there are no single family dwelling districts without a small business or apartment house center located within a half mile or a few blocks at least, convenient for everybody. About one-third of Portland, near the business and industrial districts, has been set aside to permit apartments as well as single family homes, enough room in fact to house a million and a half people, within walking distance of most of the business and work in the city. (1920, 277)

A final difference between early and later zoning is that the content of use zones—what was included and excluded—was much less restrictive. Compared to the use segregation typical of zoning today, there was actually quite a bit of mix allowed when zoning first appeared. For example, the most restricted residence district in Baltimore's 1924 zoning ordinance allowed boarding houses, dormitories, apartments over garages, hotels, and lodging houses (Greenfield 1924). Unrestricted home occupations were usually allowed; until 1947 in Oak Park, Illinois, home occupations were allowed in single-family residence districts (Village of Oak Park 1947). Thomas Adams wrote in 1922 that residences should not be excluded from light industrial districts (Adams 1922), and Nolen advocated for "differentiated districts, each with the services needed for it greatest efficiency" (Nolen, cited in Hason 1977, 46). In Chicago, the "residential" district was for single-family homes, but neighborhood businesses were also allowed. The district permitted "homes, apartments, hotels, clubs, churches schools, libraries, museums, hospitals, nurseries, truck gardens, or railroad stations." Further, the rules allowed "doctors, dentists, artists, hairdressers, manicurists and dressmakers" to set up shop in the residential use zone (Ward and Zunz 1992, 20). In business districts, everything was allowed except for industry that produced noxious odors or products. There were also provisions for mixed-use buildings: manufacturing could be done within a building in a business district, as long as it didn't take up more than 25 percent of the building's floor space.

At first, zoning proponents made only small refinements to this permissive mixing. For example, Bassett argued in "The Remarkable Adaptability of Modern Zoning" that in a residential area, butcher shops were bad, but dry goods retail was good (Bassett 1925b, 129), presumably because the former tended to be smelly. Gradually, however, rules within zones became more restrictive. What seems especially unfortunate from our twenty-first-century perspective is that rules began to exclude small, neighborhood-serving businesses like grocery stores from residential neighborhoods. In the early 1900s, there was concern about stores and garages fitting in, even when these uses occupied relatively unobtrusive and contextually appropriate building types, as shown in figures 4.6–4.8.

Newark, New Jersey's Commission on Building Districts and Restrictions argued that small businesses were interrupting sleep patterns, creating excessive dust ("an unavoidable incident of every business") and violating everyone's sense of smell with their "offensive odors" (Newark, New Jersey, 1919, 26). A 1925 zoning report argued that "business mixed up with residence" meant that more police protection would be required (Baltimore BZA 1925, 87). Again, the issue was whether mix could be accommodated not by mixing within zones, but by distributing a balanced arrangement of single-use zones.

European cities were accustomed to home-based businesses behind residences,

West 8th Street—Basement of private
house converted into public laundry.

West 8th Street, between Fifth and
Sixth Avenues—Conversion into stores.

Fig. 80—STORES INVADING RESIDENCE STREETS.

The English-basement or high-stoop type of residence is so easily converted into
stores that it is almost an invitation for business to invade residence streets.

Figures 4.6–4.8. In the studies leading up to the
nation's first comprehensive zoning ordinance in
New York City in 1916, these photos were used as
examples of the harmful invasion of nonresidential uses in residential areas.
Source: NYC Board of Estimate and Apportionment (1913).

and shops of various kinds (millwork, for example) were not considered to be health
threats (Logan 1972). But in U.S. cities, residents pushed for an ever-expanding list
of uses to be treated as nuisances. Other approaches had been implemented—for ex-

ample "frontage-consent" ordinances had been used to block certain uses like retail if a group of owners on a block refused to give consent (Schwieterman and Caspall 2006, 13). That approach proved legally difficult. Zoning provided a more efficient way to rid neighborhoods of unwanted uses.

Restrictions on use became increasingly rigid. One single mother in Atlanta requested a zone change in 1937 so that she could operate a "small fectionary business" to support herself and two children, and, she argued, keep them from "committing crimes since I have to work" (Atlanta General Council 1937, cited in Flint 1977, 368). Her application was denied. One explanation for this hard line is that planners feared it would be impossible to limit retail expansion without drawing strict boundaries. Lawrence Veiller, the housing advocate and social progressive, at first reluctant to embrace zoning, later came to see it as essential for this reason. He described the benefit of keeping stores out of residential areas as follows:

> How are we to treat [the] case where a man has invested his money in an attractive dwelling with the idea of permanently living there for the rest of his days; then suddenly he finds his property values injured, the whole character of the street endangered, because someone has chosen to construct a small retail store in one of the houses? One store of this kind leads to another, and within a short time the residences are driven out. (Veiller 1914, 10)

The argument was also made that these restrictions were good for business too. First, it prevented lower-class establishments like livery stables and junk shops from opening next door, thereby ensuring the owner that "he will be surrounded by other stores of his same class." Second, it created a strengthened business street, where businesses were "forced to stay on them" and residents would be "compelled" to shop on the nearest business street (Bassett 1922c, 5). If the rogue businesses started to "short-circuit the trade" by infiltrating a residential corner, and if this business was successful and others followed, "this hurt the car-line street where the business ought to be." There was some flexibility in this rule, however. If several stores came into a block fronting a main thoroughfare or street-car line, that street was likely showing its "normal destiny" and should be zoned for business (Bassett 1922a, 316, 324). The needs of modern retailing reinforced this. A 1938 article in the *Planners' Journal* by Mackesey and McKeever claimed that "unbiased research in merchandizing methods" had shown that "the concentration of shops in a compact shopping area [is] desirable socially and economically," and superior to "the nonconforming store in a residence district." This kind of thinking put an end to zoning allowances for the corner store in residential areas. And planners seemed to have no faith in the ability of design to solve any incompatibility issues. There were increasing calls that residential areas be protected from commercial uses with "physical buffers in the form of open space" (Mackesey and McKeever 1938, 46, 48).

Gradually, the balancing of business streets in proximity to residential neighborhoods was lost. By the end of the 1920s, Clarence Perry was bemoaning the inconvenience being caused by "remoteness from markets" due to zoning out all business. Planners struggled to balance the problem of "inconvenience" and the "danger of a business invasion" (Perry 1929, 83), but in the end, wide segregation of uses prevailed.

This is not to say there were no advantages. Neighborhoods that had been converting to business use and then industrial use were no longer tipping completely in the direction of becoming industrial: the rules of zoning prevented wholesale change and its corresponding loss of property value. To some this was a matter of social progressiveness: loss of property value meant loss of revenue for the public coffers to fund things like schools and community centers. This revenue loss could be significant, and it was well documented. Lawson Purdy, president of the Board of Taxes and Assessments for New York City who had a major role in crafting New York's 1916 ordinance, reported that a single block in New York was assessed in 1911 for $17 million and in 1916 for $7 million, all on account of the intrusion of industry. Then too, there was still the belief that functional segregation benefited the poor. Lawson Purdy and colleagues used this rationale:

> We find that retail stores on streets devoted to multi-family dwellings for very poor people is usually amiss. It increases the vehicular traffic. We have come to a point where in order to provide playgrounds for our poor children for certain hours of the day, we shut off vehicle traffic on a street and let them play in the street in safety and in peace. That could hardly be done if you had stores on the street. (Purdy et al. 1920, 20)

In some cities, the goal of blocking business development in residential neighborhoods was slow to materialize, as many stores had been "grandfathered" in. This changed, however, as legal support for functional separation became more widespread. Writing in 1940, Edward Bassett noted how the courts had, in the 1920s, resisted residential-only districts thinking they were based on aesthetics, but had since been provided proof of the value of zoning—evidence of "fire risk, noise, dust and insects" (Bassett 1940, 12). And even if the courts resisted, there were other strategies. One was condemnation to assemble land for large-scale redevelopment projects, followed by a requirement that only residential uses could be built back. Jane Jacobs claimed that 1,110 stores had been lost in this way in the redevelopment plans to house 50,000 people in New York City (Jacobs 1956). One store owner later sued for the right to locate a store in a residential neighborhood based on a proximity argument—that is, that no other stores were close by (*Kushner v. Lawton*, 1953, cited by Williams 1956).

Effects

In the early decades of the twentieth century, people pushed for land-use separation because they were fearful of a variety of negative social and economic effects—but were those fears realized? One case to review is the zoning of the Flatbush section of Brooklyn, New York, which Edward Bassett had held up as a model of the "inter-dependent community." John B. Creighton, president of one of the single-family districts, Fiske Terrace Association, complained in a 1916 statement to the New York Commission on Building Districts that the private deed restrictions for the subdivision, shown in figures 4.9, 4.10, and 4.11, had run out in 1915 "and immediately two apartment houses were erected on Ocean Avenue which we regard as rather spoiling Ocean Avenue." He worried that the zoning for apartments would "cheapen values." His fears were never realized. Zoning did allow apartment house development along Ocean Avenue adjacent to Fiske Terrace, but the subdivision was not "spoiled," and Fiske Terrace remains a highly valued single-family neighborhood, with typical home sales above $1,000,000. It is surrounded by higher-intensity uses, creating something else that is valued—a diversity of housing types in relatively close proximity. Here in Brooklyn can be seen the effects of Bassett's model of zoning—an "inter-dependent community" of "home districts" near "apartment houses."

Figure 4.9. Current zoning for Fiske Terrace (highlighted).
Source: New York City Department of City Planning.

Figure 4.10. Just behind the apartment buildings that line Ocean Avenue, shown in figure 4.11, are the homes of Fiske Terrace in the Flatbush area of Brooklyn, New York.

Figure 4.11. Ocean Avenue frontage, with the Fiske Terrace subdivision behind. Residents of Fiske Terrace worried that zoning for apartment buildings would "cheapen values," which did not turn out to be the case.

There are other examples showing that fears of housing type mix were unrealized. In figure 4.12, apartments and single-family homes coexist quite nicely along East 23rd Street between Clarendon Road and Avenue D in Brooklyn. This section was shown in the Building Commission's run-up to the NYC 1916 zoning ordinance under the headline "The Apartment House Invading Detached House Sections." The original photo is shown in figure 4.13. In this section of Brooklyn, many streets were designated "E" on the Area Maps, and open space lot requirements were used to discourage apartment buildings.

Figure 4.12. Apartments and single-family homes coexist quite nicely along East 23rd Street between Clarendon Road and Avenue D, in Brooklyn.

Figure 4.13. An image of the same street from the 1916 NYC Board of Estimate and Apportionment report.

"Step down zoning"—a term used at the time to describe what Bassett was proposing—did not work out as well in Los Angeles. Figure 4.14 shows the original zoning scheme and figure 4.15 shows the area now. The intersection of Casitas Avenue
and Woodbury Street (formerly Atlanta Avenue) is now an uncoordinated mix of
single-family homes and commercial buildings. No intervening apartment house
zone emerged.

Remnants of a finer-grained intersection of residential and business uses, encouraged by zoning, can be seen in many cities. Figures 4.16–4.19 show the 1923 zoning
and current conditions for a neighborhood in Seattle. Two maps controlled it all in
1923: one map regulating height and area, the other regulating use. Remnants of business zoning in Seattle are still evident (shown in figs. 4.18 and 4.19), although some
buildings have been converted to housing. The small size of the strip business districts

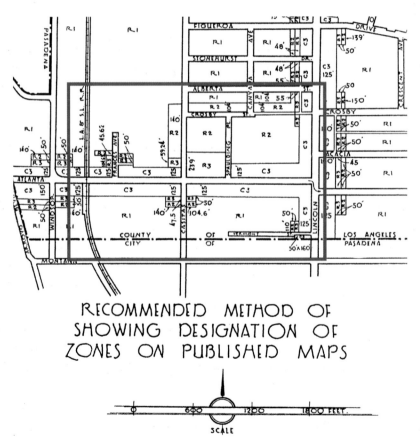

Figure 4.14. "Step-down zoning" was proposed for this area in Los Angeles in the 1920s.
Source: Zoning Study Group (1928).

Figure 4.15. The section of Los Angeles outlined in red on figure 4.14. The intersection of Casitas Avenue and Woodbury Street (formerly Atlanta Avenue) is now an uncoordinated mix of single-family homes and commercial buildings. No intervening apartment house zone emerged.

that ran one lot deep on either side of the street matched the scale of the businesses—modest, single-story buildings that fit in well with the neighborhood.

Sometimes, the result of "spot zoning"—which is the zoning of one or more parcels separately, creating a small, often isolated district—was diversity, as in the Chicago neighborhood shown in figure 4.20. The figure shows apartments (outlined in red) embedded in an otherwise predominantly single-family neighborhood. Their adjacency to the park is an example of good spatial logic, as it gives the apartment residents access to outdoor space. This also happens to be one of the most socially diverse neighborhoods in Chicago, made possible by the mixture of housing types.

Figures 4.21 and 4.22 show an example from Portland, Oregon. Here the 1920 zoning ordinance (fig. 4.21) and its result (fig. 4.22) can be seen. The area was zoned for businesses and apartments adjacent to single-family homes, creating an area that remains vibrant today.

Unfortunately, as zones grew in size and distance apart, it became impossible to hold on to the proximal arrangements 1920s planners had proposed. The earlier attempts to use zoning to create interdependent communities seem novel in the face of suburban rules that now vigorously block the mixing of housing types. The most

Figure 4.16. Use map for Seattle's 1923 zoning ordinance.
Source: City of Seattle (1923).

LEGEND
☐ FIRST RESIDENCE DISTRICT
▨ SECOND RESIDENCE DISTRICT
▨ BUSINESS DISTRICT
▨ COMMERCIAL DISTRICT
▨ MANUFACTURING DISTRICT
▨ INDUSTRIAL DISTRICT

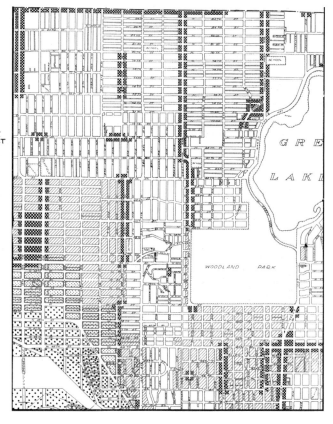

Figure 4.18. Intersection from neighborhood shown in figures 4.16 and 4.17, Seattle's 1923 zoning map. Remnants of business zoning in Seattle are still evident, although some buildings have been converted to housing.

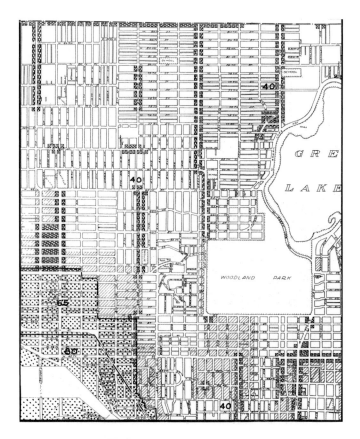

Figure 4.17. Height and area map for Seattle's 1923 zoning ordinance.
Source: City of Seattle (1923).

Figure 4.19. Intersection from neighborhood shown in figures 4.16 and 4.17, Seattle's 1923 zoning map. Remnants of business zoning in Seattle are still evident, although some buildings have been converted to housing.

Figure 4.20. A section of Chicago, Illinois. Apartments (outlined in red) embedded in an otherwise predominantly single-family neighborhood.

Figure 4.21. Original zoning map for a section of Portland, Oregon. *Source:* Cheney (1920), p. 278.

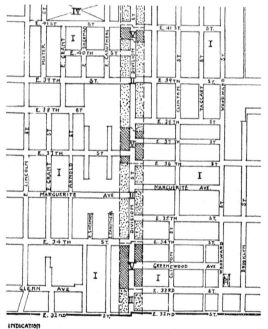

Figure 4.22. Current view of figure 4.21. The area was zoned for businesses and apartments adjacent to single-family homes, creating an area that remains vibrant today.

common rules include the following: only one family is allowed per lot; no single-family attached housing is allowed; all lots must have street frontage, which means bungalow courts, mews, or courtyard housing is prohibited; duplexes on corner lots are not allowed; no density increases on lots adjacent to commercial are allowed; no transitional zones or midblock zoning district lines are allowed, which would rationalize higher densities in locations closer to services.

Planners were cognizant of the need for some mixing of uses, but over the course of the twentieth century, zoning seemed increasingly incapable of producing a healthy form of it. What happened to zoning changes in Tampa, Florida (figs. 4.23 and 4.24) and the resultant effect on the ground (fig. 4.25) is illustrative. In 1966, the area had just two zoning districts, shown in figure 4.23: R1-A, single-family residential, and C-1, commercial. The R1-A was the *most* restrictive residential zone in Tampa in 1966. C-1, according to the 1966 code, was "designed primarily to meet the needs and conveniences of the surrounding neighborhood by providing shopping and service areas for the consumers of the tributary neighborhood."

By 2010, this same area of Tampa had four districts, as shown in figure 4.24. There was now the RS-50, residential single-family zone, now the *least* restrictive single-family district; the RO-1 zone, which permits office and residential; the CG

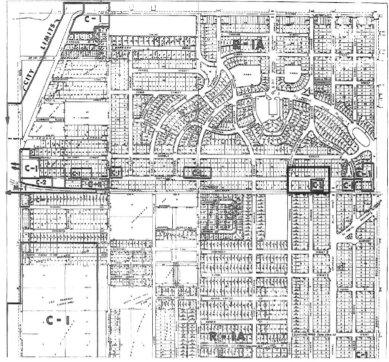

Figure 4.23. Tampa zoning, 1966. The area had just two zoning districts.

commercial-general zone, which allows "a variety of retail and commercial service activities"; and the PD Planned Development zone, intended to encourage "maximum land development opportunities." Figure 4.25 shows what was built. Building frontage is random, setbacks are arbitrary, and the area is an antipedestrian series of strip malls. These problems are, in part, the result of an overconcern for use requirements and an inattention to form. Off-street parking requirements, in keeping with concerns about use, doubled between 1966 and 2010.

There are other examples of how zoning's increasing complexity undermined a healthy form of land-use mixing. The zoning changes of one small town in central Illinois, Urbana, home of the University of Illinois, illustrate the typical progression (City of Urbana 1990). The first zoning ordinance was passed in 1936. Up until 1950, there were no minimum lot widths and no lot areas required per unit. The 1950 ordinance contained only six zoning districts: two for residential, two for business, two for industrial. The 1979 ordinance changed this simplicity dramatically, introducing sixteen districts and two overlay zones. Though the setback requirements were reduced, apartments in single-family areas were no longer allowed, and mini-

Figure 4.24. Tampa zoning, 2010. The area now has multiple zoning districts.

Figure 4.25. Inset area, showing the results of inattention to form. Building frontage is random, setbacks are deep, and the area is an antipedestrian series of strip malls.

mum lot sizes and floor area ratio rules were introduced. Apartment buildings that had coexisted beautifully with single-family houses were made illegal. The main drivers of this downzoning were "neighborhood preservationists." Planners had wisely urged that multifamily housing in single-family neighborhoods that were close to campus should be maintained because they would help with the redevelopment of obsolescent single-family housing, counter sprawl, meet a growing demand, and strengthen Urbana's downtown. A decade later, under pressure from some long-time residents, planners labeled these assumptions "faulty" (City of Urbana 1990, 14).

A section of Baltimore provides another example of the effects of zoning intended to stimulate commercial development and "mixed use." The same area is shown in two zoning maps, figure 4.26 from 1921 and figure 4.27 from 2010 (note the addition of highways through the neighborhood). Between these years, the heart of this neighborhood was changed to "B-3-2." Baltimore's zoning ordinance states: "The B-3 Community Commercial District is designed primarily to accommodate business, service, and commercial uses of a highway-oriented nature." Such services "do not involve local shopping and are not characteristic of business shopping areas" (Baltimore 2010). Also added was an R-8 zone, which allows everything from single-family homes to apartments.

Figures 4.28 and 4.29 show what became of the "highway-oriented commercial" zone. Although the change was likely an effort to stimulate any kind of investment, due to the significant loss of jobs in Baltimore, zoning was unlikely to have helped. Thankfully, a new approach to zoning in Baltimore is in the works: for starters, the city is rewriting its zoning code to allow more urban farms.

Rules that require functional separation are still the norm. In many cities, there is the occasional "mixed-use district" or overlay, but for the most part, residential areas are to be kept strictly residential. The Phoenix zoning code (in tandem with the Phoenix Subdivision Ordinance) explains that the purpose of "residence districts," which constitute most of the city, is "to preserve these areas from the distractions and adverse impacts which can result from immediate association with nonresidential uses." Uses other than residences, therefore, are labeled "distractions," rather than essentials that satisfy the needs of daily life. While each dwelling unit is to be guaranteed "access to . . . vehicular and pedestrian circulation systems" and the ability to "pursue residential activities with reasonable access to open space, and streets or roads," there is no consideration of what might be at the end of that road, or what residences are connected to—apart from open space. The only nonresidential categories explicitly mentioned as needing to be accessible are "light and air," "open

Figure 4.26. Zoning for an area in Baltimore, 1921.

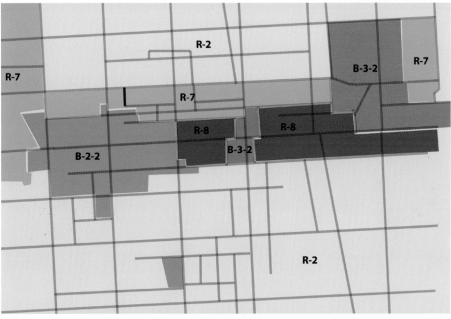

Figure 4.27. Zoning for the same area as of 2010. Note addition of the B-3 Community Commercial District, "designed primarily to accommodate business, service, and commercial uses of a highway-oriented nature."

Figure 4.28. Area shown in figures 4.26 and 4.27.

Figure 4.29. Intersection from the same area, showing an R-8 zone.

space," and "a variety of outdoor areas" (Section 608, "Residence Districts," of the City of Phoenix zoning code). The underlying assumption is that everyone has the time and means to assemble what they need for daily life from far-flung destinations.

Daily activities cannot be carried out on the premises, in home occupations or accessory buildings, as these uses are severely constrained in the Phoenix code. For example, accessory buildings in residence districts have the same yard requirements as main buildings, meaning that the property owner will need a large yard to accommodate an additional unit. There is to be no selling of products or services. One can sleep, eat, and park vehicles, engage in a "hobby, avocation or pastime," and have a home occupation as an "architect, lawyer, off-site sales businesses, accountant, real estate agent, telemarketing sales, and psychologist." But under no circumstances would it be possible to operate a barbershop, beauty parlor, veterinary office, dog grooming service, massage parlor, or restaurant. There can be no employees unless they are part of the owner's family. There can be no mechanical equipment "except that normally used for domestic, hobby, standard office, or household purposes," no outdoor display, for example on the side of a building, and no "exterior indication of the home occupation." The business can only be small, as "not more than twenty-five percent of the total area under roof on the site shall be used for any home occupation." If the home occupation is to be in an accessory building, a special use permit is required, which is not easily obtained.

Besides the fact that most zoning discourages mixed-use development, or confines it to limited areas, the mixing of uses is thwarted in multiple, indirect ways. One example is the prohibition of alcohol sales within a certain distance of a school, park, or church. Consider the added challenge such a rule creates wherever the goal is to increase density, land-use mix, and generally to bring buildings, uses, and people closer together (Slone and Goldstein 2008).

5. Form

"Urban form" is a term often loosely applied to mean any physical dimension of urbanism, but it is used in this chapter to distinguish three-dimensional character. Form is controlled by rules establishing building lines, setbacks, and lot coverage, but it can also be a function of street width, building type, and building height. The regulation of building details can be a significant aspect as well, such as rules about facade embellishment or window size. Above all, form defines space. Rob Krier identified twenty-four different ways in which buildings create spatial definition, asserting that the failure to recognize these effects "shows a society in cultural crisis" (2003, 329).

Elements of Form

One of the more interesting aspects of rules affecting form is how the intentions of rules have changed. After the turn of the twentieth century, regulations impacting form seemed no longer a conscious effort, but instead were an indirect outcome of other objectives: traffic flow, fire prevention, public health, or parking provision, among other goals. What makes this transition from form-direct to form-indirect rule so important now is the current attempt to revive, via form-based codes, the earlier approach. One may ask whether it is legitimate, or even possible, to revive the conscious, form-giving intent of past eras.

This chapter discusses three interrelated categories of rules that affect form. First are rules about street width. While motivated by a variety of different objectives, from public health to aesthetics to traffic flow, street widths have a significant impact on urban form. Second, and often directly tied to the first, are rules that regulate building height. The effect of these rules is immediately visible and unambiguous, at least before modern codes instituted complex formulas and bonus systems that seemed to affect height only indirectly. Third are rules that control frontage by establishing building lines and setback distances. These rules were most often motivated by the desire for civic decorum. Fire and public health concerns were also factors, but their effect, even if unintended, was still the "outdoor room"—the enclosure and definition of space that is the product of building setback. Where there is an aesthetic dimension, in which form is regulated for its own sake (i.e., for the purpose of a deliberate urban aesthetic experience), it stands in stark contrast to today's establishment of rules on the basis of traffic flow and other assumed efficiencies.

Street Width

Street width regulations were often directed at stemming encroachment, which seemed to be the natural inclination. One historian of medieval cities reasoned that the abundance of statutes dictating street widths, buildings, and frontage lines in medieval cities was a matter of trying to keep street encroachments to a tolerable level (Saalman 1968). The first building regulations in England in 1189 had the intent of curbing encroachment, and covered issues like obstruction of views, blockage of light, party walls, and projections (Larkham 2001). In some cities in Italy in the fifteenth century, laws regulated building projections by zones, with more strict control on primary streets. In Amsterdam, sixteenth-century decrees regulated even the maximum size of front steps in an effort to keep streets accessible. Dutch decrees also limited lean-tos, benches, and the display of goods, suggesting problems with street encumbrances (Wheelock 2000). London's Rebuilding Act of 1667 prohibited building projections and required consistent setbacks and cornice lines on designated principal streets. A set of eighteenth-century Prussian laws allowed building freedom only if the building did not lead to "disfigurement of the towns or public squares" (Allgemeine Landrecht 1794, quoted in Arntz 2002, 7).

In part the tendency to invade street space had to do with the fact that citizens often had some responsibility for construction, drainage, and lighting of streets. In Paris in the fourteenth century, for example, households were required by law to clean the streets in front of their dwellings (Girouard 1985). This had the effect of encouraging encroachment into the street, since residents felt a sense of entitlement in exchange for this responsibility. It would also have fueled a desire by citizens to keep streets narrow and minimize frontage in order to reduce cost. Dutch towns in the fifteenth century required that owners maintain the road in front of them, but it was later decreed that owners had to pay for an actual road-maker, presumably owing to the fact that roads had become "a pretty wavy affair" (Wheelock 2000, 18).

Street width regulations were also based on practical objectives of traffic flow. In Islamic towns, main streets had to be wide enough to allow two loaded beasts of burden to pass (Arntz 2002; Hakim 1986). There was a law in medieval Germany requiring streets to be the width needed for two carts to pass each other, a consideration that similarly determined street widths throughout the American West. Another practical concern was fire prevention. After the great fire of London in 1666, the London Building Act of 1667 specified wide streets in part to keep fires from jumping across them. This was a significant danger—during the medieval period, buildings sometimes encroached so far into the street that "it was literally possible to shake hands between opposite windows" (Morris 1979, 73).

Widening streets for health reasons was a related objective. Starting in the seventeenth century, it was believed that wide streets helped ventilate the city and keep it healthy, based on the "miasma theory" that stagnant air causes disease (Girouard 1985, 227). In Dublin in the eighteenth century, a Wide Streets Commission made sure street widths remained between 75 and 100 feet, and Girouard (1985) argues that since these widths went well beyond what was needed to accommodate carriage traffic, the commission must have been motivated by health reasons, or even visual ideals.

Width rules might have varied by location or primary function—a sort of "A" and "B" street hierarchy. The Roman emperor Augustus imposed a law that specified street widths ranging from 40 to 15 feet, depending on location relative to the central core. Pompeii's main streets were 30 feet wide, while its side streets were 15. London's Rebuilding Act of 1667 used varying street types based on location and width, to specify three building height categories. This was similar to rules imposed in France after the Revolution, when four categories of width were created based on street length and primary function. Streets in London were later regulated by the 1844 Metropolitan Building Act, which required them to be at least 40 feet wide, whereas alleys and mews could be 20 feet wide. The Act was faulted for applying only to new streets. It did nothing to open up the city on existing streets where buildings could be "erected to unlimited heights on old streets of any width" (Knowles and Pitt 1972, 64).

L'Enfant envisioned street width rules for Washington, D.C. based on location: grand avenues like the one leading to the White House were to be 160 feet wide, streets leading to public buildings or markets were to be 130 feet wide, and all other streets were set at 110 feet wide (Brown 1900). Later in the nineteenth century, German planners thought that streets outside of the city center, whether main streets or side streets, should be regulated differently from the center (Williams 1914). Other cities differentiated between inner and outer parts of a town, as for example the 1891 building rules in Frankfurt am Main, Germany. In German subdivision regulations of the same period, there were zone designations for main streets that "were to be lined with buildings of suitably impressive architecture" (Logan 1972, 101).

A common practice was to regulate street widths and building height in tandem. There is evidence that this rule was in place at one of the earliest known planned cities, Mohenjo-Daro in present-day Pakistan (Churchill 1945). Seventeenth-century London imposed an "elaborate prescription" of housing height and form based on the type and width of a street (Baer 2007b). Royal proclamations in France in 1783–84 introduced rules that made house height a function of street width, and forbade any roof greater than half the width of the house, a rule motivated by the desire to maintain scenic views. By the time of Baron von Haussmann's 1859 decree regulating building height in relation to street width, such rules were considered "more an evolution than a revolution" (Cognot and Roux 2002, 10).

Early urban designers like Camillo Sitte in the late nineteenth century spent a good deal of time working out the proper relationship between buildings and streets (Kostof 1991). These relationships were a defining feature of almost all of the early German zoning codes. In Stuttgart, an 1897 ordinance stipulated that building height was limited to street width plus 2 meters (6.5 feet). If a street was less than 16 meters (52.5 feet), buildings were capped at four stories (Logan 1972, 101). London's Building Act of 1894 contained absurd anomalies: a street 49.5 feet wide required buildings not more than 49.5 feet tall, whereas a street 50 feet wide could have a building 80 feet tall. Relative width seemed a better practice. Karlsruhe, Germany, fixed building height at 1.25 times street width, while Rome fixed it at 1.5 times the width. This practice transferred to the United States. Initially, the rules were contained in building codes. A page from an 1898 compilation of New York building codes is shown in figure 5.1.

In the early twentieth century, building height rules in U.S. cities were almost always a function of street width—even tenement house rules set in 1885. This transferred to early zoning codes. The "multiple of street width rule" for New York's 1916 zoning code established five classes of height districts at the street line, and then setbacks in prescribed ratios at distances further back. This was intended to allow "greater freedom" in building design, while still ensuring "a uniform angle of light down into the center of the street" (New York City Board of Estimate and Apportionment 1916, 33).

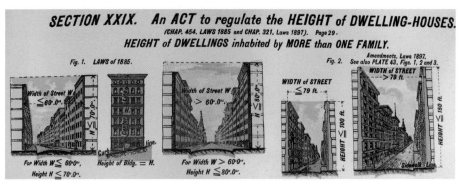

Figure 5.1. Graphic from a New York building code, 1898.

Gradually in the United States, however, street width became more about surrounding use and accommodating traffic than any civic considerations about height–width relationships. Charles Robinson, who wrote several early twentieth-century textbooks on the new city planning field, wanted the percentage of area devoted to streets for any given city to be raised from 10 percent, typical of ancient and medieval cities, to a more "modern" standard of 25 to 40 percent (Robinson 1916, 28–29). This was in contrast to Raymond Unwin's famous dictum that "the less area devoted to streets the better" (quoted in Kostof 1992).

Yet Robinson was attuned to the wastefulness of excessively wide streets. His main objective was to have less standardization of rules and more case-by-case assessment. His contemporaries agreed. Thomas Adams, a leading planner of the early twentieth century, wrote: "it is not proper to fix definite standards of width for streets" (Adams 1934, 150), leaving him vacillating between what he acknowledged were two "absurd" conditions: "needlessly wide streets" and streets "choked with traffic" (30). In their defense, early city planners like Robinson and Adams did understand that streets were, to quote another contemporary, "an index of character" (Augur 1923), meaning, a measure of urban quality. Yet if character was to be defined by street width and "the picturesqueness of winding narrow ways," it seemed unlikely that this could ever be enforced by a rule.

Building Height

Rules governing building height, whether or not connected to street width, have a long history. There was a height rule of 66 feet under the Roman emperor Augustus in 15 BC (Southworth and Ben-Joseph 2003). A famous book of German building regulations known as the *Sachsenspiegel*, produced in the early 1200s, specified laws governing minimum distances between buildings and maximum heights (Arntz 2002). Like street width rules, the intent was generally to keep the city from getting overbuilt, which was the inclination of property owners. In nineteenth-century Germany, for example, owners sought to maximize the value of property by building taller buildings in response to the 1875 Law of Building Lines. Developers of the Berlin Meitskaserne "filled every inch of property with huge buildings; . . . inhabitants had no benefit whatever of the light and air of the ample streets, as they breathed through narrow courtyards and less" (Kostof 1992, 206).

There are some instances where the opposite concern led cities to impose rules that increased building height because they were not being built up enough. For example in the eighteenth century, German cities imposed regulations on *minimum* height (Kostof 1991). After World War II, residential buildings in German cities were required to be at least four stories high in an effort to make cities more urban and dense, especially at the core. Something similar is now being proposed via some types of form-based codes.

In the late 1900s, in response to the skyscraper—disdained for blocking light and air and increasing congestion—U.S. cities started to impose height limits that generally ranged between 100 and 200 feet. Boston was the first, imposing a height limit of 125 feet in 1891 (a later 1903 regulation was upheld by the U.S. Supreme Court in 1909). Building height was set at 80 feet along some main thoroughfares, and 125 feet on all other streets—thus establishing an "A" and "B" district (New York City Board of Estimate and Apportionment 1913), a form of zoning now being revived (see, e.g., Duany, Plater-Zyberk, and Speck 2000) but missing from most contemporary zoning codes. Building height was limited in Washington, D.C., in 1899 by height districts (fig. 5.2), to be no higher than the capitol. By 1913, twenty-one U.S. cities had height restrictions (New York City Board of Estimate and Apportionment 1916).

Chicago's building heights laws were literally up and down: 130 feet (about ten stories) was the limit in 1893, 260 feet in 1902, back down to 200 feet in 1910, back up to 260 in 1920—the result of political power shuffles. Height rules affected more than the profile of a skyline. Interior courtyards in the center of a building (in the form of either an "O-plan" or a "U-plan") emerged in order to maximize rentable space under height limits (Schwieterman and Caspall 2006, 81). Under New York's tenement house laws, height limits combined with rules about lot coverage to coerce the familiar dumbbell shapes into existence. Some thought that these rules erred by prioritizing health over aesthetics. Triggs, an urban historian and planner, argued that

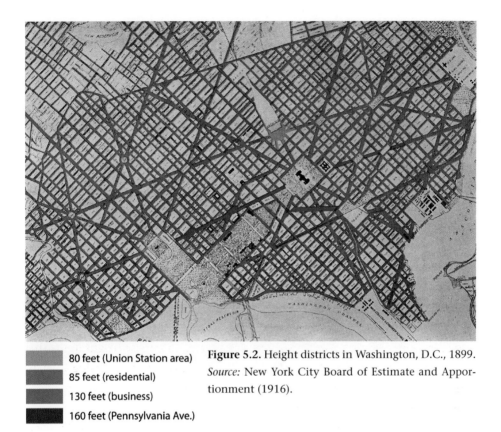

80 feet (Union Station area)
85 feet (residential)
130 feet (business)
160 feet (Pennsylvania Ave.)

Figure 5.2. Height districts in Washington, D.C., 1899. *Source:* New York City Board of Estimate and Apportionment (1916).

tall buildings looked better on narrower streets, and that in the case of building height regulations, "the aesthetic idea is opposed to that of hygiene" (Triggs 1909, 241).

There were proposals for addressing the need for light and air that did not simply restrict building height. The architect Frank Flagg conceived of a city of towers, where the first five or six stories of a building would cover the whole lot, but the upper stories could cover only a quarter of the lot. The only limit on the height of the tower would be structural constraints. Flagg's ideas were meant to ensure sufficient light and air for office workers as well as the urban residents on the streets below, and his ideas influenced the provisions of New York's 1916 zoning ordinance. One of his buildings is shown in figure 5.3, Singer Tower, 149 Broadway, New York, New York, constructed in 1908 and demolished in 1967.

Homer Hoyt postulated that building height ordinances were promoted by three types of interests: owners of property away from the central core who wanted business "to expand laterally rather than vertically"; owners of skyscrapers who wanted to secure their monopoly; and owners of older buildings who feared tax increases

Figure 5.3. Singer Tower, New York (now demolished). An early proposal to ensure sufficient light and air for office workers as well as the urban residents on the streets below. *Source:* Historic American Buildings Survey, Library of Congress; from the "Built in America" website: http://memory.loc.gov/

(Hoyt 1933, 153). Then too there were commercial landowners who supported the "safety and serenity" of "older traditions" (Weiss 1992a, 57) who tended to disapprove of skyscrapers. City Beautiful proponents were ardent supporters of the aesthetic need to limit building height so that buildings of civic importance could be accentuated against commercial buildings, the latter fulfilling their proper function as "background" (New York City Board of Estimate and Apportionment 1913, 224). Complicating these motivations, property values could be seen as increasing or decreasing with building height limits, depending on one's point of view.

The 1916 New York code spurred the introduction of rules about the "bulk" of buildings—their height and area—on a mass scale. George Ford, who coauthored the New York code, thought that the effect would be like Paris—a city of mainly four- or five-story buildings. Architects of the time agreed that the effects of the zoning law were positive from a design point of view, giving "an incalculable value to the silhouette of the city" (Knight 1924, 11). In part this was a result of rules that limited verticality to towers and ziggurats. In Chicago, towers that were less than 25 percent of the lot could rise to any height, given leeway because, by advertising business growth, they were thought to express civic pride. Chicago's initial building height rule of 1893 was replaced in 1923 with a new rule that gave no height limit to towers, but stipulated that towers could not occupy more than one fourth of the lot, and that space within the tower could not be more than one sixth of the building. New York had a similar allowance. Hoyt thought it much too permissive: "if all the land in Chicago were built to the limit allowed by the zoning law, the entire population of the United States could be housed in the city" (Hoyt 1933, 440). By 1933, buildings were limited to forty-six stories (Hoyt 1933, 296).

The idea of setback rules that varied by height was not original. A precursor to New York's setback regulations was London's 1894 Building Act, shown in figure 5.4.

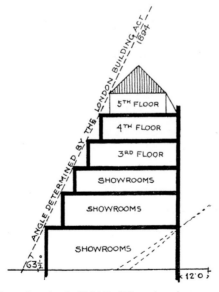

Figure 5.4. Graphic from London's 1894 Building Act. A precursor to New York's setback regulations in 1916.
Source: Triggs (1909), p. 244.

The relationship between code and building form is nowhere clearer than in New York's skyline, the result of the 1916 zoning code (Boyd 1920; Corbett 1923; Willis 1993). Some view the height and bulk rules that created New York's profile, exemplified by the Empire State and Chrysler buildings, as by far the most important innovation of the code, and indeed the volumetric approach created a whole new stepped-back aesthetic in buildings that was emulated across the country (Weiss 1992b). The maximum building envelope under the rules would have created sloping walls, but these were straightened up for practical reasons. Architects worked within the rules to define their style, but they thought it a mistake to conclude that the code "of itself creates beautiful buildings. It merely offers the architect an opportunity to prove his ability" (Boyd 1920, 206–7).

Because height rules were based on a formula that combined street width and zoning district, the dimensions and proportions of the ziggurat skyline varied widely. The famous architectural delineator Hugh Ferriss envisioned the possibilities of urban form under the new set of rules in a series of drawings published in *Pencil Points* magazine in 1923. The effects were clear, and they verified Thomas Adams's contention that "a zoning ordinance is really an extension of a building ordinance" (Adams 1935, 96).

For all of the effects on form, stepped-back building height rules were not motivated by aesthetics. They were intended to improve light and air on the street, and secondarily, street and sidewalk capacity. The landmark study by the Regional Plan of New York and Its Environs, *Buildings: Their Uses and the Spaces About Them*, was motivated by the view that "overcrowding of land with buildings is the chief problem in all cities" (Adams 1931, 22). The effect of rules on building form, especially setbacks, were considered in detail, as shown in figure 5.5. Among planners, there was also concern that districts with taller, bulkier buildings would overburden the transportation system. These considerations trumped any consideration of the relationship between building bulk and sense of place. Similarly, Frederick Law Olmsted Jr.'s "principles which should control limitations in bulk of buildings" were based on health and efficiency, not placemaking or skyline aesthetics (Olmsted 1931, 22).

Planners and most of the general public were fearful of the skyscraper, that it would "wreck, as it pierces, the neighborhood atmosphere," contributing to "the destruction of individuality" and loss of "the character of the community, difficult to define but clearly appreciable" (Hubbard and Hubbard 1929, 178). Buildings that rose too high were lambasted as "freaks" and "pirates" that stole light and air—New York City's 1915 Equitable Building was so out of scale that it was one of the main instigators of zoning. Chicago produced a report in 1923 that chronicled "the effects of

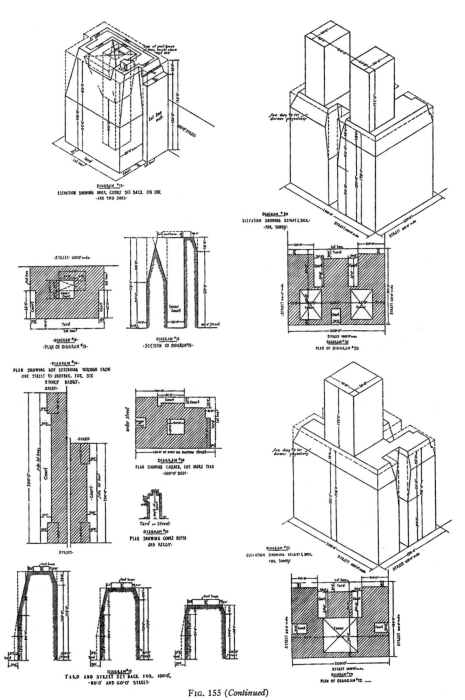

Fig. 155 (*Continued*)

Figure 5.5. Graphic from the Regional Survey, vol. 6 (Adams 1931). Building form determined by setback rules.

dark and poorly ventilated rooms upon the persons who occupy them" (Nichols 1923, 38; see box 5.1). They were essentially arguing to constrain capitalism, and they had a strong point: buildings with windows on the lot line could have their windows completely blocked off by an adjoining building, a situation that could only be remedied by limiting the height and area covered by buildings. Figures 5.6 and 5.7 are photos that were included in the 1916 Building Commission study, showing how windows would be "blocked up." Figure 5.7 was included to make the point that the blocking of windows was a problem even for the "high-class apartment house."

These concerns could not withstand the strong economic pressure of downtown property owners, however, who interpreted limitations on height and bulk as limitations on rents and values. This is one reason variances on height limit were granted often. Tulsa, Oklahoma, had a height limit of just 60 feet in the 1920s, but somehow managed to build two buildings over 250 feet and many close to 200 (Hubbard and Hubbard 1929).

Box 5.1. "The Effects of Dark and Poorly Ventilated Rooms Upon the Persons Who Occupy Them"

1. Physiological
   a. Loss of color
   b. Loss of appetite
   c. Loss of weight
   d. Eye strain and inefficient vision
   e. Nervousness
2. Mental effects
   a. Depression of spirits
   b. Irritability
3. Moral effects

("May it not be true that the irritability which comes to one who feels the supply of light insufficient to convenient working, results in a distinct lowering of moral standards?")

Source: Nichols (1923), p. 38.

Frontage

Technically, frontage includes both the public elements of curb, sidewalk, and planting, and the privately maintained elements of building facade and setback, within which there might be a variety of elements (such as a porch or stoop). The focus here is on rules that define the building wall—setbacks, building lines, and facade

Figure 5.6a and b. Photos from the 1916 Building Commission study showing the problem of windows being blocked by adjacent buildings.
Source: New York City Board of Estimate and Apportionment.

Figure 5.7. The blocking of windows was a problem even for "the high-class apartment house."
Source: New York City Board of Estimate and Apportionment.

treatment. This includes, as well, rules that affect the spaces between buildings, which can impact the quality of frontage.

Up until the absorption of frontage rules into zoning in the 1920s, the control of frontage was handled separately and was mostly a matter of maintaining visual order. Rules might have been ostensibly about improving "the general appearance of the street" (Van Nest Black 1935, 22), but the control of harmonious frontage also had the effect of defining space and creating a viable public realm in front of a row of buildings. In this pursuit, rules were applied to both attached buildings in dense urban cores and detached buildings in smaller-scale places like Williamsburg, Virginia. Behind the facade, of course, anything could happen, and building quality could be quite lax (Arntz 2002). And where rules prioritized uniformity above all else, the results could be bleak. A notorious example was the bye-law street in England, which, coupled with standardized terrace or row housing, was more about reducing costs than achieving visual harmony, and the conditions became oppressive.

Uniform frontage was required for centuries in Europe. The rules could be enduring: in Winchester, England, building frontage rules remained unchanged from the eleventh to the twentieth centuries (Kostof 1992). Frontage rules established in the thirteenth century enforced Gothic, similar-sized windows (a colonelli) on all frontage surrounding the public space in Siena's Piazza del Campo (Girouard 1985; Schevill 1909). The earliest German regulations concerning frontage were from the same period. Seventeenth-century England was full of regulations aimed at facade treatment. Various royal proclamations and building acts in London contained rules that controlled such things as the material of front-exposed walls, the encroachment of overhanging windows, the width of balconies, and the allowed height of the ground floor above the street (Baer 2007a).

Rules mandated visual harmony. Edinburgh's New Town, an eighteenth-century classical city, required extraordinary conformance to detailed regulations on building frontage and facade treatment (Youngson 2002). Haussman's rules for building forms along Parisian thoroughfares in the mid-nineteenth century enforced classical, uniform street facades that accentuated the grandeur of boulevards and avenues. Other European cities followed suit. The Frankfort Building Ordinance of the late nineteenth century, which required oversight by the "building police," dealt with many aspects of urban frontage, regulating street and building lines, setbacks, facade treatment, and "court space." Rules about roofs, window placement, vertical roof projections, and overhangs were all directed at ensuring a unified public realm. The rules were both precise and context based. One rule stipulated the following: "New structures shall not cover more than ¾ of the lot back of the building line, but on corner lots improved with one building ⅚ is allowed" (cited in Williams 1922, 230).

The desire for harmonious frontage prompted William Penn to declare in the seventeenth century, "let the houses built be in a line, or upon a line, as much as may be" (Hazard 1850, 530). The United States has its own history of frontage control. In the 1600s, Cambridge, Massachusetts, famously required buildings to stand back 6 feet from the street. Jefferson and L'Enfant had similar rules about street frontage in their plans for laying out Washington, D.C., in the late 1700s: "houses shall range even and stand just six feet in their own ground from the street" (Reps 1965, 126). George Washington allowed more discretion: "all buildings on the streets shall be parallel thereto, and may be advanced to the line of the street, or withdrawn therefrom, at the pleasure of the improver" (Tindall 1914, 122). Williamsburg, Virginia, was built under a 1699 act that stipulated that residents "shall not build a House less than tenn Foot Pitch and the front of each House shall come within six Foot of the Street and not closer." Houses on the main street were to "all front a like." Vacant lots were not allowed, and the buyer was required to build a "good Dwelling House containing twenty Foot in Width and Thirty Foot in Length" if it was located on the "main Street of tenn Foot Pitch" within 24 months (Davies 1958, 6). In New York, seventeenth-century surveyors were instructed to make sure that "a Regular Order and Uniformity may be kept and observed in the Streets and Buildings" (cited in Osgood et al. 1905, 226).

Frontage rules were also applied to detailing the "devices of transition" (Kunstler 1998, 141) between the public, semiprivate, and private realms: arcades, porches, shopfronts, and the like. The social and environmental value of requiring a covered public walkway (which would have significant cooling effect) was contained in rules guiding city building in sixth-century Palestine (Hakim 2001). In Bern, Switzerland, arcades were precisely regulated by building codes and were required for the fronts of all houses on main streets as early as the sixteenth century (Braunfels 1990). In the New World, the *Laws of the Indies* prescribed arcades around central plazas for sociability, trading, and protection from the elements.

Rules that restricted building materials and facade details could be imposed for fire safety reasons, but there were also aesthetic goals. In fifteenth-century Nuremburg, Germany, codes stipulated how much ornamentation a building could have, how many oriel windows were permitted, and how buildings should be lined up to create an "undeviating building line" (Kostof 1992, 201). During the same period,

French building regulations limited ornamentation (falling entablatures were a significant problem) and promoted a classically proportioned, flat building line. English law dictated in 1618 that windows had to be taller than they were wide, and sometimes brick arches over windows were required (Ayers 1998). Rules that paid attention to these kinds of details lasted for centuries. Late nineteenth-century Parisian law gave exact dimensions "for every decorative element, including columns and pilasters, friezes, cornices, consoles and capitals" (Evenson 1979, 149).

Initially, it was thought that zoning might incorporate this level of detail. As an example, when New York's zoning code was being discussed prior to its 1916 adoption, New York's Health Commissioners gave public testimony on the need for zoning to regulate cornices because of their effect on "the simplicity, beauty and architectural attractiveness of buildings and the streets" (New York City Board of Estimate and Apportionment 1916, 105). But zoning never really appropriated frontage rules for these purposes.

The closest the United States got to uniform frontage was the establishment of a building line. New Haven had established building lines around 1870 along many of its streets, but Cappel documented how buildings encroached across these lines (Cappel 1991). Building lines were more common by the 1890s, although there was still no legal basis for them (Davies 1958). This began to change by the 1920s, when building lines were established in subdivision regulations. Front-yard setbacks, which are functionally the same thing, were codified into zoning ordinances rather than subdivision regulations. Bettman saw this as a "conflict in theory," since the zoning ordinance was subject to amendment, whereas platting maps were recorded and more permanent (Hubbard and Hubbard 1929).

Constant legal tangles over setback rules made enforcement difficult. Box 5.2 lists court cases as of 1928 just on the issue of required front-yard setbacks. The exact dimensions of front-yard setback requirements were established on the basis of what was already there, largely due to inertia. According to one 1927 publication, the usual method of establishing front-yard setbacks was to calculate the average front-yard depth of more than one-half of the structures on either side of a street. Figure 5.8 shows how the calculations were made in Memphis, Tennessee. In another example from a 1935 textbook (fig. 5.9), rear yards were to be a certain percentage of the entire lot depth. Side yards were optional, reserved only for the most restricted areas (Baker 1927).

Uniform frontage in Baltimore's 1925 zoning ordinance was thought to produce the kind of house that would "go far toward solving all social problems of the city,"

Box 5.2. Court cases on the issue of front-yard setbacks, as of 1928

FRONT YARDS
In favor of validity of building line or setback provisions.

Matter of Wulfsohn v. Burden, 214 App. Div. 824, 210 N. Y. S. 941, 241 N.Y. 288, 150 N.E. 120; Herman v. Walsh, Sup. Ct., Kings County, N.Y. L. J. Dec. 7, 1926, 220 App. Div. 773; Friedlander v. 465 Lexington Ave. Inc., Sup. Ct., Westchester County, Mt. Vernon Argus Jan. 6, 1927, 222 App. Div. 689 (N.Y.); Matter of 465 Lexington Ave. Inc. v. Burden, Sup. Ct., Westchester County, June 9, 1925 (N. Y.); Pritz v. Messer, 112 Ohio St. 628, 149 N.E. 30, 113 Ohio St. 706, 150 N.E. 756; State ex rel. Ball v. Harris, C.P. Ct., Trumbull county, Jan. Term, 1926, Harris v. State ex rel. Ball, 23 Ohio App. 33, 155 N.E. 166; Weiss v. Guion, 17 Fed. (2d) 202 (Ohio); Kaufman v. City of Akron, c.P. Ct., Summit County, Jan. 6, 1927 (Ohio); Gorieb v. Fox, 145 Va. 554, 134 S.E. 914, 273 U.S. 687, 47 Sup. Ct. R. 448, 274 U.S. 603, 47 Sup. Ct. R. 675.

CONTRA.—Willison v. Cooke, 54 Colo. 320 130, P. 828; Smith v. City of Atlanta, 161 Ga. 769, 132 S. E. 66; Morrow v. City of Atlanta, 162 Ga. 228, 133 S. E. 345; Opinion of Justices, 124 Me. 501, 128 A. 181; State ex rel. Penrose Inv. Co. v. McKelvey, 301 Mo. 1, 256 S. W. 474; City of St. Louis v. Evraiff, 301 Mo. 231, 256 S. W. 489; Michel v. Village of South Orange, 3 N.J. Misc. 243, 127 A. 794; Vatter v. Kaltenback, 3 N.J. Misc. 665, 129 A. 926, 131 A.

900; Eaton v. Village of South Orange, 3 N.J. Misc., 956, 130 A. 362; Heller v. Village of South Orange, 3 N.J. Misc. 1076, 130 A. 534; Franklin Realty & Mortgage Co. v. Village of South Orange, 4 N.J. Misc. 109, 132 A. 81, 134 A. 917; Michel v. Village of South Orange, 4 N.J. Misc. 302, 132 A. 337; Scola v. Senior, 130 A. 886 (N.J.); Ricci v. Meyer, 135 A. 666 (N.J.).

See City of Little Rock v. Reinman, 107 Ark. 174, 155 S. W. 105, Reinman v. City of Little Rock, 237 U.S. 171, 35 Sup. Ct. R. 511; Barbier v. Connolly, 113 U.S. 27, 5 Sup. Ct. R. 357 (Cal.); State ex rel. Civello v. City of New Orleans, 154 La. 469, 97 S. 661; State ex rel. National Oil Works of Louisiana v. McShane, 159 La. 723, 106 S. 252; Tighe v. Osborne, 149 Md. 349, 131 A. 801; Tighe v. Osborne, 150 Md. 452, 133 A. 465; Siegemund v. Bldg.

Com'r of City of Boston, 156 N.E. 852 (Mass.); State ex rel. Better Built Homes & Mortgage Co. v. McKelvey, 301 Mo. 130, 256 S. W. 495; Rudensey v. Senior, 4 N.J. Misc. 577, 133 A. 777; Lincoln Trust Co. v. Williams Bldg. Corp., 183 App. Div. 225, 169 N. Y. S. 1045, 229 N. Y. 313, 128 N. E. 209; Matter of Hecht-Dann Const. Co. Inc v. Burden, 124 Misc. 632, 208 N. Y. S. 299; White's Appeal, 287 Pa. 259, 134 A. 409; Eubank v. City of Richmond, 110 Va. 749, 67 S. E. 376, 226 U.S. 137, 33 Sup. Ct. R. 76; Hayes v. Hoffman, C. C., Milwaukee County 1926, 192 Wis. 63, 211 N. W. 271.

Source: Bassett and Williams (1928).

with the added benefit that a fine, ordered frontage, because it would promote healthy living conditions, would mean that "labor turn-over and labor problems would be rare" (Baltimore BZA 1925, 96). This was because frontage control was believed to be an important aspect of ensuring that attached housing for the working classes was dignified. It would help satisfy the goal of "light, air and privacy" and produce "real homes" even if they were attached (Parrish 1917, 9). Thomas Adams supported this view, believing that front and side yards "are not essential if houses are not more than two rooms deep and if ample space for light and air is provided in streets and rear yards" (1934, 163). Veiller took this further and wrote that if row housing was needed to maintain affordability, rear yards should be eliminated, the community should take control of backyards, and they should be developed as parks, playgrounds, and gardens (Veiller 1917, 28).

Rules about lot coverage can also affect frontage. In the early decades of the twentieth century, lot coverage rules tended to be simple and, at least initially, not very

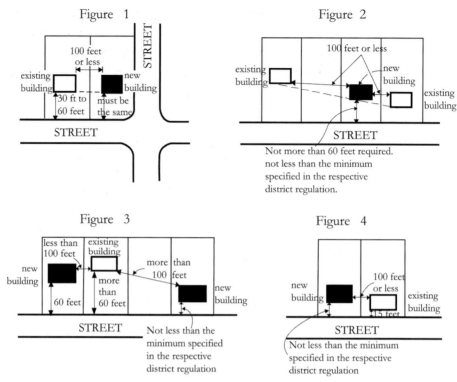

Figure 5.8. Setback rules from the Memphis zoning ordinance, c. 1923.

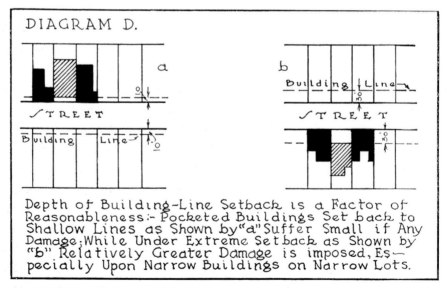

Figure 5.9. How setbacks were determined.

Source: Van Nest Black (1935).

constraining. Building shape was mostly determined by these rules, such as the requirements from St. Louis, Missouri's 1923 zoning ordinance, shown in table 5.1.
The zones refer to height and area districts. The simplicity (and low level of restric-
tiveness) of this approach was changed by 1935, when St. Louis's zoning ordinance
specified front- and side-yard setbacks rather than lot coverage.

Table 5.1. St. Louis lot coverage rules, 1923

	Proportion of plots that may be covered			
	Corner plots		Other plots	
Zone	First storey	Above first storey	First storey	Above first storey
	Per cent	Per cent	Per cent	Per cent
A	100	100	100	*
B	100	90*	100	80*
C	100	75*	100	60*
D	60†	50	50t	40

* Rear yard of at least 10 feet required.
† Rear yard of at least 15 feet and side yard of at least 4 feet required.
Source: The Architect, January 19, 1923, p. 60.

By the 1930s, the building line of the subdivision ordinance and the setback rule
of zoning—really one and the same in terms of effect—seemed to become more
about exclusion and the maintenance of low-density residential character than anything else. Commercial buildings that had long been part of the uniform street wall
were now disdained because they projected their "plate-glass front to the street line,"
which had the effect of "cutting off the frontages" of houses set further back (Hubbard and Hubbard 1929). Through zoning, there was an attempt to surround everything from the downtown skyscraper to the single-family home in the suburbs with
open space. Because ventilation was affected by the "height, size, shape and character of buildings and their distance apart," the maintenance of uniform frontage became less important (New York City Board of Estimate and Apportionment 1916,
28). New York's 1916 Building Commission claimed that buildings too high and too
close together affected not only physical health but "the mental condition." What
this meant in terms of rules was worked out in great detail. The graphic in figure
5.10 is from the authoritative *Regional Survey of New York and Its Environs* (Heydecker

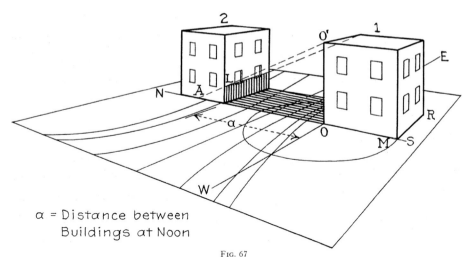

α = Distance between
Buildings at Noon

FIG. 67
DIAGRAM ILLUSTRATING HOW CLOSELY ONE HOUSE CAN BE PLACED TO ANOTHER WITHOUT INTERFERING WITH THE
SUNLIGHT PENETRATION OF THE LATTER

Figure 5.10. Graphic from the *Regional Survey of New York and Its Environs* (Heydecker and Goodrich 1929), showing the scientific basis for the notion that taller buildings needed to be spaced farther apart.
Source: Heydecker and Goodrich (1929).

and Goodrich 1929). The illustration provides a scientific basis to the notion that taller buildings needed to be spaced farther apart.

Setback rules, in other words, were no longer about uniform or dignified frontage. Buffer-yard and setback rules in subdivision ordinances meant that buildings were pushed farther apart, weakening the relevance of a frontage requirement and obliterating the need for a uniform building line. Baltimore zoning officials used setback rules to ensure "open spaces on the front, rear and sides of buildings" in order to allow "access of light to streets and buildings." Quoting New York officialdom,

> every dwelling and tenement should be so located and so planned as to provide in every living or sleeping room at least such an amount of direct sunlight or its equivalent as would be supplied by the sun shining for one-half hour at its maximum, or noon, intensity through windows of the prevailing dwelling-house size, facing south at the winter solstice, December 21st. (Heydecker and Goodrich 1929, 200)

The breakdown of frontage became a matter of scientific principle. Hoover's commission reviewed the scientific evidence and set the standard, declaring that it was "essential" that each unit have light from an angle of 27 degrees, which would require "space between house fronts of twice the height of the taller building" (Gries and Ford 1931, 123). Add to this the finding that tuberculosis was "twice as great among tenement dwellers as among those living in separate houses" (Baltimore BZA 1925, 31), and there seemed little point to trying to enforce spatial definition with frontage rules. Now, setback rules might be based on something as irrelevant to spatial definition as a utility easement that prohibits improvements on the ground above (Slone and Goldstein 2008).

The Loss of Form

Besides street width, building height, and frontage, rules aimed at improving aesthetics created particular urban forms. While Girouard wrote that the medieval period had "only a few recorded instances of aesthetic awareness" (1985, 76), others have argued that regulations concerning such things as bridge ornamentation, street trees, the protection of admired buildings, and the cleanliness of canal banks—rules in place by the sixteenth century—were intended to protect the aesthetics of the public realm (Kistemaker 2000). There is no doubt that this attention was driven by the need to maintain civic beauty for the wealthy classes. It was well known that streets and blocks were regulated to provide "pleasant areas for well-off population groups" (Logan 1972, 107).

But attention to form as an aesthetic goal, to be enforced by rules, was lost in the early decades of the twentieth century. Through its two standard state-enabling acts issued in the 1920s, Herbert Hoover's advisory committee on zoning helped shift the rationale for form-generating rules from being a matter of civic intent to being a matter of scientific requirement. The commission promoted building lines, setbacks, and front-yard requirements for the purpose of accommodating open space and "the proposed future boundaries" of streets—and nothing more (Gries and Ford 1931, 38).

Though a minority, some noteworthy planners did object. Russell Van Nest Black thought the whole emphasis on future street widening was "exaggerated." He warned that street design was more important than street widening and should be "directed toward preservation of the livability and usefulness of land abutting or fronting upon streets, and toward the preservation of the livability and usefulness of neighborhood areas served by streets" (Van Nest Black 1935, 166).

Nineteenth-century Austrian architect Camillo Sitte would have argued the same. But he was not against rule making. He played a strong role determining how building mass and form could be derived from a system of rules. He helped to create a comprehensive ordinance regulating the Berlin suburbs in 1892 (Logan 1972). But in the United States, concerns about the ability of rules to create "architectural uniformity" (Comey 1912, 116) did not translate to code, in part because there was no support from the American legal community. Bassett believed that the proper place for such concerns was deed restrictions, not municipal regulation.

The famous 1909 *Welch v. Swasey* case (214 U.S. 91, 1909), which allowed Boston to impose building heights, presumably for aesthetic reasons, established that matters of taste and beauty could be motivations in city rules but only in an auxiliary way. For the next half century, the use of aesthetics as a basis for rules was continually tried, and sometimes upheld (Smardon and Karp 1992), until finally, in 1954, the Supreme Court decision in *Berman v. Parker* gave planners the ability to apply rules to values that were "spiritual as well as physical, aesthetic as well as monetary." This reasoning was further supported in 1978 by the *Penn Central Transportation Company v. New York City* case (438 U.S. 104), when the U.S. Supreme court ruled that the protection of Grand Central Terminal did not constitute a "taking" and thus did not require compensation.

And yet, because zoning was constantly being challenged in the courts, zoning advocates always felt the need to pin zoning on "safety, health and morals" rather than aesthetics, taste, civic decorum, and good design. Even then, as one planner observed, "the imagination is at times pretty severely stretched" (Baker 1927, 18). When a city in Nebraska tried to forbid gas stations on its main street in 1924 because the stations "would be an everlasting eyesore and disgrace," they were told they were being "unreasonable," and the ordinance was struck down (American City 1924, 205). When a municipality in New Jersey wanted to require its commercial buildings to be a minimum of two stories rather than a more informal, less substantial one-story structure, their ordinance was found to be baseless (Bassett 1923, 12).

Effects

New York's series of tenement house laws show the effect of rules on building form. Figure 5.11 is an image of present-day New York, showing the forms resulting from three different rules: 1867, which required only a window in each room; 1879, which required an airshaft, and 1901, which required a courtyard. The old tenement law of 1879 created a "dumbell"-shaped building because of the required airshaft, but this created problems because the airshaft became a place where residents dumped their garbage.

An example of the effect of the new tenement law of 1901 is shown in figures 5.12, 5.13, 5.14, and 5.15—all views of an apartment building on Manhattan's upper west side (*1913 Supplement to the World's Loose Leaf Album of Apartment Houses* 1913). Figure 5.13 shows the 1913 advertisement for the building, called the Dorothea. It

Figure 5.11. East 4th Street, between 1st and 2nd Avenues, on the Lower East side of Manhattan, New York City. The image shows the effects of three types of rules.

has six bays across, and instead of an airshaft, an interior courtyard, as required by the new law. The law resulted in larger buildings, often constructed on combined or corner lots to meet the space requirements for internal courtyards.

The 1928 Chase LaSalle Street Building in downtown Chicago (designed by the architectural firm Graham, Anderson, Probst, and White, the descendant firm of Burnham and Root), shown in figure 5.16, is another example of form affected by rules. Here form was affected by height rules: the building has twenty-two floors in the shape of an open square, designed this way because it maximized rentable space under the 1920 height limit of 260 feet.

Courtyards were an important solution to the blocking of windows in dense urban areas. To satisfy the demands of a wealthier clientele, dimensions often exceeded what was required by law. A development in Brooklyn with a courtyard shows a potential solution to the problem of blocked light and air and included an interior children's playground (fig. 5.17). Unfortunately, the development was later severed by a highway, shown in figure 5.18, rendering the innovation somewhat irrelevant.

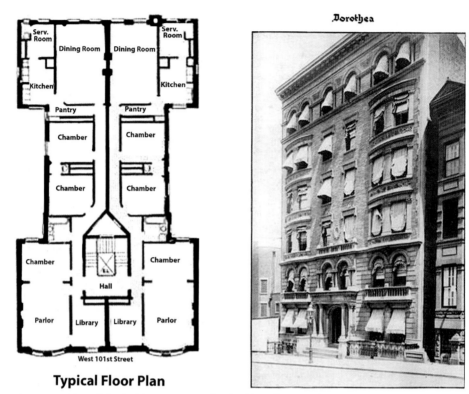

Typical Floor Plan

Figures 5.12 and 5.13. Advertisement for the Dorothea in 1913, 331 West 101st Street, in New York City. The building's form shows the effect of the new tenement law of 1901.
Source: 1913 Supplement to the World's Loose Leaf Album of Apartment Houses (1913).

Figure 5.14. Street view of the Dorothea today.

Figure 5.15. Aerial view of the Dorothea today.

Figure 5.16. The Chase LaSalle Street Building in Chicago. The O shape maximized rentable space under the 1920 height limit of 260 feet.

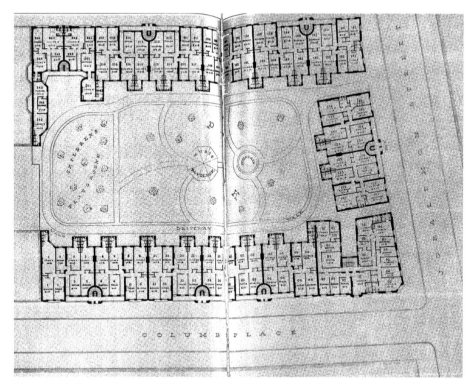

Figure 5.17. Plan for housing in Brooklyn, New York, c. 1910. Courtyards were an important solution to the blocking of windows in dense urban areas.
Source: White (1912).

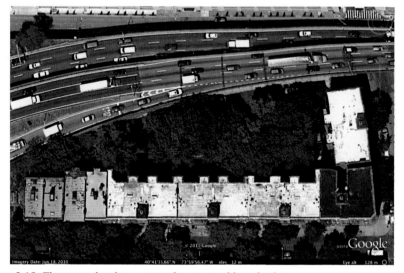

Figure 5.18. The same development today, severed by a highway.

The "volumetric approach" of the New York City skyline produced a stepped-back aesthetic that was copied in places like Boston (fig. 5.19), St. Louis (fig. 5.20), Sacramento, Cincinnati, Knoxville, Memphis, Milwaukee, and Minneapolis. When the International Style became popular several decades later, architects used plazas and low-rise buildings at the base of towers to meet the setback requirements, producing an entirely different building style under the same set of rules. One example of this is the 1958 Seagram Building, shown in figure 5.21.

Rules on allowable density and height could change entire cities and neighborhoods. In Baltimore in 1904 a one-block zone around the Washington Monument of Baltimore set a building height limit of 70 feet, while the rest of the city had a limit of 175 feet. The effects of this are clearly shown in a current view of Baltimore, figure 5.22. Clearly visible in figure 5.23 are the effects of height limits in Boston (described in fig. 5.24). In the 1913 ordinance (fig. 5.24), there was an "A" district (125 foot

Courtesy of Parker, Thomas & Rice, Arch'ts.
Henry Bailey Alden, Assoc. Arch't.
BOSTON, United Shoe Machinery Building

Courtesy of St. Louis City Plan Commission
Mauran–Russell & Crowell, Arch'ts. I. R. Timlin, Assoc. Arch't
SAINT LOUIS, Southwestern Bell Telephone Building

Figures 5.19 and 5.20. Cities all over the United States emulated New York's stepped-back zoning. *Left:* United Shoe Machinery Building, Boston, Massachusetts, 1929. *Right:* Southwestern Bell Telephone Building, St. Louis, Missouri, 1929.
Source: Hubbard and Hubbard (1929), p. 179.

Figure 5.21. With large setbacks at the base, box-shaped skyscrapers of the International Style could also be constructed under the 1916 NYC zoning ordinance. Shown is the Seagram Building in New York City, completed in 1958.
Source: By Noroton (talk) 03:19, 1 May 2008 (UTC) (Own work) [Public domain], via Wikimedia Commons.

max.) and a "B" district (80 foot max., except on streets wider than 64 feet) for building heights. The foreground buildings in figure 5.23 constituted the "A" district and include Burnham's 1912 department store, Filene's, now a Boston Landmark.

The Lake View neighborhood on the north side of Chicago is an example of the effects of downzoning to stop an area from densifying. Figure 5.25 shows what the area looked like in 1925, before zoning. As Schwieterman and Caspall (2006) point out in their study of Chicago zoning, the 1957 zoning ordinance, shown in figure 5.26, put low-density (R1) and high-density (R7) zones right next to each other. The

Figure 5.22. Building heights within one block around the Washington Monument in Baltimore, Maryland, were restricted to 70 feet.

Figure 5.23. The effect of height limits can be seen in Boston, Massachusetts.

neighborhood then became dotted with high-rises, visible in the current view (fig. 5.27). In response to strong neighborhood complaints that zoning was too permissive and allowed too much density, the area was downzoned in 1979. The core of this neighborhood was blocked from further high-rise development.

Street regulations also affect urban form in very visible ways. In the United States, rules governing streets are the exclusive province of transportation engineers, who focus almost solely on the flow of cars and the prevention of accidents. Codes for street design are therefore de facto consequences of manuals published by the

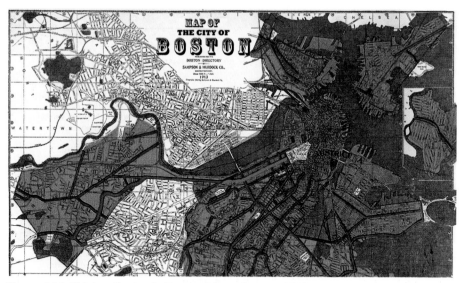

Figure 5.24. Heights districts in Boston, Massachusetts, 1913.
Source: New York Board of Estimate and Apportionment (1913).

Figure 5.25. The Lake View neighborhood, Chicago, in 1925, before zoning's effect.
Source: Chicago Historical Society.

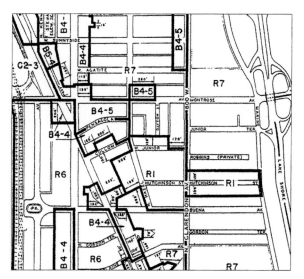

Figure 5.26. The zoning map of the Lake View neighborhood, Chicago, 1957, put low-density (R1) and high-density (R7) zones right next to each other.
Source: City of Chicago.

Figure 5.27. The Lake View neighborhood in 2010, showing results of permissive zoning. The area outlined in red was later downzoned, following resident complaints.

Institute of Transportation Engineers (ITE) (see, e.g., Hammond and Sorenson 1941; ITE 1964). Southworth and Ben-Joseph chronicled this changing relationship between street standards and urban design (2003). They showed how residential street standards became institutionalized in the United States in the 1930s when the Federal Housing Administration (FHA) adopted street standards in conjunction with its lending activities. Between 1950 and the mid-1980s, the standards of the ITE became the law of the land in virtually every part of the United States, which remains the situation today.

When street standards became the domain of traffic engineers, it effectively ended concern for termination points, or consideration of the relationship between street width and urban form. For comparison, figure 5.28 shows a section of the Hohenzollernring boulevard in Cologne, which was laid out to fit the rule of a width to length ratio of 1:20 (in this case, 36 to 700 meters) (118–2,297 feet), considered an appropriate rule of thumb by early twentieth-century planners (e.g., Triggs 1909). Note that the street segment provides a termination point by deflecting.

Figure 5.28. Streets like the Hohenzollernring boulevard in Cologne, Germany, were required to either terminate or deflect after a certain distance.

But, as mentioned earlier, considerations of width to length or termination point, important for creating a human-scaled, high-quality urban form, play no part in rules governing street dimensions in most of the United States. An example is shown in figure 5.29 and table 5.2. The table lists Pima County subdivision rules on street segment length, which are more lenient than anything actually built. Figure 5.29 shows an area in Tucson, Arizona, located in Pima County, where the allowed width to length ratio is 1:38. Note, however, that unlike the Cologne example, there is no termination or deflection point, only a cross street. The length of arterials in the figure is about 3,000 meters (roughly 2 miles). Streets are allowed to continue on, indefinitely, implying that the sole use of the street is for traffic flow.

Initially, the main concern for those designing streets in the United States was whether building cubage would overtax the capacity of streets to move people and traffic efficiently. Street widths were thus classified "in accordance with planned street uses" (Hubbard and Hubbard 1929, 152), even in residential subdivisions. There was no relationship at all between street width and building height. Required widths in new subdivisions were specified in a city's major street plan, and city planners usually pushed for streets to be "generously broad." This was interpreted as a

Figure 5.29. Streets in Pima County, Tucson, Arizona, are permitted to continue on indefinitely.

Table 5.2. Pima County subdivision rules

Parameter	Local street	Residential collector	Major collector
MANDATORY CRITERIA			
Volume (veh/day)	< 1,000	1,000–2,500	2,500–10,000
Segment length (mi)	< ¼	¼–1	1–3
Design speed (mph)	25	25–30	40
Direct access to property	Yes	No*	No
RECOMMENDED CRITERIA			
Major terminus	Collector or local street	Arterial or major collector	Arterial
Minor terminus	Local street or turnaround	Residential collector or local street	Arterial, residential, or major collector
System continuity	Low	Medium	High

*Direct access to property can be provided if the maximum segment length is limited to ¼ mile *and* the design speed is 25 mph.

matter of farsighted thinking, whereby planners could be "proud of our forethought for the traffic which the future is to bring" (Robinson 1916, 29).

Rules for excessive street width reinforce a sense of openness and detachment, even on smaller residential streets. Figure 5.30 shows a section of Tucson, Arizona, and the varying street width rules enforced, derived from the ITE manual (listed in table 5.3). Figure 5.31 shows just how wide the narrowest "local" street is, and how the notion of spatial definition is rendered meaningless under these requirements.

The loss of a connection between rules and spatial definition was obvious already by 1929, when the Regional Plan of New York and Its Environs published its study quantifying how buildings should be spaced apart, depending on their height and type (Heydecker and Goodrich 1929). It was a prescription for detachment. Figure 5.32 is a page from the study, combined with aerial images showing contemporary examples of what these rules have meant for urban form.

This validation of detachment, when combined with parking demands, made the issue of spatial definition obsolete—detached buildings set amid parking lots would never be able to provide a sense of enclosure. Buildings were no longer encroaching across the building line, as had been the case for centuries; they were instead receding from it. In the 1920s, for example, Akron, Ohio, was considered a

Figure 5.30. Varying required street right-of-way widths in a Tucson, Arizona, subdivision.

Figure 5.31. Outside of Tucson, Arizona, there is no possibility of enclosure with a manda-tory 45 foot street right-of-way width, which is the narrowest allowed.

Table 5.3. Street standards in Pima County, Arizona

Street class	Right-of-way (feet)	Travel lanes (feet)
Local street	45	12
Residential collector	60	14
Major collector	90–120	12
Urban arterial, six-lane divided	75–150	11 or 12

Source: Pima County (2005).

model to be studied because of its 20 miles of building lines along nonresidential streets, codified in the subdivision platting regulations. Figure 5.33 is a page from the ordinance, showing how build-to lines for retail business were established. Today, underdevelopment, disinvestment, and the accommodation of parking lots have made Akron's building lines barely recognizable, as shown in figures 5.34 and 5.35.

With the loss of focus on the public realm, building lines yielded to the pressures of car-based urbanism. This was facilitated by the fact that, unlike rules on frontage that had been in place for centuries, zoning, with its focus on use requirements, seemed incapable of considering spatial definition. Frontage was reduced to setback, which became little more than a device for lowering density. Rules affecting frontage became a matter of addressing traffic problems. This could have a devastating effect. In Detroit, Michigan, rules called for buildings to be "held back to the building line" so that street widening could eventually occur. The 1920s photo shown in figure 5.36 was meant to demonstrate the building line, but with temporary one-story structures that could be torn down to accommodate future widening (a common practice). As figure 5.37 shows, Detroit got a lot more than street widening. So much was torn down for parking lots that it is difficult to compare these views—but note the church steeple, which can be seen in both photographs.

Another variant of building line regulation was the "vision clearance" rule (Hubbard 1925, 105). To prevent "blind corners," zoning was openly described as a "traffic safety measure" (Fisher 1924) that could be used to provide a better range of vision at street intersections. Figures 5.38 and 5.39 show the effects in Kenosha, Wisconsin, in the 1920s and currently, where setback requirements in a 1920s zoning ordinance were enacted to provide "vision clearance." The setback rules had the effect of creating four chamfered corners. Unfortunately, as figure 5.39 shows, the setback rules now seem irrelevant in the context of wide arterials dominated by parking.

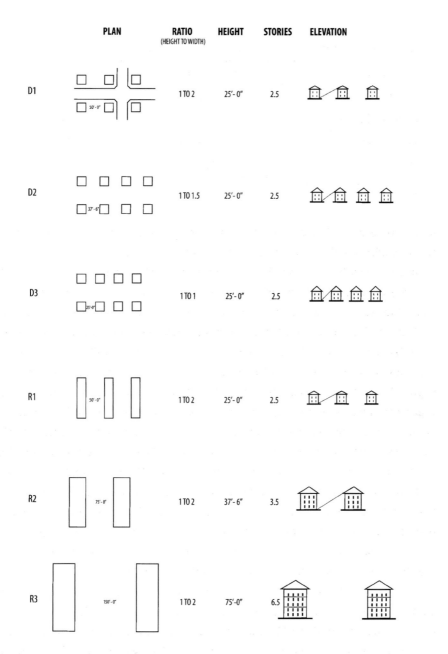

DIAGRAM ILLUSTRATING HOW BUILDINGS OUGHT TO BE SPACED TO PROVIDE SUITABLE LIGHT

W. D. HEYDECKER   1928

Figure 5.32. Reproduction of a graphic from the *Regional Survey of New York and Its Environs* (Heydecker and Goodrich 1929). The study showed how buildings should be spaced apart, depending on their height and type.

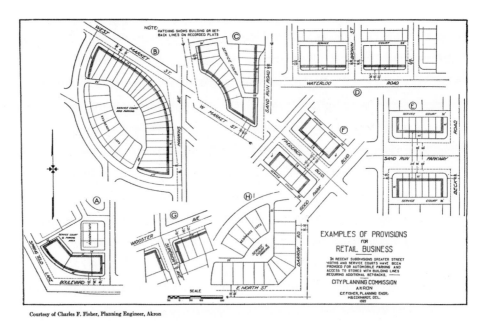

Courtesy of Charles F. Fisher, Planning Engineer, Akron

Figure 5.33. Akron, Ohio, platting regulations, showing build-to lines for retail business. *Source:* Hubbard and Hubbard (1929), p. 158.

As these setback rules increased, they guaranteed weak intersections with no spatial definition, and thus little social value. The effects are easily seen at the intersection of suburban arterials. Here buildings are regulated as objects within space, not as elements that define space. The effect of Gilbert, Arizona's code, shown in figure 5.40, is a good example. The rules state that the intersections of arterials, because of their "importance" and because they serve as "major focal points of activity in the community" require a 250 foot by 50 foot landscape buffer along the street frontage. Important intersections, in other words, are to be hidden and shielded with "landscape." Buildings are an encumbrance, not a mark of importance. The figure shows a "neighborhood convenience" zone that, on the plus side, requires that "parking shall not be allowed to encroach in the setback." However, what *is* required is a landscape triangular area, "thirty-three feet from the intersection of the curb lines" (Gilbert, Arizona 2011, 103).

Rules about curb radii can have a significant effect on urban form by determining block edge configuration. This in turn affects the speed of turning vehicles and the distance required to cross a street on foot. A smaller radius produces tighter blocks, slower vehicles, and shorter distances for pedestrians. Akron, Ohio, had a 5 foot curb radius rule in its 1920 platting regulations (Menhinick 1929) shown in figure 5.41. A similarly compact form is found in a section of Richmond, Virginia (fig.

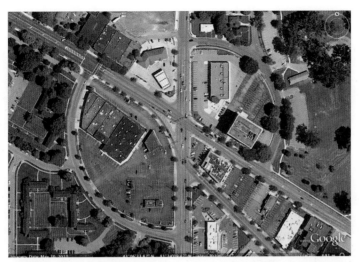

Figure 5.34. Area "B" from figure 5.33.

Figure 5.35. Area "C" from figure 5.33.

5.42), where the rules allowed a 10 foot curb radius and a 40 foot street width. Akron and Richmond can be compared to the 30 foot curb radius rule in Gilbert, Arizona (fig. 5.43), which creates a very different, and much more car-oriented, environment. In Tampa, Florida, the requirement of a 50 foot curb radius for commercial driveways (fig. 5.44) guarantees a dispersed urban form. Curb radius rules for Tampa are listed in table 5.4. Note how the requirements for driveways in Tampa are wider than the requirements for street intersections in Akron and Richmond.

Figure 5.36. A 1935 photo of downtown Detroit, Michigan, showed how temporary one-story structures could be torn down to accommodate future street widening
Source: Van Nest Black (1935), p. 70.

Figure 5.37. The same area of Detroit (fig. 5.36) today. Note church steeple in both images.

Courtesy of Kenosha City Planning Commission

An apartment house corner, showing setback

Figure 5.38. At street corners, setback rules provided "vision clearance," such as this example in Kenosha, Wisconsin, 1920s.
Source: Hubbard and Hubbard (1929), p. 182.

Figure 5.39. Kenosha, Wisconsin, today. Corner setback rules were rendered irrelevant with wide arterials and street-facing parking lots.

Figure 5.40. An intersection in Gilbert, Arizona. According to the rules, important intersections are to be hidden and shielded with "landscape."

Figure 5.41. Akron, Ohio, had a 5 foot curb radius rule in the 1920s.

Figure 5.42. Richmond, Virginia, allowed a 10 foot curb radius.

Figure 5.43. Gilbert, Arizona, has a 30 foot curb radius requirement.

Figure 5.44. Commercial driveway in Tampa, Florida, requiring a 50 foot curb radius. The requirements for commercial driveways in Tampa are wider than the requirements for street intersections in Akron and Richmond.

Table 5.4. Curb radius rules in Tampa, Florida

Type of street being accessed	Type of street intersecting	Corner radius minimum (feet)	Driveway type	
			Res. (feet)	Commercial or industrial (feet)
Local	Local	15	25	30
Local	Collector	25	25	30
Local	Minor/principal arterial	25	25	30
Collector	Local	25	35	40
Collector	Collector	35	35	40
Collector	Minor/principal arterial	35	35	40
Minor/principal arterial	Local	25	50	50
Minor/principal arterial	Collector	35	50	50
Minor/principal arterial	Minor/principal arterial	35	50	50

Source: City of Tampa

Figure 5.45 shows an example from Gilbert, Arizona, of the effects of setbacks and landscape buffering requirements (the effects of buffering requirements were discussed under "pattern" in chapter 3, but they also significantly impact form). The corresponding rules from the Land Development Code are listed in table 5.5. In addition to the deep setbacks required in commercial zones, the rules state: "landscape area shall not be encumbered by parking areas, buildings, driveways or other improvements." Elsewhere the code states, "a minimum twenty-foot wide landscape strip shall be established along all major arterial streets." In this example, parking cannot be within the landscape area, but it can be in front of a building. The ordinance states: "parking areas are permitted within the building setback provided that they do not encroach into or reduce the required landscaped bufferyard." Of course, these requirements are partly for the purpose of providing, within the public right-of-way, filtration acreage for storm water management. An issue to be considered is the degree to which these practices undermine walkable urbanism.

Apparently unaware of the damage this could cause, planners in the 1920s praised zoning ordinances that required lots to have "an area left open for automo-

Figure 5.45. Another intersection in Gilbert, Arizona. The rules state that parking cannot be within the landscape area, but it can be in front of a building.

bile storage" (Hubbard and Hubbard 1929, 182), a legacy that has significantly damaged the pedestrian quality of streets. But parking requirements have also been detrimental because they outlaw certain building types. For example, figure 5.46 shows the many U-shaped courtyard housing types popular in Chicago in the period from 1900 to 1930, a building type with significant advantages in terms of maximizing access to green space and creating a sense of privacy in an otherwise high-density setting (Polyzoides, Sherwood, and Tice 1997). These cannot be built today because of the off-street parking requirement of one space per unit. The corresponding zoning for this area, shown in figure 5.47, has many "RM" (multiunit) zones. These require one off-street parking space per unit, a rule that effectively blocks new courtyard housing development.

Rules determining street width, building height, setback, and lot coverage have produced an urban form that, in twenty-first-century America, has little ability to define space. Instead, rules have prioritized traffic flow and parking provision, health effects and fire prevention, often based on reasoning that no longer holds. Planners are now attempting to revive past traditions and innovate with new types of rules. They are using rules to reestablish the importance of spatial definition, now understood to be an essential part of the walkable—and more livable—city.

Table 5.5. Table from the Unified Land Development Code, Subdivision Regulations, Gilbert, Arizona

Proposed zoning classification	Minimum building setback (feet)	Maximum building height (feet)
N-S, Neighborhood Service	40	15
NCC, Neighborhood Convenience	40	15
C-1, Light Commercial*	100	30
C-2, General Commercial*	100	30
PSC-1, Planned Neighborhood Shopping Center*	100	30
PSC-2, Planned Shopping Center*	100	30
I-B, Industrial Buffer	75	30
I-I, Garden Industry	Not allowed adjacent to residential	
I-2, Light Industry	Not allowed adjacent to residential	
I-3, General Industry	Not allowed adjacent to residential	
R-2, Two-Family Duplex Residential	100	36
R-3, Multifamily	100	36
R-4, Multifamily	100	36

*Not allowed adjacent to R1-20 or larger lots.
Source: City of Gilbert, Arizona

Figure 5.46. The north side of Chicago, Illinois, showing the many U-shaped courtyard housing types popular in Chicago in the period from 1900 to 1930.

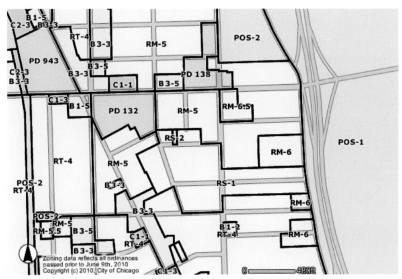

Figure 5.47. Zoning designations for the area shown in figure 5.46. The "RM" (multiunit) zones require one off-street parking space per unit, a rule that effectively blocks new courtyard housing development.

Source: City of Chicago zoning ordinance.

6. Reform

Reforming City Rules

Proposals to reform city rules swing in two directions—either pushing toward greater flexibility, or pushing toward greater predictability. In either approach, the end game is a better kind of urbanism, a more livable, walkable, enduring kind of place. This chapter reviews both approaches and then considers the possibility of their integration, or at least, balance.

Flexibility

The rage of developers, architects, and planners against city rules as too oppressive has been brewing for almost a century now. In 1909, Raymond Unwin, the great British town planner, described the building regulations he was confronting as little more than "needless harassment and restriction of really good building" (1909, 388). Lewis Mumford, writing in 1923, viewed the application of zoning as "narrow, uncertain and ineffectual" (Mumford, cited in Toll 1969, 258). He was not a fan of prescriptive rule making in general, writing that because the *Laws of the Indies* prescribed exact dimensions (e.g., plazas were to be 400 by 600 feet), they produced towns that "looked backward, not forward" (Mumford 1961, 330). Clarence Perry (1939) lambasted zoning as inflexible and incapable of creating attractive cities. An article in the *Harvard Law Review* in 1959 complained that "Procrustean rules" like zoning were offering "little chance for imaginative architecture and planning" (Goldston and Scheuer, 1959, 243). Part of the problem was that there was a substantial lag time between code innovation and code implementation. New York City's 1916 zoning code was based on nineteenth-century concepts, and its decidedly antiurban 1961 revision was based on 1940s and 1950s thinking (Grava 1993).

By the 1950s, the critique of city rules—especially zoning—forced city planners to enact reforms, and most of the largest cities in the United States undertook complete revisions of their zoning ordinances during this period (Williams 1956). Their concern was primarily that zoning did not contemplate adaptive mechanisms, and to that end, their remedies focused on injecting pliability. To be modern was to be flexible. This seemed a natural response to the problem that many rules had been instituted in such a static way, with no contemplation of how an area might evolve. While it had always been possible to get a variance, the process was burdensome and could involve substantial cost. The thinking of zoning's original proponents, to quote Newark, New Jersey's planners in 1919, was that "we must have zoning to protect what we have got" (Newark, New Jersey, 1919). A more flexible approach was needed, one designed not to cast existing conditions in stone but to help them evolve.

Many professional planners had been cognizant of the need for more flexibility from the beginning. At the Second National Conference on City Planning and Congestion of Population, held in 1910, Frederick Law Olmsted Jr. said that regulation should always be in a state of "flux and adjustment—on the one hand, with a view to preventing newly discovered abuses, and, on the other hand, with a view to opening a wider opportunity of individual discretion at points where the law is found to be unwisely restrictive" (1910, 14). Flexibility was achieved by prioritizing *procedure*. John Nolen's proposed zoning act for Washington, D.C., for example, was all about process and included nothing about prescribed form (Bettman and Nolen 1938), signaling confidence that the kind of places produced would be good ones, if only the right procedures were followed. Of course, it would fall on city planners' expertise to supply the right vision. Charles Robinson had recommended putting every aspect of urban development in the hands of planners who would offer "the central viewpoint" and who would "take, beyond the cavil of petty politics or local interest, the community standpoint" (1901, 245).

An array of techniques and legal mechanisms were developed to enable greater flexibility. First there was the "special use" or "conditional use" permit, introduced just after World War II. Special exceptions might be granted to allow, for example, hospitals and public garages in a neighborhood if a voting board could be convinced that it was in the public's (or their) best interest. Next came "performance standards" in zoning, first introduced in Chicago for manufacturing districts in 1957, in which development is regulated through the measurement of its impacts on adjoining properties. In the 1960s, performance standards were famously adopted in Petaluma, California, and Ramapo, New York. Although these innovations were the precursors of growth management and later smart growth regulation (Nolon 2003), performance zoning never did catch on, as the administrative overhead required made them impractical to implement (Baker, Sipe, and Gleeson 2006).

Other attempts to increase flexibility include the planned unit development (PUD) and related variants (PD, PCD, etc.), overlay zoning, floating zones, the floor area ratio (FAR), and, in the United Kingdom, Simplified Planning Zones (SPZs). Manchester, New Hampshire's 1963 revision to its zoning ordinance was intended to "keep abreast of modern city development concepts" by introducing buffers, reducing land-use mix, requiring off-street parking, and introducing the "new technique" of the floor area ratio (FAR). Complicated overlay zones, planned unit ordinances, and other installations of discretionary review—even as part of a legal code—meant that there was plenty of room for interpretation. Discretionary review became built-in (Lai 1988; see also Punter 1999).

Moving from as-of-right rules to discretionary review increased complexity. New York's 1961 zoning document ballooned from 261 to 835 pages by adding more precise rules designed to tweak the right effect, in the process trading taller buildings for plazas and other "amenities." Discretion triggered additional layers of review, creating "a costly and time-consuming negative synergism" disliked by many (including most architects) for its tendency to open the door to manipulation, favoritism, and unfairness (Salins 1993, 167). Thus, in the attempts to make rules more flexible, they became more unwieldy.

After midcentury there was renewed attention on the development plan, and rules for redevelopment ("urban renewal") were made flexible enough to allow the piecing together of public–private ventures. This resulted in "logical" associations that conflated "large concentrations of people" with "large open spaces." Traditional zoning and subdivision controls, up until then, seemed incompatible with this idea. Planners wanted "immunity" from building-line and yard area requirements, as well as "freedom" to combine multifamily housing with single-family dwellings, neighborhood business districts, and even industrial land. Planners were trying to relax the rules they had labored hard to create only a couple of decades earlier (Goodrich, Shurtleff, and Black 1938, 131).

Scientifically based rules from the 1920s gave way to new ideas about urban form itself: modernist urbanism, the movement launched by the Congrès internationaux d'architecture modern (CIAM) in the 1920s that advocated land-use segregation, high-rise towers in parks, and a rejection of the pedestrian street. The planner Carl Feiss declared in 1943 that "the civic facade, so important to Camillo Sitte, is no longer our primary problem" (1943, 8). By the 1950s, planners declared that controls on yards, setbacks, and heights, especially in large-scale developments, were "an irrelevant nuisance" (Williams 1951, 99).

This shift was especially visible in American downtowns. Exact dimensions were no longer prescribed. Instead, rules facilitated negotiation—the exchange of plazas, amenities, and protected structures for taller buildings. Chicago's 1957 law and New York City's 1961 code instituted this kind of system, relying on the Floor Area Ratio rather than any hard and fast rules about form (Weiss 1992b). Park Avenue and 52nd Street in New York, shown in figure 6.1, is an example of the form resulting from complicated rules about air rights and zoning lot mergers. Marcus (1984) described how these rules changed the shape of New York—with purchased air rights, tall buildings that exceeded zoning began to loom over smaller, protected historic structures. Chicago's 1957 law, which provided bonus densities for amenities, resulted in a number of tall buildings attached to public plazas. By the 1990s, Seattle was offering twenty-six bonus density possibilities. The negotiations in American downtowns became so complex that tying form to code became almost irrelevant. Large-scale development was the result of "discretion, negotiation and compromise" more than any hard and fast rules about what good form actually is (Punter 2000, 305; see also Goldberger 1991).

The call for flexibility in regulation continued through the 1960s, '70s, and '80s— for example, in Kevin Lynch's *The Image of the City* (1960), and Babcock and Weaver's *City Zoning* (1979). Planning theorist Andreas Faludi railed against the inflexibility of zoning and called for codes that would instead provide "an essential element in a dynamic planning system" (1986, 255). Another response was to draft tailor-made ordinances aimed at protecting or changing particular development types. It had become clear that zoning by itself was incapable of protecting what was valued in the built environment (Scheer 2011), so cities created ordinances to offer this protection. Chicago, for example, created the Landmark Preservation Ordinance (1968), the Lakefront Protection Ordinance (1973), and later, the Townhouse Standards amendment (1998) and the Strip-Center Ordinance (1999).

The ability to change a zoning ordinance, or be granted a variance from it, was part of the system from the beginning, but the process was cumbersome. From 1942 to 1952 in Chicago, for example, there were 4,000 applications submitted for zoning map amendments (Schwieterman and Caspall 2006). Miami's first zoning ordinance,

Figure 6.1. Park Avenue and 52nd Street in New York; form resulting from complicated rules about air rights and zoning lot mergers.

adopted in 1934, endured 5,000 amendments until a new ordinance rezoned the city in 1960. In 1982, a new, award-winning ordinance introducing such innovations as "mixed-use" was implemented, but later denounced as "incomprehensible." One decade later, a new ordinance was implemented, designed to simplify the rules. But it also increased parking requirements and setbacks for residential homes and had to be amended "innumerable times," creating "a hodge-podge without regard for smart growth and quality of life" (City of Miami 2010). One cannot escape the irony that hodge-podge development was exactly what planners thought zoning would rectify.

Every city has a Board of Zoning Appeals that is, as the Des Moines zoning engineer argued in 1926, a "safety valve . . . without it the zoning, like a boiler without a safety valve, would blow up sooner or later" (Taubert 1926, 30). At first, the number of variances requested was in the hundreds, annually. In 1926, New York City was processing about five variances per week. Chicago had 252 requests to the board of appeals in 1935. According to one estimate, requests were granted about 50 percent of the time (Flint 1977). Bassett had praised the variance process for its remarkable flexibility and ability to allow board discretion. He did not object to the granting of variances for "esthetic" reasons—"Why not?" was his reply (Bassett 1926a, 127). By the 1970s, the number of variances requested had grown to the thousands for large cities (Babcock and Bosselman 1973).

Some planners considered variances to be a form of discretionary review (Punter 2000). Planners came to rely on them to get their nonconventional projects through, and this practice remains. One study estimated that thirty separate variances would be needed to build a traditional neighborhood development (TND) in Austin, Texas (Planners Advisory Service 1998). The notion that variances would be needed to enable an entire development type (such as TND) rather than as a way to alleviate individual hardship is a somewhat inverted application of the variance idea.

Zoning could also be overridden by preexisting conditions. In 1931, it was estimated that half the population living in tenements in New York City were living in buildings constructed prior to the New Tenement Law of 1901, and thus in violation of it (Bassett 1931). Planners were frustrated by the issue of nonconformity and seemed to have little patience for what had evolved organically before rules (when the market had determined the location of, for instance, nonresidential uses in residential areas). Most cities had thousands of these nonconforming properties. Despite objections, nonconforming uses were almost always grandfathered in. The idea was that, through restrictions on future expansion, nonconforming uses would gradually disappear. When this failed to happen, planners started proposing various retroactive elimination schemes (Ives 1937).

The granting of conditional use permits, amendments, and variances has been a mixed bag. Too often the process has been open to political games involving power and retribution. Weaver and Babcock recalled how business interests were unlikely to let "silly" rules get in their way, that zoning was never to be seen as "an inhibiting factor in the development of the business and commercial centers of our major cities" (1980, 5). Small-scale builders, on the front lines of appeals and variance requests, were often disadvantaged. Lacking the leverage of jobs and tax revenue, they were required to carefully negotiate whatever level of variance the system would bear. If amendments and variances proved difficult, they sometimes became adept at using design tricks to circumnavigate the rules. For example, developers learned how to connect buildings at the corners in order to avoid side-yard setback rules.

The ultimate in flexibility, of course, would be to eliminate rules. In recent years, there have been musings about the value of getting rid of zoning entirely and letting the market guide development (Levine 2005). A crucial point, which is sometimes lost, is that sprawl is not the result of *no* rules, it is often the result of too many rules. The rules that mandate parking spaces, setbacks, lot size, lot coverage, buffers, on-site stormwater retention—all of these and more are working in favor of sprawl and against compact, diverse, walkable urbanism. One suggestion has been to adopt "open-ended" regulations, whereby rules are only adopted if they "do not limit the rights of other property owners or the community and impacts are mitigated" (Staley and Claeys 2005, 202). Unfortunately, our experience with no zoning—namely, Houston—is hardly a model to emulate (Buitelaar 2009). Land use patterns there have tended toward homogeneity and sprawl, not good urbanism (Lewyn 2005; Siegan 1972). On the other hand, if it is true that the biggest effect of zoning's removal would be that "apartment house developments" would penetrate "high-class residential districts," as Toll argued it would (1969, 300), that might be just the kind of free-market effect reformers have been looking for.

The elimination of rules entirely is unlikely in most American cities, given the American predilection for the rule of law. But there is flexibility—still commonly implemented via the PUD (which, as mentioned earlier, also goes by other names depending on the jurisdiction). Overlay zoning and floating zones are used to provide additional options, where a developer can choose between conventional zoning or some other set of rules. The floor area ratio remains a very popular method of flexible control as well, providing choice in terms of lot coverage and building height.

A significant downside of the negotiated, flexible approach to rules is that it can easily result in bad form and bad politics. Melville Branch deemed the granting of zoning waivers in exchange for amenities an indication of planning failure (Branch 1986). In the Chicago Tribune's investigation of zoning reforms that were supposed to take place after a sweeping overhaul in the late 1990s—in a series aptly entitled "Neighborhoods for Sale" (Chicago Tribune 2008)—reporters uncovered a world of corruption, political paybacks, and a complete disregard for community input.

But the main problem with flexibility is its track record: it has often resulted in sprawl disguised as "planned unit development," or "innovative" arrangements that are really nothing more than lifeless open spaces, insular and disconnected superblocks, or antipedestrian thoroughfares. The Prairie Shores development in Chicago, shown in figure 6.2, was the outcome of flexible zoning requirements—the creation of a "mixed use redevelopment project" based on a post–World War II approach to design that was believed to be highly innovative. The planned development approach, instituted in Chicago in 1957, meant that "two parties sat down

Figure 6.2. Prairie Shores development, Chicago, Illinois, a "planned development" where height, density, parking, setbacks, and other features were negotiated instead of rules.

to negotiate over height, density, parking, setbacks, and other features," which, it was hoped, would result in "innovative site plans" (Schwieterman and Caspall 2006, 45). The result of such negotiations tends to be modernist urbanism.

There are plenty of examples of how the flexibility planners tried to introduce—whether labeled the PUD, the planned area development (PAD), or the planned community district (PCD)—just didn't pan out. Figure 6.3 shows a development in Phoenix, Arizona, resulting from a combination of the C-2 and PCD zones. Only the requirements of the C-2 zone seemed to have been applied, since there are no specific design requirements associated with the PCD zone. Figure 6.4 shows an area of

Phoenix built under the rules of the PAD-15 zone. This development fell well within the requirements, but to what positive effect? The main advantage seems to have been that zoning was applied by area rather than by individual parcel. But without guidelines for urban form, the rules did nothing to create a better place. The successful PUD is usually considered to be one that allows flexibility, a streamlined approval process, and a strong community association, not necessarily any particular pattern and form (see, e.g., the criteria for a successful PUD in Moore 1985, published by the Urban Land Institute).

Figure 6.3. Model of a development in Phoenix, Arizona, resulting from a combination of the C-2 and planned community district (PCD) zones.

Figure 6.4. Model of a development in Phoenix, Arizona. built under the rules of the planned area development (PAD) zone.

Predictability

The response to these effects has been a desire for greater predictability—a reversal of the previous half-century of calls for greater flexibility. Since at least the 1980s, planners have been in pursuit of regulation that produces more exact outcomes, with preemptive arguments like "to specify the details of design is not necessarily to restrict architectural creativity" (Cook 1980, 156). If the goal is the production of a more pedestrian-oriented public realm capable of supporting diversity, reformers want rules that will reduce the risk of getting something that falls far short. They argue that codes can be a powerful means to reforming the built environment and providing more stable investment opportunities.

To the extent that codes shield designers from the vagaries of bureaucracy or politics, explicit rules can mean more, not less, freedom. Codes can make "the good easy" (Duany and Talen 2002), by for example, proactively prescribing a walkable city where appropriate. Reformers now want to enact rules for the purpose of creating specific kinds of places, patterns, and forms, not for the purpose of avoiding lawsuits (Ben-Joseph 2004). This requires not only translating desired forms into code but also leveraging the review process so that desired forms of development in desired locations get special, expedited treatment. The U.S. Green Building Council's Leadership in Energy and Environmental Design—Neighborhood Development (LEED-ND) certification can be used in this way, whereby if projects locate in ND-eligible areas, or meet the requirements of LEED-ND certification, the review process can be accelerated. This is likely to involve streamlining rules—that is, combining zoning, subdivision regulations, public facility standards, and landscape ordinance requirements into a single code.

Andres Duany laid out the rationale for this type of coding in a laundry list entitled "Notes Toward a Reason to Code" (Duany 2004, 32–33). He deemed codes essential because they assure "a minimum level of competence" in getting buildings to define rather than occupy space. He argued that this can be achieved by taking advantage of our national tendency to adhere to rules and follow bureaucratic procedure, an inclination that can actually protect the public realm from politicians, fire marshals, corporate interests, engineers, the architectural avant garde, and "the vicissitudes of ownership." Codes can also coordinate the rules of disparate professions and the idiosyncracies of individual designers, getting them to act "with unity of purpose," without which "there is nothing but the unassembled collection of urban potential." Codes provide a measure of stability necessary to compete with other stable, predictable investment opportunities in the form of office parks and shopping centers.

What Duany is referring to has come to be known as the form-based code (FBC; see Katz 2004; Parolek, Parolek, and Crawford 2008). FBCs emerged in recent decades as the best option for implementing a three-dimensional vision of desired urban pattern and form in a transparent, predictable way—an approach that doesn't hide behind arcane text that no one can understand, or that results in forms and patterns no one particularly wants. FBCs are much different than conventional zoning, subdivision regulations, and the myriad of "flexible" techniques instituted from a previous generation of code reformers because FBCs code a *plan* (see Katz 2004). FBCs implement this plan by controlling form explicitly—recalling a time when planners were expected "to know what kinds of forms—of buildings, of ground, perhaps of vegetation" are needed, and then "to provide for these forms and for their arrangement in the best way to serve human needs, not forgetting that one of these needs is always beauty" (Hubbard 1937, 1).

Enclosure is a primary concern of form-based coding. Spatial definition is seen as the antidote to "antisocial" rules that ignore the space-creating qualities of buildings (Kunstler 1998, 136). FBCs address enclosure by reinstating building lines, prohibiting blank walls, requiring permeability (e.g., buildings must have street-level windows), requiring narrower street widths and shorter turn radii, and regulating public and private frontage. There could be a requirement that garages be set back further than the primary facade of a house, and that buildings not turn their side to a main street.

FBCs also try to reinstate a meaningful spatial pattern of zones by varying regulations based on locational intensity, ranging from more rural to more urban qualities (the specific approach is known as transect-based coding; however, FBCs make use of intensity patterns with or without transect terminology; see Duany, Sorlien, and Wright 2008; Duany and Talen 2002). This attention to pattern is readily seen in the regulating plans of FBCs. An example is shown in figure 6.5. Higher-intensity zones typically line commercial streets, while less intense zones transition, sequentially, away from the commercial areas. Typically, smaller unit sizes, street widths, and lot area requirements are associated with zones "closer in"—that is, in more urbanized locations.

FBCs address homogeneity by aiming for a much greater diversity of land uses within a smaller number of zones. Often zones have a land-use designation that is "restricted, limited, or open," which coincides with a significantly more inclusive interpretation of allowable uses. FBCs also permit a greater variety of housing unit types, applying frontage, setback, building type, and other form-related rules to help

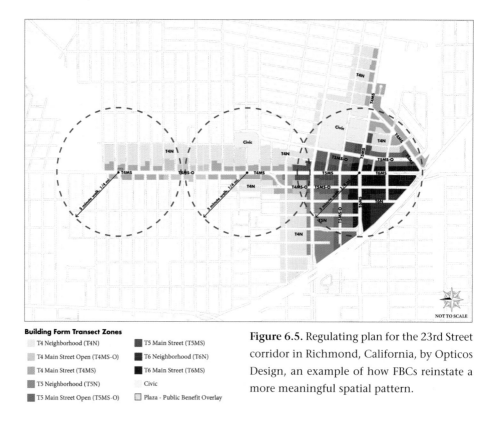

Building Form Transect Zones

☐ T4 Neighborhood (T4N)	■ T5 Main Street (T5MS)
☐ T4 Main Street Open (T4MS-O)	■ T6 Neighborhood (T6N)
☐ T4 Main Street (T4MS)	■ T6 Main Street (T6MS)
■ T5 Neighborhood (T5N)	☐ Civic
■ T5 Main Street Open (T5MS-O)	☐ Plaza - Public Benefit Overlay

Figure 6.5. Regulating plan for the 23rd Street corridor in Richmond, California, by Opticos Design, an example of how FBCs reinstate a more meaningful spatial pattern.

successfully integrate townhomes, duplexes, and single-family residences in relatively close proximity.

FBCs seek to promote connectivity—and therefore mitigate separation—in a number of ways. One strategy is to ensure that stormwater management and landscape buffering requirements do not undermine the needs of connectivity in more urbanized locations. Connectivity is also addressed by limiting parking requirements, limiting curb cuts, allowing shared driveways, and requiring that streets, paths, and routes intersect rather than dead-end. Codes might require (rather than suggest) through-block connections, coordinated bike routes, pedestrian crossings, and allowances for future street extensions.

Duany and Plater-Zyberk's 1982 master-planned community of Seaside, Florida, initiated the first wave of FBCs, specifying building height, setback, permitted encroachments, and parking (then termed a zoning code; see Mohney and Easterling 1991; Krieger 1991). There were initially five types of standards: a regulating plan, urban regulations, architectural regulations, street sections, and landscape regulations. Subsequently, the Congress for the New Urbanism advocated that codes focus on the visual harmony of the public realm by requiring continuous urban frontage. By the late 1990s, the goal of radically transforming development regulations in favor of form-based coding was in full swing. The governor of Maryland, Parris Glendening, held a conference in 1999 on the theme of rehabilitating codes, proposing a "smart growth model ordinance" as well as a new building code. Since then, FBCs have taken on their own complexity, where cities now merge FBCs with priority areas or overlay zones, or hybrid zones that have some form-based emphasis mixed in with conventional use-based coding. The result may be a mixture, as in New York City, where two types of rules are enforced: contextual, where buildings define space, or noncontextual, where buildings simply exist within it.

Transect-based codes such as the SmartCode are a subset of FBCs. These regulations vary depending on locational intensity, ranging from rural preserve to urban core (Duany, Sorlien, and Wright 2008; Duany and Talen 2002). Petaluma, California, which had earlier experimented with code innovation in the 1960s, and the first U.S. city to have a plan for controlling growth in the 1970s, was the first city to adopt a SmartCode, in 2003. Miami, Florida, approved a transect-based code in 2010, the first FBC adopted for a large American city. Denver, Colorado, became the second. Other large cities like Baltimore, Dallas, Houston, and Orlando are in the process of adopting FBCs (Borys and Talen 2010; Steuteville 2010). Sarasota County was the first countywide FBC. As of 2011, there were 200 adopted FBCs in the United States, and an additional 126 codes currently in the developmental stage. Of the 200 adopted, not all are yet adopted, and less than 20 percent can point to projects that have been built or approved under the code. Of those adopted, nearly half are of the transect-based, SmartCode variety.

Most FBCs are very graphic in their presentation. This is in direct contrast to previous generations of codes that were not only excessively long and bureaucratic but failed to provide any clues as to how rules would translate into physical form. Katz argued that the graphic approach of FBCs encourages more public participation because citizens can "see what will happen where" (Katz 2004, 18). Miami21 used graphics to show the effects of the old code ("11000") vis-à-vis the new code, shown in figures 6.6, 6.7, 6.8, and 6.9. The figures are interpretations of different aspects of the code, provided by two architectural teams. As seen in figures 6.6 and 6.7, the Miami21 code allows higher lot coverage and requires less open space, resulting in a different, more pedestrian-friendly street-level presence. Figures 6.8 and 6.9 show how the rules affect a single-family residence and a duplex. In both cases, the lot

11,000 - Building Rendering   Miami 21 - Building Rendering

Figure 6.6. Effects of the old code ("11000"), versus **figure 6.7**, effects of the new code (Miami21).
Source: Oppenheim Architects.

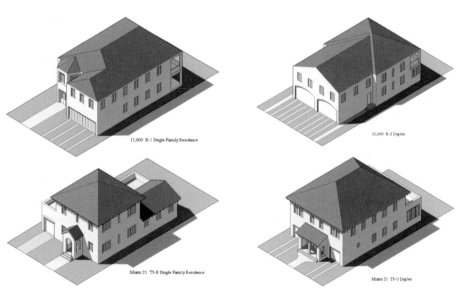

11,000 R-1 Single Family Residence   11,000 R-2 Duplex

Miami 21 T3-R Single Family Residence   Miami 21 T3-O Duplex

Figures 6.8 and 6.9. Effects of the new code (Miami21) versus the old code ("11000") for a single-family residence in the T-3 zone *(left)*, and for a duplex in the T-3 zone *(right)*.
Source: Martinez and Alvarez Architects.

area required per unit is lower, lot coverage is higher, and garage doors are minimized by making use of a single garage door with tandem parking. In the T-3 zones, shown in these figures, front porches have a setback of only 10 feet, while the principal front of the building has a setback of 20 feet (in this way, porches are permitted to "encroach" within the front setback).

Whether termed a form-based code or not, the emphasis on form, pattern, and mixed use pervades all code reform efforts of the last two decades (Morris 2009; Tracy 2004). There are traditional neighborhood development ordinances, mixed-use and live/work codes, transit-oriented development ordinances, transit area codes, transect-based codes, smart growth codes, sustainable codes, transit-supportive codes, urbanist codes, and green building codes of various stripes (Clarion 2008; Crawford 2004; Morris 1996). Groups like the U.S. Green Building Council (http://www.usgbc.org/) and the Development Center for Appropriate Technology (http://www.dcat.net/) are trying to reform existing codes to be more "sustainable," which, in terms of regulating the built environment, essentially means the promotion of mixed use and attention to form and pattern (in addition to removing bans on solar panels, or creating incentives like density bonuses for green roofs and water-conserving landscape standards). Meanwhile, at the state level, new kinds of regulations have been adopted to encourage local governments to use codes to reign in sprawl (Knaap et al. 2007).

Planners believe that the approach will spur revitalization. San Francisco created the Rincon Hill Downtown Residential Mixed Use District (RH-DTR) (figs. 6.10 and 6.11) at the southern edge of downtown San Francisco to encourage high-density mixed-use development. A page from the code is shown in figure 6.12. The code was a translation of the City's 1971 Design Plan—an attempt to recapture an urban form believed necessary for pedestrian-friendly cities. The code is proactive: active uses are required on all street frontages. One hundred percent lot coverage is permitted, setbacks are minimal, aboveground parking is not permitted, and off-street parking is not required. To provide some light and air, setbacks above a given height are required. The regulations have been compared to the Vancouver model, whereby high-rise towers are surrounded by human-scaled, pedestrian-friendly townhouses and small-scale retail.

Unsurprisingly, the planner's desire for predictability through FBCs has been met with resistance from the design community. Architects have often been unhappy with "beauty-by-law methods" (Mackesey 1939, 98), seeing rules as preventing good urban form, not inspiring it. Claims of rigidity are now surfacing in relation to FBCs, and FBCs have been pejoratively described as "an excellent way to preserve static neighborhoods" (Scheer 2011). Architects are likely to see FBCs as an indication that planners think architects can't be trusted to make good decisions. They may see codes as stifling ingenuity and potentially, public life. They may believe that codes go too far, inhibit creativity, thwart the ability to adapt to changing circumstances,

Figure 6.10. The Rincon Hill Downtown Residential Mixed Use District (RH-DTR), at the southern edge of downtown San Francisco, was established to encourage high-density mixed-use development.

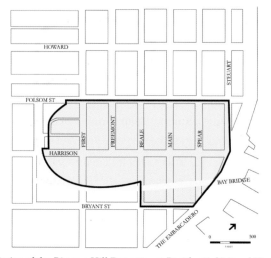

Figure 6.11. Boundaries of the Rincon Hill Downtown Residential Mixed Use District (RH-DTR).

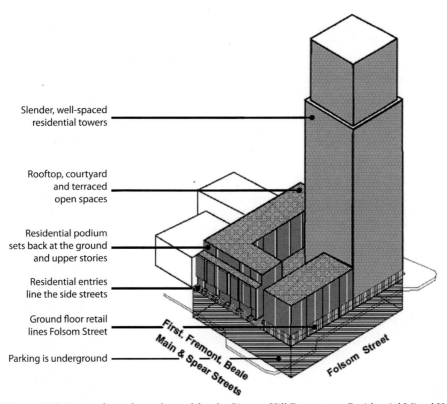

Slender, well-spaced
residential towers

Rooftop, courtyard
and terraced
open spaces

Residential podium
sets back at the ground
and upper stories

Residential entries
line the side streets

Ground floor retail
lines Folsom Street

Parking is underground

First, Fremont, Beale
Main & Spear Streets

Folsom Street

Figure 6.12. A page from the code used for the Rincon Hill Downtown Residential Mixed Use District (RH-DTR).

fail to respond to locality or context, and ignore environmental concerns. They may doubt the ability of codes to make better places or improve the quality of design, arguing instead for the promotion of "architectural patronage" and an expansion of design competitions as a means of promoting better place making (Punter 2000, 306).

Carmona, Marshall, and Stevens conducted an extensive review of design codes and summarized the critiques, among them interference with creativity, too much focus on product, misplaced belief that objective criteria exist, and belief that codes can compensate for poor design skill. All of these add up to a strong reaction against any constraints on the "creative design process" (2006, 228).

This resistance to FBCs mirrors the critique of the first zoning rules in the United States—concerns that eventually led to the flexible approaches reviewed earlier. Writing in 1901, Robinson concluded, "Rules and suggestions can be based only on practical considerations. The rest must be in the designer's heart" (1901, 126). This meant that, while early planners promoted a theory of systematized planning (Birch 1980), they often failed to extend the system to matters of design, place, and character. As a result, urban form languished under rules that paid little attention to the quality of urban form. Instead, matters of design were to be handed over to professions outside of planning. The pillars of modern zoning—Bassett, Williams, Bettman, and Whitten—coauthored in 1935 a city planning textbook that weighed in on the proper place for consideration of the "elements of city construction"—blocks, streets, and the like—warning city planners not to "try to set forth rules for obtaining the best appearance of these elements when coordinated. This is another field—that of the landscape architect and the architect" (Bassett et al. 1935, 4). Planners were left to conceive of rules as something separate from desired patterns and forms.

Searching for Balance

The task before planners—then, as now—is to find a way to balance predictability and flexibility. Planners will have to find a way to accommodate the need for predictable outcomes with the need for freedom to pursue multiple paths toward a common goal based on the needs and challenges of the community. The key questions are uncomplicated: can an approach that steers clear of prescription create attractive, well functioning cities? And can prescriptive rules allow creativity and innovation where they are needed?

The growing popularity of FBCs is exposing this tension clearly. To FBC advocates, added layers of discretionary review in the name of flexibility not only permit poor design but promote a loss of connection to social purpose, essentially obscuring the underlying motivation to create a rule. Critics of FBCs, on the other hand, see them as promoting hegemonies devoted to corporate capitalism, or worse, conservative ideologies about traditional family type. Balancing these opposing perspectives will be no small challenge. The failure to integrate top-down (formal, predetermined) and bottom-up (organic, incremental) approaches in planning has been a problem since the profession was created over a century ago, resulting in an ongoing tension that seems to "see-saw cyclically over time" (Collins and Collins 2006; from Konvitz 1985, xv).

Many urban planners and designers seem conflicted over their desire for predictability and flexibility as simultaneous requirements. The perspective of urban morphologists exposes this—on the one hand, they are happy with the turn toward urban form and building type in the reform of codes. They applaud the use of "typomorphology" (Moudon 1994, 289), where urban form is appreciated through the

lens of urban structure and space. Like FBC advocates, they regret that urban designers and architects often underplay the importance of street, block, plot, and
building, preoccupied instead with "the relatively ephemeral nature of the architectural superstructure" (Samuels 2008, 59). But urban morphologists are unhappy that
the appreciation of form is not backed by greater understanding of the dynamics
and multiple scales inherent in the built landscape. They see an underappreciation
of the historical trajectory of places ("static analysis leads to a static vision"), and a
lack of attention to the regional or citywide scale of regulation (Scheer 2008, 141).
There is a concern that the types being coded no longer have an underlying social,
cultural, or economic rationale for being—for example, perimeter blocks forced upon
suburban forms are being put in place for reasons completely separate from their
historical basis. Scheer argues that FBC advocates seem not to appreciate scales beyond the lot, block, and neighborhood, making their motives unacceptably idealis-
tic and ultimately incapable of "holding back the forces of urban development and
transformation" (Scheer 2011). In other words, if FBC advocates persist in their promotion of space-defining forms regardless of generative conditions, they will be in
danger of creating historic relics.

While urban morphologists argue that space-defining forms were not instituted
for the purpose of sociability and good civic design but were instead established to
fit the most common development types (Scheer 2011), proponents of FBCs believe
there is something deeper at stake. They view rules that created consistent frontages
as justified in their own right because of their critical contribution toward a
pedestrian-scale, high-quality public realm, regardless of earlier causal factors unre-
lated to civic goals. They are confident in the universality of certain principles of
form, human scale, and the legitimacy of rekindling past traditions.

FBC proponents also believe that their codes are responsive to locational context. Intensity and character of place vary spatially, and FBCs can reinforce that variation through the intelligent application of context-sensitive codes. In some ways
this reflects what the original framers of zoning had in mind. They erred by separating pattern from form, but they did understand that urban character and intensity vary by location. The continuity of this idea supports current reform efforts.

An obvious solution to the tug-of-war over predictability versus flexibility is a
coding approach in which only the most essential elements get coded. The idea
would be to permit a culturally distinctive response within a coding framework, a
paring down of rules to just the essentials. Such codes might stipulate a few key principles that, from there, "let it go" (Jacobs 2002, 139; see also Ben-Joseph 2009). The

idea would be to have "a small dose of prescribed rules" and a "large measure of performance outcome" (Ben-Joseph 2009), or, as Carmona describes it, an approach whereby codes regulate "the essentials of urbanism" while at the same time help to "mediate the tyrannies of practice" (Carmona 2009, 2643). The idea is not new. The planner Tracy Augur called for this approach in the 1920s, arguing that planners should "designate a few things which cannot be done and leave the rest to individual initiative" (Augur 1923, 17). In Europe, Unwin had earlier proposed an approach allowing "something of that elastic character which belongs to natural restraints,"(1909, 387) and "a little give and take, a little averaging of one part with another" (1909, 393). Some FBCs like the SmartCode attempt this balance by being parametric, defining minimum and maximum ranges rather than absolutes, in the hopes of leading to greater visual variety.

An alternative proposal for balancing certainty with flexibility is to focus on coding land use in a more intelligent way. Toronto's "split zones" system is one idea. A property might have a maximum floor area ratio of 5.0 overall, but there might be a cap of 4.0 for residential and 2.0 for commercial. Thus maximum buildout can be achieved only if uses are mixed. The approach allows landowners "flexibility to make choices about use within the framework of the marketplace" (Wickersham 2001, 560).

Another strategy might be to start with a base code and then allow the code to be added to in modular fashion. To some degree the *Laws of the Indies* operated this way, as there was a significant amount of local variation in the application of a basic set of rules (although this could also be interpreted as a matter of simply ignoring the rules, rather than adapting them). The SmartCode pursues this approach by encouraging add-on subunits called modules. There are now over thirty transect-based modules, in process or completed, that supplement the base SmartCode. There are modules for affordable housing, bicycling, flood hazard mitigation, visitability, and signage (http://www.transect.org/). Since all modules conform to a transect-based system of urban-to-rural segmentation, critics of FBCs might find these modules, too, unacceptably prescriptive.

Urban morphologists have suggested regulating typological pattern, not style or details about materials, colors, and window sizes, as a way of balancing certainty and adaptability. Regulating details, according to Scheer and Scheer (1998), is a legacy of historic preservation and need not apply to coding urban form in general. A focus on a few simple rules, like how a building sits on the lot, frontage type, and whether to allow attached or freestanding buildings, would avoid irritating levels of control that ultimately create bland buildings and prevent "the happy accidents and individual quirks" that create a more vibrant street and a more vital place (1998, 153).

Perhaps none of these suggestions for balancing flexibility and predictability are an advance over what was proposed more than a century ago in Germany. The following is text from the nineteenth-century General Building Law of Saxony (quoted from *The Improvement of the Dwellings and Surroundings of the People: The Example of Germany*, by T. C. Horsfall 1904; also reprinted in Robinson 1901, 236).

a. The position of the blocks of building, as well as of the lines of streets and the building-lines, must be adapted to the configuration of the land, and must be such that an adequate supply of sunshine in the rooms occupied is secured.

b. The dimensions of the various blocks of building must be such as to allow of the proper utilization of the ground for building.

c. The width of the streets and footpaths is decided by the requirements of local traffic, and must be suitably graduated in accordance with the nature of the streets, as main streets, by-streets, or streets used only for dwellings. In the case of the streets of detached or semi-detached buildings, where there is not proper through traffic, the part of the road used for vehicles need not exceed a width of twenty-six feet. In the case of the streets for which through traffic may be expected eventually, especially tram-lines, and a widening of the street must be anticipated, there must be front gardens of suitable depth on both sides. Private roads, which give access to the backs of buildings for several blocks, must not have a less width than nineteen and the half feet.

d. Gradients in the streets must be distributed as evenly as possible.

e. In determining the directions of streets care must be taken to provide short and convenient connections between streets and the chief centres of traffic.

f. [Sites] for churches and school buildings, as well as public playgrounds and recreation grounds, must be provided in sufficient number.

g. In deciding what shall be the kind of building allowed, and as to whether factories and workshops shall be allowed, the existing character of the district, or part of a district, and its needs must be taken into account.

Here is a code consisting of a few simple rules and baseline dimensions, coupled with a wide latitude for local interpretation. But would this kind of code work in places that lack a more unified building culture, in which concepts of "suitability" and "character" lack definition? Do we really know what we'd be getting if accepted custom (if it exists) were substituted for explicit regulation? What evidence is there of shared attitudes about the built environment, instilling confidence that greater leeway would create good places? In debating this, some have asked why modern codes, even if "comprehensive and precise," are unable to deliver an ordered urban framework previously achieved by just a few simple rules (Braunfels 1990, 1). Are cities too disparate and lacking in commonality among competing actors and interests to ever hope for something good to emerge from a simple code?

Absent vernacular building traditions, cultural agreement, or technological limits, FBCs must now build consensus around what Ben-Joseph termed "place-based norms" (2005, 24). But do such norms exist? Is the continued reliance on conventional codes and the failure to enact more widespread change—despite a universal dislike of codes—an indication that norms about place are missing? Or, are intrinsic norms simply obscured under the weight of intractable codes, waiting for some mechanism to reinvigorate them? With endless technological possibilities and continuous social and economic change constantly challenging cultural agreement, can code reformers be called upon to help reestablish, and then help codify, an innate collective wisdom?

Code reformers are banking on the notion that collective norms about urban pattern and form can be reawakened. Although not often stated, this conviction is based on an intransigent belief in the existence of universal principles, of an urban form that transcends style and taste and is based on a certain degree of human hard-wiring. This belief gives FBC advocates the confidence to argue that place-based norms are only uncovered by engaging the public in the code-making process (Parolek, Parolek, and Crawford 2008). Principles persist because they have demonstrated success in being able to support how humans function in, and relate to, their environment. Rejecting both the reliance on individual designers and an ideology that requires that all buildings be "of our time" (the zeitgeist; see Krier 2009), code reformers are hoping to recapture an essential kind of urbanism whose basic outlines in terms of pattern and form transcend idiosyncratic tastes and market-led product types (Duany 2004; xi–xiii in this book) and instead focus on producing a high-quality, pedestrian-oriented public realm of the kind one would find in parts of many older American cities, like Boston, New Orleans, Chicago, or Annapolis. It is possible, in short, to know what good cities are, and how rules can produce them.

But finding the balance between predictability and flexibility—between the tendency to want to enforce a specific physical goal and the need to allow a more fluid discovery of design sensibilities—will also require a legal framework that looks at rules as an interdependent system (Slone and Goldstein 2008, 25). So-called generative codes are in this spirit. Generative coding was popularized by Christopher

Alexander and colleagues (1987), whose work on the organic city-making process followed in the tradition of Jane Jacobs's process-oriented ideals. The approach rejects predetermined forms and patterns in favor of "the stepwise process by which a form might emerge from the evolutionary actions of a group of collaborators" (Mehaffy 2008, 57). Rules might be based on respecting the public realm, respecting one's neighbor, acknowledging the inevitability of change, and respecting local customs, through which urban form evolves "naturally," as a "self-regulating and adaptive system" (Hakim and Ahmed 2006, 19).

Code reformers need to find a way to reconcile rules that guide these decision-making processes with rules that prescribe form. They need to clarify what is negotiable, and what cannot be compromised. They need to operationalize a code that allows certain freedoms within a framework of prohibitions that not only prevents damage to neighbors but promotes a better public realm. Rules that are "bottom-up" and "self-regulating" might be welcomed in a society defined by rugged individualism, self-reliance, and entrepreneurialism, but it will first be necessary to demonstrate that a valued public realm, supportive of connection and diversity, is capable of being created that way.

Perhaps the codes currently in use in some of the best urban places America has to offer can be looked to for inspiration. The rules in parts of Denver; Salem, Massachusetts; and San Francisco (figs. 6.13, 6.14, and 6.15) reaffirm historic, walkable character. Their rules are summarized in boxes 6.1, 6.2, and 6.3. Here are codes requiring that a build-to line maintain frontage, that main entrances face the street, that weather and wind protection be provided for pedestrians, that blank walls are not allowed, that windows need to be at street level, that street trees must be provided, that it is okay to have porches and bay windows, that café tables and sidewalk sales should be encouraged, that lighting and signage must be scaled to pedestrians rather than cars, and that parking lots and garage doors should not face the street. These are rules adjusted to different contexts, but all have the overriding goal of creating buildings that define space, that prioritize the needs of the pedestrian, and that try to minimize the negative effects of cars. If none of these commonsense elements is likely to be built without coercion, can planners be forgiven for wanting to write them into the rules?

Figure 6.13. The rules for a section of Denver, Colorado, reinforce walkable urban character; see box 6.1.

Box 6.1. Main Street district abutting a multiunit, low-density residential district: Residential and commercial uses permitted

- Buildings shall be built to within 1'6" of the zone lot line along public streets.
- Minimum percent of lineal street frontage that shall be occupied by the ground floor of any building: Main street: 75 percent, side street: 25 percent
- Structures shall be set back 5 ft. from the zone lot line shared with the residentially zoned lot.
- Maximum building height: 38 ft.
- No parking shall be allowed between the building and the street.
- Minimum glazed lineal building frontage in the zone of transparency (ground floor): Main street: 60 percent, side street: 25 percent
- Window glazing shall be clear and shall transmit at least 65 percent of visible daylight.
- Off-street parking requirement: 1 parking space per 500 sq. ft. of nonresidential uses
- Maximum sign area: 80 sq. ft.

Figure 6.14. Rules for a section of San Francisco, California; see box 6.2.

Box 6.2. North Beach Neighborhood Commercial District (NCD): Functions as a neighborhood-serving marketplace, citywide specialty dining district, and a tour ist attraction, as well as an apartment and residential hotel zone

- Height and bulk limit: 41–65 ft.
- Maximum lot size: 5,000 sq. ft.
- FAR: 1.8
- At least ½ of the total width of such new or altered structures at the commercial street frontage shall be devoted to entrance commercial uses space, windows or display space at the pedestrian eye-level. Such windows shall use clear, untinted glass for decorative or architectural accent.
- When width of all awnings is 10 ft. or less along the direction of the street, the projection of such awnings shall not exceed 6' vertical distance from the top to the bottom of such awnings.
- Street trees shall be installed in a minimum of one 24 in. box tree for each 20 ft. of frontage of the property along each street with any remaining fraction of 10 ft. or more of frontage requiring an additional tree. Such trees shall be located either within area on the lot or within the public ROW along such lot.
- Minimum parking spaces for restaurants: 1 for each 200 sq. ft. of occupied floor area, where the occupied floor area exceeds 5,000 sq. ft.
- Minimum parking spaces for commercial service spaces: 1 for each 1,000 sq. ft. of occupied floor area, where the occupied floor exceeds 5,000 sq. ft.
- Parking reductions may be granted if anticipated auto usage of residents and visitors is low.

Figure 6.15. Rules for a street in Salem, Massachusetts; see box 6.3. Photo courtesy of City of Salem.

Box 6.3. Central development district: Residential and commercial uses permitted

- Minimum lot area: 2,000 sq. ft.
- Minimum lot width: 30 ft.
- Maximum lot coverage: 100%
- Maximum building height: 70 ft., 6 stories
- Floor area ratio: 6:1
- Nonresidential uses shall not be required to provide off-street parking since the community will accept the responsibility for nonresidential parking in this district.
- Nontenant, occupant, or owner having the care of any building or lot of land bordering on any street, lane, court, square, or public place within the city shall allow any bushes, shrubbery, or any other form of plant growth to obstruct the safe passage of any pedestrian on any such street, lane, court, square, or public place.
- No new street or way, except a footway, shall be laid out and accepted by the city council of a less width than 40 ft.

7. Conclusion

In twenty-first-century America, there is wide agreement that a new approach to city building is sorely needed. Cities need to be less wasteful and more efficient, less land consumptive and more compact, less dispiriting and more vital. Many are looking to rules to be the instigators of this sea change. In the quest for sustainable cities, as Americans rescale, localize, and rein in complex financial systems and large-scale production builders, there is a need for a system of rules that supports a more enlightened approach to city making.

History shows that the effect of rules on pattern, use, and form has not been trivial. It has meant the difference between accessibility and inaccessibility, inclusion and exclusion, efficiency and waste. Mostly, rules in America have produced "a social fabric of stifling monotony" (Whyte 1958). This has had far-reaching consequences: income segregation, racial segregation, concentrated poverty, spatial mismatch between jobs and housing, urban sprawl, traffic congestion, among other things (Ihlanfeldt 2004). Where social institutions made progress in breaking down barriers to integration, city rules like zoning thwarted the translation of that progress in broader terms. Zoning's role in perpetuating school desegregation problems is but one example (Nechyba 2001; Wells et al. 2004).

This situation became worse over time. As zoning gained more widespread acceptance in the courts, as well as within American society more generally, rules took on a more broad-brush quality. The smaller-scale zoning of the early twentieth century, which often supported a finer-grain land-use mix, gave way to something much coarser and less nuanced. Economics played a strong role in this too. As development became larger in scale, zoning was made to support the single-use, production community building favored by developers (Weiss 1987). This is not how zoning was originally conceived. In fact, it is possible to view zoning as something that developed incrementally out of a long-evolving desire to maintain public welfare and a sense of order, not necessarily as a result of pro-development interests in line with the "city efficient" era (e.g., Kolnick 2008; Wolf 2008).

Can conventional rules about pattern, use, and form still be interpreted as a way of promoting the common good, as initially intended? Are minimum building and lot sizes meant to keep poor people out, or, as social reformers first claimed, are they meant to increase the living conditions of the poor? Are minimum lot and block sizes a form of snobbery, or are they intended to provide a more humane quality of life for all? Are rules that limit density potentially good for everyone, maintaining certain minimum standards of light and air, or does the limitation on density simply increase housing cost and encourage sprawl? Are limitations on use still needed to ensure that harmful uses stay away from residences, or are these rules simply contributing to automobile dependence, which is itself harmful?

Often rules have been devoted more to preventing than to requiring. There is rarely a situation where certain uses are proactively *required* in order to complete a neighborhood or make an area more serviceable for residents, or where rules require the combining of one type of use with another in order to stimulate economic growth (zoning for mixed-use or transit-oriented development [TOD] are recent phenomena designed precisely to create that kind of integration). Under the current system, rules promote positive objectives only by prohibiting the bad, not requiring the good.

The history of rules discussed in this book has shown that U.S. divergence from European practice has been mostly damaging to American cities. Although couched as an effort to keep bad things away from people, use-related rules, which were not a significant aspect of European codes, devolved into an ideology about cities that prioritized a narrow sense of order over urban diversity and interchange. The legacy of this is that, today, not only is mix never required—it is rarely allowed. City rules have obstructed a well-functioning mix that could put people and services within proximity, or that could mix housing types so that resources would be more equitably distributed.

As the story of zoning unfolded, the rules designed to prevent disinvestment and sprawl instead became their precursor. By the 1960s, this was impossible to ignore. Leading planners were practically screaming off the pages of planning journals and books about the failed experiment that was zoning. There was Reps's epic *Requiem for Zoning* (1964), Babcock's *The Zoning Game* (1966), Mandelker's *The Zoning Dilemma* (1971), and

Siegan's *Land Use without Zoning* (1972). Carl Feiss asked whether planners had been "lulled into a coma of mass acceptance" of an "incomprehensible" tool that was fostering "unlimited sprawl" (Feiss 1961, 121–22). Siegan asked whether land was being regulated "merely for the sake of regulation," apparently because people must be assuming that even if zoning was "unreasonable, inequitable, and irrational," it was better than nothing (Siegan 1972, 21).

For decades now, there have been thorough explorations of the inefficiencies, social inequities, and added costs of conventional zoning codes (Dowall 1984; Levine 2005; Pendall 2000). From the economist's point of view, zoning is the embodiment of Madisonian "plans of oppression" (McDonald and McMillen 2004, 343), driven by principles of exclusion and protection of self-interest. Zoning has been deemed anything but sustainable: it "guarantees the maximum consumption of units of time, energy, hardware, and land for the execution of the daily functions of the whole of society" (Krier 2009, 103). Yet it remains. How much of society's reluctance to throw bad rules out is a matter of failing to understand its ill effects? How much have the underlying purposes of rules been obscured as a result of being "modified by bureaucracies, adapted to political exigencies, and otherwise thoroughly watered down for ease of application and administration" (Relph 1987, 74–75)?

Now instead of calling for zoning's demise, urban planners and designers have recognized it as a powerful tool not to be abdicated, but to be transformed for better purpose. Just as zoning was seen in the Progressive Era as a powerful tool for *decongesting* the city, city rules are now being seen as a powerful tool for *reconcentrating* it. Can a change in the rules be enlisted once again to create the cities Americans want? There is some hope that this is possible. Unlike federal tax laws or finance regulation, city rules like zoning and subdivision regulations are locally controlled and more within reach. This makes them the most reasonable and realistic avenue for fundamentally changing the way cities are built.

Advocates of code reform can take comfort in the fact that rules intended to support great cities draw from an extensive history. The decentralization and separation that corrupted city rules, put in motion at the First National Planning Conference in 1909, can be viewed as a blip in the historical record. What emerged out of the initial American experience with rules was that Americans became expert at legalizing separation—creating divisions between pattern, use, and form, between flexibility and predictability, between rule and outcome. But this does not accurately reflect what city rules have often accomplished.

This book has tried to make those effects clear. It has attempted to unravel the connections between rule, effect, and motivation, and in many cases, legitimize the frustrations and anger directed at rules. It is perilous to continue to ignore the sheer illogic of the system of rules a century has cobbled together. What is to be done with a system that puts homes next to highways, that won't allow a church to feed the homeless, that blocks neighborhoods from having grocery stores because of use restrictions, or that allows an entire community to exclude the poor?

These inequities signal moral imperatives, but rule changes will also be motivated by very practical reasons. Rules that might have once helped production builders realize greater profit are no longer necessarily seen as being good for business. There is now a major housing imbalance brewing—61 percent of existing housing stock is in the form of single-family, detached dwellings, yet two thirds of housing demand in the coming years, fueled by millennials and baby boomers, will be in the form of one- or two-person households (Leinberger 2008; Myers 2007). What is needed are rules that won't get in the way of accommodating the needs of a new generation, especially when those needs are in line with sustainability goals. Rules are going to have to help small units and compact urbanism thrive. At the very least, they shouldn't get in the way.

How much are rules out of sync with current public sentiment? It is likely that at least some segments of the American population—and certainly almost all urban planners—have moved away from a mindset devoted to maintaining homogeneous neighborhoods. Land-use diversity, at least in controlled form, is unlikely to be viewed as a threat to American society. What neighborhood of single-family homes wouldn't welcome a small grocery store, café, or barber shop? Small retailers that fulfill daily needs are much more likely now to be perceived as an amenity than as a disamenity. People still want, above all, to protect the value of their property, but now this value may be enhanced not by sameness but by controlled diversity and with an urban form capable of maintaining it (Talen 2008). Being able to walk to a store or to house one's relatives in an accessory unit will be powerful forces working to change conventional rules. Mixed use has a market value.

Americans are once again putting great stock in rules. No longer just a way to "minimize human unhappiness" (Kunstler 1998, 123), rules are now meant to address multiple dimensions of urban life, everything from mental health, food access, housing options, and urban agriculture to bicycle use—a wide array of urban conditions that are both cause of, and effect on, place quality. There is a recasting of rules aimed at "public health, safety, welfare, morals," or even nuisance, to now address climate change, energy use, physical activity, and an aging population. In many ways, the creation of "place"—and all that it implies—is the new health and safety motivation.

Under this broadened set of objectives, some may wonder whether too much is being asked of rules. This would not be unusual. In 1925, the Baltimore Board of Zoning Appeals wrote in their annual report that zoning "ought to make our cities better places in which to live and to make of people better Americans" (Baltimore BZA 1925, 24). It was unfortunate that the pronouncements and expectations about what rules could accomplish were never subjected to evaluation about whether cities were actually becoming "better places in which to live." Can planners put new purpose into making an explicit connection? Could the promise of a new system of rules—rules devoted to human scale, diversity, sustainability, and beauty rather than exclusion, sorting, and efficiency—motivate that effort?

For this to happen, there would need to be a more explicit idea about what the city should be. One can imagine that this *telos*, this understanding of what the human habitat is and should be, is what guided earlier generations of rule makers to precisely regulate urban pattern and form. It was there in the initial efforts of American planners to transfer social and moral purpose to zoning and subdivision regulation, and it was there when Thomas Adams wrote in 1932 that the zoning of residential areas was about getting people to care about the larger neighborhood context of which the resident was a part. Unfortunately, as planners acquired the tools and the legal authority to encourage people to behave as if they cared about the world outside of their own homes, the laws seemed more and more directed at securing private realms, not public ones.

Gaining better, more sustainable cities—places that are walkable, diverse, compact, and beautiful—will require strong public support and, along with it, a new approach to the rules of city making. New economic and environmental realities—global warming, economic recession, demographic change—are reining in the urban free-for-all that allowed previous generations to spread cities out and neglect the public realm. Undergirding this effort will be the need to become more cognizant of the effect of rules on the condition of urbanism, and more cognizant of underlying intentions. Will planners now be able to present as clear a consensus and vision about what the effect of rules should be as urban planners did a century ago?

References

Ackerman, Frederick L. 1935. "Zoning." *Journal of the American Planning Association (AIPJ)* 1 (1): 21–22.

Adams, Thomas. 1922. *Modern City Planning: Its Meaning and Methods*. National Municipal Review vol. 11, no. 6. New York: National Municipal League.

Adams, Thomas. 1931. *Regional Survey of New York and Its Environs*. vol. 6, *Buildings: Their Use and the Spaces about Them*. New York: Regional Plan of New York and Its Environs.

Adams, Thomas. 1932. "A Communication: In Defense of the Regional Plan." *New Republic* 71 (July 6): 207–10.

Adams, Thomas. 1934. *The Design of Residential Areas: Basic Considerations, Principles and Methods*. Harvard City Planning Studies, Volume VI. Cambridge, MA: Harvard University Press.

Adams, Thomas. 1935. *Outline of Town and City Planning: A Review of Past Efforts and Modern Aims*. London: J. & A. Churchill.

Adams, Thomas, and Harland Bartholomew. 1935. "Zoning: Discussion." *Journal of the American Planning Association (AIPJ)* 1 (3): 65–66.

Adams, Thomas, Harold M. Lewis, and Theodore T. McCrosky. 1929. Regional Survey of New York and Its Environs, vol. 2. *Population, Land Values and Government*. New York: Regional Plan of New York and Its Environs.

Addams, Jane. 1902. "The Housing Problem in Chicago." *Annals of the American Political Science Association* 20:111.

Alexander, C., H. Neis, A. Anninou, and I. King. 1987. *A New Theory of Urban Design*. New York: Oxford University Press.

American City Magazine. 1912. "Editorial Comment: The Housing Problem." *American City*, July, 1–8.

American City Magazine. 1924. "An Ordinance Forbidding Gasoline Filling Stations Held to Be Void as Being Unreasonable." *American City*, February, 205.

American Planning Association. 1996. *Modernizing State Planning Statutes*. Growing Smart Working Papers, vol. 1. Planning Advisory Service Report, no. 462/263. Chicago: American Planning Association.

Anderson, Nels. 1925. "Zoning and the Mobility of Urban Population." *City Planning* 1 (3): 155–59.

Arntz, K. 2002. *Building Regulation and the Shaping of Urban Form in Germany*. Working Paper, no. 85, School of Planning and Housing, University of Central England. Birmingham, England: University of Central England (Birmingham City University).

Atlanta General Council. 1937. "Petition to Rezone," by Louise Binvis, 30 September, Document Files, 1937, p. 727. Cited in Barbara J. Flint, 1977, *Zoning and Residential Segregation: A Social and Physical History 1910–40*. Chicago: University of Chicago Press.

Augur, Tracy Baldwin. 1923. The laws and regulations relating to platting of land in the United States as affecting the desirability of lows for dwelling purposes. *Landscape Architecture* 15 (26): 51–52.

Ayers, J. 1998. *Building the Georgian City*. New Haven, CT: Yale University Press.

Baar, Kenneth. 1992. The national movement to halt the spread of multifamily housing, 1890–1926. *Journal of the American Planning Association* 58 (1): 39–48.

Babcock, Richard F. 1966. *The Zoning Game*. Madison: University of Wisconsin Press.

Babcock, Richard F., and Fred P. Bosselman. 1973. *Exclusionary Zoning: Land Use Regulation and Housing in the 1970s*. New York: Praeger.

Babcock, Richard F., and Clifford L. Weaver. 1979. *City Zoning, the Once and Future Frontier*. Chicago, IL: Planners Press.

Bacon, Albion Fellows. 1911. *What Bad Housing Means to the Community*. National Housing Association publication 6, January. New York: National Housing Association.

Baer, William C. 2007a. "Planning for Growth and Growth Controls in Early Modern Northern Europe: Part 2: The Evolution of London's Practice 1580 to 1680." *Town Planning Review* 78 (3): 157–77.

Baer, William C. 2007b. "Planning for Growth and Growth Controls in Early Modern Northern Europe: Part 1: The Continental Experience." *Town Planning Review* 78 (2): 203–23.

Baker, Douglas C., Neil G. Sipe, and Brendan J. Gleeson. 2006. "Performance-Based Planning: Perspectives from the United States, Australia, and New Zealand." *Journal of Planning Education and Research* 25 (4): 396–409.

Baker, Newman F. 1927. *Legal Aspects of Zoning*. Chicago: University of Chicago Press.

Baltimore Board of Zoning Appeals (BZA). 1925. *Second Annual Report of the Board of Zoning Appeals*. Baltimore: City of Baltimore.

Baltimore, City of. 2010. Zoning Code of the City of Baltimore. http://www.baltimore city.gov/Portals/0/Charter%20and%20Codes/Code/Art%2000%20-%20Zoning.pdf.

Bartholomew, Harland. 1932. *Urban Land Uses: Amounts of Land Used and Needed for Various Purposes by Typical American Cities*. Harvard City Planning Studies, vol. 4. Cambridge, MA: Harvard University Press.

Bassett, Edward M. 1922a. *Zoning*. Technical Pamphlet Series no. 5., National Municipal Review Supplement. New York: National Municipal League.

Bassett, Edward M. 1922b. "Home Owners Make Good Citizens." *Baltimore Municipal Journal*, March 10, 6.

Bassett, Edward M. 1922c. "Zoning versus Private Restrictions." *Baltimore Municipal Journal*, January 6, 2.

Bassett, Edward M. 1922d. "Zoning Protects the Small Storekeeper." *Baltimore Municipal Journal*, March 24, 5.

Bassett, Edward M. 1923. *Present Attitude of Courts toward Zoning.* New York: National Conference on City Planning.

Bassett, Edward M. 1925a. "Exploitation of Home Districts by Apartment Houses." *City Planning* 1 (2): 60–61.

Bassett, Edward M. 1925b. "The Remarkable Adaptability of Modern Zoning." *City Planning* 1 (2): 129.

Bassett, Edward M. 1926a. "Remarkable Scope of Variances." *City Planning* 2 (2): 127–28.

Bassett, Edward M. 1926b. "Zoning Trip." *City Planning* 2 (3): 212–15.

Bassett, Edward M. 1931. "Control of Building Heights, Densities and Uses by Zoning." In *Regional Survey of New York and Its Environs,* vol. 6, *Buildings: Their Use and the Spaces about Them.* New York: Regional Plan of New York and Its Environs.

Bassett, Edward M. 1940. "Upheaval in New York City Zoning." *Planning and Civic Comment* 6 (3): 10–13.

Bassett, Edward M., and Frank B. Williams. 1928. "Zoning Cases in the United States." New York: Regional Plan of New York and Its Environs.

Bassett, Edward M., Frank B. Williams, Alfred Bettman, and Robert Whitten. 1935. New *Model Laws for Planning Cities, Counties, and States.* Cambridge: Harvard University Press.

Baumeister, Reinhard. 1876. *Town Expansions Considered with Respect to Technology, Building Code and Economy.* Berlin: Ernst & Korn.

Ben-Joseph, Eran. 2004. "Future of Standards and Rules in Shaping Place: Beyond the Urban Genetic Code." *Journal of Urban Planning and Development* 130 (2): 67–74.

Ben-Joseph, Eran. 2005. *The Code of the City: Standards and the Hidden Language of Place-Making.* Cambridge, MA: MIT Press.

Ben-Joseph, Eran. 2009. "Designing Codes: Trends in Cities, Planning and Development." *Journal of Urban Studies* 46 (12): 2691–2702.

Ben-Joseph, Eran, and Terry S. Szold, eds. 2004. *Regulating Place: Standards and the Shaping of Urban America.* New York: Routledge.

Berry, C. P. 1915. *Digest of the Law of Restrictions on the Use of Real Property.* Chicago: George I. Jones.

Bettman, Alfred. 1925. "The Fact Bases of Zoning." *City Planning* 1 (2): 86–95.

Bettman, Alfred. 1926. "The Present State of Court Decisions on Zoning." *City Planning* 2 (1): 24–28.

Bettman, Alfred, and John Nolen Jr. 1938. "Recent Trends in Zoning Legislation." *Journal of the American Planning Association* 4 (6): 135–38.

Birch, Eugenie Ladner. 1980. Advancing the art and science of planning: Planners and their organizations, 1909–1980. *Journal of the American Planning Association.* 46 (1): 49.

Borys, Hazel, and Emily Talen. 2010. *The Codes Study.* http://www.smartcodecomplete .com/learn/code-study.html

Boyd, John Taylor, Jr. 1920. "The New York Zoning Resolution and Its Influence upon Design." *Architectural Record* 48 (3): 193–208.

Branch, Melville C. 1986. "Don't Call It City Planning: Misguided Densification in Large US Cities." *Cities* 3 (4): 290–97.

Braunfels, Wolfgang. 1990. *Urban Design in Western Europe: Regime and Architecture, 900–1900.* Translated by Kenneth J. Northcott. Chicago: University of Chicago Press.

Bressi, Todd W. 1993. *Planning and Zoning New York City: Yesterday, Today and Tomorrow.* Rutgers, NJ: Center for Urban Policy Research.

Brown, Glenn. 1900. *History of the United States Capitol.* Washington, DC: Government Printing Office.

Buitelaar, Edwin. 2009. "Zoning, More than Just a Tool: Explaining Houston's Regulatory Practice." *European Planning Studies* 17 (7): 1049–65.

Burgess, Patricia. 1994. *Planning for the Private Interest: Land Use Controls and Residential Patterns in Columbus, Ohio, 1900–1970.* Columbus, OH: Ohio State University Press.

Cappel, A. J. 1991. "A Walk along Willow: Patterns of Land Use Coordination in Pre-zoning New Haven (1870–1926)." *Yale Law Journal* 101 (December): 617–42.

Carmona, Matthew. 2009. Design coding and the creative, market and regulatory tyrannies of practice. *Urban Studies* (46) 12: 2643–67.

Carmona, Mathew, Stephen Marshall, and Quentin Stevens. 2006. "Design Codes: Their Use and Potential." *Progress in Planning* 65 (4): 209–89.

Cavaglieri, Giorgio. 1949. "Outline for a History of City Planning. From Prehistory to the Fall of the Roman Empire: IV. Etruscan and Roman." *Journal of the Society of Architectural Historians* 8 (3): 27–42.

Cheney, Charles H. 1920. "Removing Social Barriers by Zoning." *Survey*, May 22, 275–78.

Chicago Tribune. 2008. "Neighborhoods for Sale: Zoning Reality, Reform Divide." *Chicago Tribune*, August 20. http://www.chicagotribune.com/news/nationworld/chi-zoning-no-say-box20aug20,0,2469980.story. Accessed September 7, 2011.

Churchill, Henry S. 1945. *The City Is the People.* New York: Harcourt, Brace.

Citizens' Housing and Planning Council of New York. 1959. *A Citizen's Guide to Rezoning.* New York: Citizens' Housing and Planning Council of New York.

City of Anchorage, Kentucky. 2011. Codes of Ordinances. http://www.cityofanchorage.org/documents/consolidatedordinancess15-2011.pdf.

City of Miami. 2010. "Miami's Zoning History." http://www.miami21.org/Miami_Zoning_History.asp.

City of Seattle, WA. 1923. Zoning Ordinance of the City of Seattle. Seattle: City of Seattle.

City of Urbana, Illinois. 1990. *Downtown to Campus Plan.* Urbana, IL: City of Urbana, Department of Community Development Services.

Clarion Inc. 2008. *Sustainable Community Development Code: A Code for the 21st Century.* Denver: Rocky Mountain Land Use Institute.

Clark, Charles D. 1938. "Federal Housing Administration Standards for Land Subdivision." *Journal of the American Planning Association (AIPJ)* 4 (5): 109–12.

Clingermayer, James C. 2004. "Heresthetics and Happenstance: Intentional and Unintentional Exclusionary Impacts of the Zoning Decision-Making Process." *Urban Studies* 41 (2): 377–88.

Cognat, Segolene, and Jean-Michel Roux. 2002. *Legislation, Regulation and Urban Form in France: From the Ancien Regime to the Present.* Working Paper Series, no. 87, International Seminar on Urban Form. Birmingham, England: University of Central England (Birmingham University).

Collins, Christiane Crasemann, and George R. Collins. 2006. *Camillo Sitte: The Birth of Modern City Planning.* Mineola, NY: Dover.

Comer, John P. 1942. *New York City Building Control 1800–1941.* New York: Columbia University Press.

Comey, Arthur C. 1933. *Transition Zoning.* Harvard City Planning Series, vol. 5. Cambridge, MA: Harvard University.

Comey, Arthur C. 1912. "Regulating the Height of Fireproof Commercial Buildings." *American City* 7 (2): 116.

Congress for the New Urbanism. 2004. *Codifying New Urbanism: How to Reform Municipal Land Development Regulations.* Chicago, IL: Planners Press.

Conzen, M. R. G. 1969. *Alnwick, Northumberland: A Study in Town-Plan Analysis.* London: Institute of British Geographers.

Cook, Robert S. 1980. *Zoning for Downtown Urban Design: How Cities Control Development.* Lexington, MA: Lexington Books.

Corbett, Harvey W. 1923. "Zoning and the Envelope of the Building." *Pencil Points* 4:15–18.

Crawford, Andrew Wright. 1920. "What Zoning Is." *American Civic Association Series* 13 (15, June 30): 1–8.

Crawford, Paul. 2004. *Codifying New Urbanism.* Chicago: Planners Press.

Cresswell, Tim. 2004. *Place: A Short Introduction.* Wiley-Blackwell.

Daunton, M. J. 1983. *House and Home in the Victorian City: Working Class Housing, 1850–1914.* New York, E. Arnold.

Davies, Pearl J. 1958. *Real Estate in American History.* New York: Public Affairs Press.

Davis, Howard. 1999. *The Culture of Building.* New York: Oxford University Press.

Diggs, Charles H. 1939. "Subdivision Design." *Journal of the American Planning Association* 5 (2): 29.

Dovey, Kim. 2009. *Becoming Places: Urbanism/Architecture/Identity/Power.* London: Routledge.

Dowall, D. E. 1984. *The Suburban Squeeze.* Berkeley: University of California Press.

Duany, Andres. 2004. "Notes toward a Reason to Code." *Perspecta 35 "Building Codes": The Yale Architectural Journal.* Cambridge, MA: MIT Press. Special insert between pages 32 & 33.

Duany, Andres, Elizabeth Plater-Zyberk and Jeff Speck. 2000. *Suburban Nation: The Rise of Sprawl and the Decline of the American Dream.* New York: North Point Press.

Duany, Andres, Sandy Sorlien, and William Wright. 2008. *The SmartCode Version 9 and Manual.* http://www.smartcodecentral.com.

Duany, Andres, and Emily Talen. 2002. "Transect Planning." *Journal of the American Planning Association* 68 (3): 245–66.

Dutt, Binode Behari. 1925. *Town Planning in Ancient India.* Calcutta: Thacker, Spink. Republished 1977 by New Asian Publishers.

Ellickson, R. C. 1973. "Alternatives to Zoning: Covenants, Nuisance Rules, and Fines as Land Use Controls." *University of Chicago Law Review* 40:681–781 [reprinted in Ackerman, *Economic Foundations of Property Law* (1975)].

Elliott, Donald L. 2008. *A Better Way to Zone: Ten Principles to Create More Livable Cities.* Washington, D.C.: Island Press.

Evenson, Norma. 1979. *Paris: A Century of Change, 1878–1978.* New Haven, CT: Yale University Press.

Faludi, Andreas. 1986. "Flexibility in US Zoning: A European Perspective." *Environment and Planning B: Planning and Design* 13 (3): 255–78.

Federal Housing Administration (FHA). 1935. *Underwriting Manual*. Washington, DC: Government Printing Office.

Feiss, Carl. 1943. "History and the Modern Planner." *Journal of the Society of Architectural Historians* 3 (1): 7–10.

Feiss, Carl. 1961. "Planning Absorbs Zoning." *Journal of the American Planning Association* 27 (2): 121–26.

Fischel, William. 2004. "An Economic History of Zoning and a Cure for Its Exclusionary Effects." *Urban Studies* 41 (2): 317–40.

Fischler, R. 1998. "Health, Safety, and the General Welfare—Markets, Politics, and Social Science in Early Land-Use Regulation and Community Design." *Journal of Urban History* 24 (September): 675–719.

Fisher, Charles F. 1924. "Zoning as a Traffic Safety Measure." *American City Magazine*, February, 144–45.

Flint, Barbara J. 1977. "Zoning and Residential Segregation: A Social and Physical History, 1910–1940." PhD diss., History, University of Chicago.

Fogelson, Robert M. 2005. *Bourgeois Nightmares: Suburbia, 1870–1930*. New Haven, CT: Yale University Press.

Ford, G. B. 1911. "Third American City Planning Conference." *Town Planning Review* 2 (3): 212–14.

Freund, Ernst. 1911. "Discussion of Certain Principles of a Uniformed City Planning Code." *Proceedings of the Third National Conference on City Planning, Philadelphia, 1911*, 245.

Geddes, Patrick. 1915. *Cities in Evolution*. London: Williams & Norgate.

Gilbert, Arizona. 2011. "Gilbert Land Development Code." http://www.gilbertaz.gov/planning/ldc.cfm.

Girouard, Mark. 1985. *Cities and People: A Social and Architectural History*. New Haven, CT: Yale University Press.

Glaeser, Edward L., and Joseph Gyourko. 2002. *The Impact of Zoning on Housing Affordability*. National Bureau of Economic Research (NBER) Working Paper, no. 8835. Cambridge, MA: NBER.

Goldberger, Paul. 1991. "Shaping the Face of New York." In *New York Unbound: The City and the Politics of the Future*, edited by Peter D. Salins, 127–40. New York: Wiley Blackwell.

Goldston, Eli, and James H. Scheuer. 1959. "Zoning of Planned Residential Developments." *Harvard Law Review* 73 (2): 241–67.

Goodrich, Ernest P. 1939. "Some Thoughts on 'Reasonableness' in Zoning." *Journal of the American Planning Association* 5 (3): 65–70.

Goodrich, Ernest P., Flavel Shurtleff, and Russell V. Black. 1938. "The Control of Population Density and Distribution through Zoning." *Journal of the American Planning Association* 4 (6): 129–31.

Grava, Sigurd. 1993. "Commentary." In *Planning and Zoning New York City: Yesterday, Today and Tomorrow*, edited by Todd W. Bressi, 103–4. New Brunswick, NJ: Center for Urban Policy Research.

Greenfield, Albert M. 1924. *Zoning Code for Baltimore: A Practical Working Arrangement of the Zoning Ordinance*. Baltimore: H. E. Houck.

Gries, John M., and James Ford, eds. 1931. *Planning for Residential Districts*. Washington, DC: The President's Conference on Home Building and Home Ownership.

Hakim, Besim. 1986. *Arabic-Islamic Cities: Building and Planning Principles*. London: Kegan Paul.

Hakim, Besim. 2001. "Julian of Ascalon's Treatise of Construction and Design Rules from Sixth-Century Palestine." *Journal of the Society of Architectural Historians* 60 (1): 4–25.

Hakim, Besim, and Zubair Ahmed. 2006. "Rules for the Built Environment in 19th Century Northern Nigeria." *Journal of Architectural and Planning Research* 23 (1): 1–26.

Haldeman, B. Antrim. 1912. "The Control of Municipal Development by the 'Zone System' and Its Application in the United States." *Proceedings of the Fourth National Conference on City Planning, Boston, Massachusetts, May 27–29, 1912*. Boston: National Conference on City Planning, 1912, 173–88.

Hall, Prescott F. 1917. *The Menace of the Three-Decker*. New York: National Association of Housing, 1–10.

Hall, Thomas. 2009. *Planning Europe's Capital Cities: Aspects of Nineteenth-Century Urban Development*. London: E & FN Spon.

Hammond, Harold Francis, and Leslie John Sorenson. 1941. *Traffic Engineering Handbook*. New York: Institute of Traffic Engineers, Association of Casualty and Surety Executives, New York. National Conservation Bureau.

Hart, J. F. 1996. "Colonial Land Use Law and Its Significance for Modern Takings Doctrines." *Harvard Law Review* 109 (April): 1252–1300.

Hartman, E. T. 1925. "Zoning and Democracy." *Social Forces*, 4 (1): 162–65.

Hason, Nino. 1977. *The Emergence and Development of Zoning Controls in North American Municipalities: A Critical Analysis*. Toronto: Department of Urban and Regional Planning, University of Toronto.

Hazard, S. 1850. *Annals of Pennsylvania from the Discovery of the Delaware*. Philadelphia: Hazard and Mitchell.

Herlihy, Elisabeth M. 1925. "Boston Zoning—Its First Birthday." *City Planning* 1 (2): 81–85.

Heydecker, Wayne D., and Ernest P. Goodrich. 1929. "Sunlight and Daylight for Urban Areas." In *Regional Survey of New York and Its Environs*, vol. 7, *Neighborhood and Community Planning*, 141–209. New York: Regional Plan of New York and Its Environs.

Hinckley, T. L. 1926. "Natural Zoning in Middletown." *City Planning* 2 (1): 56.

Hirt, Sonia. 2007. "The Devil Is in the Definitions: Contrasting American and German Approaches to Zoning." *Journal of the American Planning Association* 73 (4): 436–50.

Holliday, A. C. 1922. "Restrictions Governing City Development: II Zoning Use Districts." *Town Planning Review* 9 (4): 217–38.

Hood, R. 1927. "Tower Buildings and Wider Streets: A Suggested Relief for Traffic Congestion." *American Architect* 132 (July 5): 67–68.

Hoover, Herbert. 1926. *A Zoning Primer by the Advisory Committee on Zoning: Department of Commerce*. Washington, DC: Government Printing Office.

Horsfall, T. C. 1904. *The Improvement of the Dwellings and Surroundings of the People: The Example of Germany*. Manchester, UK: Manchester University Press.

Hoyt, Homer. (c. 1933) 1970. *One Hundred Years of Land Values in Chicago*. New York: Arno.

Hubbard, Henry V. 1937. "The Appearance of the City." *Journal of the American Planning Association (AIPJ)* 3 (1): 1–8.

Hubbard, T. K., and H. V. Hubbard. 1929. *Our Cities, Today and Tomorrow: A Study of Planning and Zoning Progress in the United States*. Cambridge, MA: Harvard University Press.

Hubbard, Theodora Kimball. 1925. "Survey of City and Regional Planning in the United States, 1925." *City Planning* 2 (2): 87–147.

Ihlanfeldt, Keith R. 2004. "Introduction: Exclusionary Land-Use Regulations." *Urban Studies* 41 (2): 255–59.

Illinois Chapter of the American Institute of Architects (AIA). 1919. "A Wise Zoning Plan for Chicago." *Western Architect* 28:118–19.

Institute of Traffic Engineers (ITE). 1964. *Recommended Practices for Subdivision Streets.* Washington, DC: Institute of Traffic Engineers.

Ives, Richard. 1937. "Some Aspects of the Problem of Nonconforming Uses." *Journal of the American Planning Association* 3 (6): 152–55.

Jackson, Kenneth T. 1985. *Crabgrass Frontier.* New York: Oxford University Press.

Jacobs, Allan. 1980. *Making City Planning Work.* Chicago: Planners Press.

Jacobs, Allan. 2002. "General Commentary." In *The Seaside Debates: A Critique of the New Urbanism*, edited by Todd W. Bressi, 136–52. New York: Rizzoli International.

Jacobs, Jane. 1956. "The Missing Link in City Redevelopment." *Architectural Forum*, June, 132.

Jacobs, Jane. 1961. *The Death and Life of Great American Cities.* New York: Vintage Books.

Katz, Peter. 2004. "Form First." *Planning* (November): 16, 18.

Kayden, Jerold. 1993. "Commentary." In *Planning and Zoning New York City: Yesterday, Today and Tomorrow*, edited by Todd W. Bressi, 106–7. New Brunswick, NJ: Center for Urban Policy Research.

Kimball, Theodora. 1923. *Manual of Information on City Planning and Zoning.* Cambridge, MA: Harvard University Press.

Kistemaker, R. E. 2000. "The Public and the Private: Public Space in Sixteenth- and Seventeenth-Century Amsterdam." In *The Public and Private in Dutch Culture of the Golden Age*, edited by Arthur K. Wheelock and Adele R. Seeff, 17–23. Translated by Wendy Shattes. Newark: University of Delaware Press.

Knaap, Gerrit, Huibert A. Haccou, and Kelly J. Clifton. 2007. *Incentives, Regulations and Plans: The Role of States and Nation-States in Smart Growth Planning.* Northampton, MA: Edward Elgar.

Knack, Ruth, Stuart Meck, and Israel Stollman. 1996. "The Real Story behind the Standard Planning and Zoning Acts of the 1920s." *Land Use Law* (February): 3–9.

Knight, Cyril R. 1924. "The Effect of Zoning on New York Architecture." *Town Planning Review* 11 (1): 3–12.

Knopf, S. Adolphus. 1909. *Tuberculosis: A Preventable and Curable Disease—Modern Methods for the Solution of the Tuberculosis Problem.* New York: Moffat, Yard.

Knowles, C. C., and P. H. Pitt. 1972. *The History of Building Regulation in London 1189–1972.* London: Architectural Press.

Knowles, Morris. 1920. *Industrial Housing.* New York: McGraw-Hill.

Kolnick, Kathy A. 2008. *Order before Zoning: Land Use Regulation in Los Angeles, 1880–1915.* PhD diss., University of Southern California.

Konvitz, Josef W. 1985. *The Urban Millennium: The City-Building Process from the Early Middle Ages to the Present.* Carbondale: Southern Illinois University Press.

Kostof, Spiro. 1991. *The City Shaped.* London: Thames & Hudson, Ltd.

Kostof, Spiro. 1992. *The City Assembled.* London: Thames & Hudson, Ltd.

Krieger, Alex. 1991. *Towns and Town-Making Principles*. Cambridge, MA: Harvard University Graduate School of Design.

Krier, Rob. 2003. "Typological and Morphological Elements of the Concept of Urban Space." In *Designing Cities: Political Economy and Urban Design*, edited by Alexander R. Cuthbert, 323–39. Oxford: Blackwell.

Krier, Leon. 2009. *The Architecture of Community*. Washington, DC: Island Press.

Kunstler, James Howard. 1998. *Home from Nowhere: Remaking our Everyday World for the Twenty-First Century*. New York: Touchstone Press.

Lai, Richard Tseng-yu. 1988. *Law in Urban Design and Planning: The Invisible Web*. New York: Van Nostrand Reinhold.

Lands, Leeann Bishop. 2004. "A Reprehensible and Unfriendly Act: Homeowners, Renters, and the Bid for Residential Segregation in Atlanta, 1900–1917." *Journal of Planning History* 3 (2): 83–115.

Larco, Nico. 2009. "Untapped Density: Site Design and the Proliferation of Suburban Multifamily Housing." *Journal of Urbanism* 2 (2): 167–86.

Larkham, P. J. 2001. *Regulation and the Shaping of Urban Form in the UK*. Working Paper, no. 83, School of Planning and Housing, University of Central England. Birmingham, England: University of Central England (Birmingham City University).

Larsen, Kristin. 2002. "Harmonious Inequality? Zoning, Public Housing, and Orlando's Separate City, 1920–1945." *Journal of Planning History* 1 (2): 154–80.

Lasker, Bruno. 1920. "The Issue Restated." *Survey*, May 22, 278–79.

Laws of Connecticut. 1672. Act Concerning Home Lots of Oct. 1672, supra note 70, at 29, 29.

Lees, Martha A. 1994. "Preserving Property Values—Preserving Proper Homes—Preserving Privilege: The Pre-Euclid Debate over Zoning for Exclusively Private Residential Areas, 1916–1926." *University of Pittsburgh Law Review* 56 (2): 367–440.

Leinberger, Christopher. 2008. *The Option of Urbanism*. Washington, DC: Island Press.

Levine, Jonathan. 2005. *Zoned Out: Regulation, Markets, and Choices in Transportation and Metropolitan Land-Use*. Washington, DC: Resources for the Future.

Lewyn, Michael. 2005. "How Overregulation Creates Sprawl (Even in a City without Zoning)." *Wayne Law Review* 50:1171; GWU Law School Public Law Research Paper, no. 170. http://ssrn.com/abstract=837244.

Linklater, Andro. 2002. *Measuring America: How an Untamed Wilderness Shaped the United States and Fulfilled the Promise of Democracy*. New York: Walker.

Lippard, Lucy. 1998. *The Lure of the Local: Sense of Place in a Multicentered Society*. New York: New Press.

Logan, Thomas H. 1976. "The Americanization of German Zoning." *Journal of the American Planning Association* 42 (2): 377–85.

Logan, Thomas Harvey. 1972. "The Invention of Zoning in the Emerging Planning Profession of Late-Nineteenth-Century Germany." PhD diss., University of North Carolina, Chapel Hill.

Loukaitou-Sideris, Anastasia, Evelyn Blumenberg, and Renia Ehrenfeucht. 2004. "Sidewalk Democracy: Municipalities and the Regulation of Public Space." In *Regulating Place: Standards and the Shaping of Urban America*, edited by Eran Ben-Joseph and Terry S. Szold, 141–66. New York: Routledge.

Lubove, R. 1962. *The Progressives and the Slums: Tenement House Reform in New York City, 1890–1917*. Pittsburgh: University of Pittsburgh Press.

Luithlen, L. 1997. "Landownership in Britain and the Quest for Town Planning." *Environment and Planning A* 29 (8): 1399–1418.

Lynch, Kevin. 1960. *The Image of the City*. Cambridge, MA: Harvard University Press.

Macdonald, Elizabeth. 2005. "Suburban Vision to Urban Reality: The Evolution of Olmsted and Vaux's Brooklyn Parkway Neighborhoods." *Journal of Planning History* 4 (4): 295–321.

Mackesey, Thomas W. 1939. "Aesthetics and Zoning." *Journal of the American Planning Association (AIPJ)* 5 (4): 95–98.

Mackesey, Thomas W., and J. Ross McKeever. 1938. "Some Aspects of the Problem of Nonconforming Uses." *Planners' Journal* 4 (2): 46–48.

Makielski, Stanislaw. J., Jr., 1966. *The Politics of Zoning: The New York Experience*. New York: Columbia University Press.

Mandelker, Daniel R. 1971. *The Zoning Dilemma: A Legal Strategy for Urban Change*. Indianapolis, IN: Bobbs-Merrill.

Manning, Warren H. 1915. "A Step towards Solving the Industrial Housing Problem." *American City* 12 (4): 321–25.

Marcus, Norman. 1984. "Air Rights in New York City: TDR, Zoning Lot Merger and the Well-Considered Plan." *Brooklyn Law Review* 50:867.

Marschner, F. J. 1958. *Land Use and Its Patterns in the United States*. Agriculture Handbook, no. 153. Washington, DC: U.S. Department of Agriculture.

Marsh, Benjamin. (1909) 1974. *An Introduction to City Planning*. New York: Arno Press.

Mattocks, Robert H. 1935. "Review of Harvard City Planning Studies Vol. 5—Transition Zoning." *Town Planning Review* 16 (3): 243–44.

McDonald, John F. 2004. "Did Suburban Zoning Become More Restrictive?" *Planning Perspectives* 19 (4): 391–408.

McDonald, John F., and Daniel P. McMillen. 2004. "Determinants of Suburban Development Controls: A Fischel Expedition." *Urban Studies* 41 (2): 341–64.

Meck, Stuart. 2002. *Growing Smart Legislative Guidebook: Module Statues for Planning and the Management of Change*. Chicago: American Planning Association.

Mehaffy, Michael. 2008. "Generative Methods in Urban Design: A Progress Assessment." *Journal of Urbanism* 1 (1) 57–75.

Melosi, Martin V. 1999. *The Sanitary City: Urban Infrastructure in America from Colonial Times to the Present*. Baltimore: Johns Hopkins University Press.

Menhinick, Howard K. 1929. "A Study of Municipal and County Regulations for Subdivision Control." *City Planning* 5 (3): 177–82.

Moe, Richard. 2000. "Civil Codes." *Preservation*, November/December, 6.

Mohney, David, and Keller Easterling. 1991. *Seaside*. London: Architecture Design and Technology Press.

Moody, Walter D. 1911. *Wacker's Manual of the Plan of Chicago*. Chicago: Chicago Plan Commission.

Moore, Colleen Grogan. 1985. *PUDs in Practice*. Washington, DC: Urban Land Institute.

Morris, A. E. J. 1979. *History of Urban Form before the Industrial Revolutions*. London: George Goodwin, 1–18.

Morris, Marya. 1996. *Creating Transit-Supportive Land-Use Regulations*. Chicago: American Planning Association.

Morris, Marya. 2009. *Smart Codes*. Chicago: Planners Press.

Moudon, Anne Vernez. 1994. "Getting to Know the Built Landscape: Typomorphology." In *Ordering Space: Types in Architecture and Design*, edited by Karen A. Franck and Lynda H. Schneekloth. New York: Van Nostrand Reinhold, 289–311.

Mullin, John Robert. 1976/77. "American Perceptions of German City Planning at the Turn of the Century." *Urbanism: Past and Present* 3:5–15.

Mumford, Lewis. 1949. "Planning for the Phases of Life." *Town Planning Review* 20 (1): 5–16.

Mumford, Lewis. 1961. *The City in History: Its Origins, Its Transformations, and Its Prospects*. New York: Harcourt Brace & World.

Myers, Dowall. 2007. *Immigrants and Boomers: Forging a New Social Contract for the Future of America*. New York: Russell Sage Foundation.

National Conference on City Planning. 1921. *Proceedings of the Thirteenth National Conference on City Planning, Pittsburgh, May 9–11, 1921*. Boston: National Conference on City Planning.

Netter, Edith M., and Ruth G. Price. 1983. "Zoning and the Nouveau Poor." *Journal of the American Planning Association* 49 (2): 171–81.

Nettlefold, J. S. 1914. *Practical Town Planning*. London: St. Catherine Press.

New York City (NYC). 1916. *1916 Zoning Resolution*. New York: City of New York.

New York City Board of Estimate and Apportionment. 1913. *Report of the Heights of Buildings Commission*. New York City: Board of Estimate and Apportionment, Committee on the City Plan.

New York City Board of Estimate and Apportionment. 1916. *Final Report of the Commission on Building Districts and Restrictions*. New York City: Board of Estimate and Apportionment, Committee on the City Plan.

New York City Department of Transportation. 2008. *The New York City Pedestrian Safety Study and Action Plan*. New York: Department of Transportation.

New York Colony. 1894. *The Colonial Laws of New York from the Year 1664 to the Revolution*. 5 vols. Albany, NY: James B. Lyon, State Printer.

Newark, New Jersey, Commission on Building Districts and Restrictions. 1919. *Proposed Building Zones for Newark*. September 16, 1919.

Nichols, Charles M. 1923. *Studies on Building Height Limitations in Large Cities, with Special Reference to Conditions in Chicago*. Chicago: Chicago Real Estate Board.

Nichols, J. C. 1926. "The Planning and Control of Outlying Shopping Centers." *Journal of Land and Public Utility Economics* 2 (1): 17–22.

Nichols, J. C. 1929. "A Developer's View of Deed Restrictions." *Journal of Land and Public Utility Economics* 5 (2): 132–42.

1913 Supplement to the World's Loose Leaf Album of Apartment Houses. New York: New York World.

Nivola, Pietro S. 1999. *Laws of the Landscape: How Policies Shape Cities in Europe and America*. Washington, DC: Brookings Institution Press.

Nolon, John R. 2003. "Golden and Its Emanations: The Surprising Origins of Smart Growth." Pace Law Faculty Publications, no. 173. http://digitalcommons.pace.edu/lawfaculty/173.

Olmsted, Frederick Law, Jr. 1910. "City Planning. An Introductory Address at the Second National Conference on City Planning and Congestion of Population, at Rochester, New York, May 2, 1910." American Civic Association Series, vol. 11, no. 4.

Olmsted, Frederick Law, Jr.. 1931. "Principles Which Should Control Limitations in Bulk of Buildings: A Discussion Applying to Districts Where Great Intensity of Building Is Most Justifiable, Especially Manhattan." *City Planning* 7 (1): 22–24.

Osgood, Herbert L., Frederic W. Jackson, Robert H. Kelby, and Hiram Smith, eds. 1905. *Minutes of the Common Council of the City of New York, 1675–1776.* 8 vols. New York: City of New York.

Parolek, Daniel G., Karen Parolek, and Paul C. Crawford. 2008. *Form-Based Codes: A Guide for Planners, Urban Designers, Municipalities and Developers.* New York: Wiley.

Parrish, Helen L. 1917. *One Million People in Small Houses—Philadelphia.* National Housing Association, no. 7, 3–12.

Peets, Elbert. 1931. "Current Town Planning in Washington" *Town Planning Review,* 219–237.

Pendall, R. 2000. "Local Land Use Regulation and the Chain of Exclusion." *Journal of the American Planning Association* 66 (2): 125–42.

Perry, Clarence. 1939. *Housing for the Machine Age.* New York: Russell Sage Foundation.

Perry, Clarence Arthur. 1929. "The Neighborhood Unit, a Scheme of Arrangement for the Family-Life Community." In *Regional Survey of New York and Its Environs,* vol. 7, *Neighborhood and Community Planning,* 2–140. New York: Regional Plan of New York and Its Environs.

Pima County, Arizona. 2005. "Subdivision and Development Street Standards." http://www.pimaxpress.com/Dev_Review/PDFs/SubDevStreetStandards.pdf.

Planners Advisory Service. 1998. *The Principles of Smart Development.* PAS Report, no. 479. Washington, DC: American Planning Association.

Plunz, Richard. 1993. "Zoning and the New Horizontal City." In *Planning and Zoning New York City: Yesterday, Today and Tomorrow,* edited by Todd W.Bressi, 27–47. New Brunswick, NJ: Rutgers University Center for Urban Policy Research.

Polyzoides, Stefanos, Roger Sherwood, and James Tice. 1997. *Courtyard Housing in Los Angeles: A Typological Analysis.* Princeton: Princeton Architectural Press.

Power, Garrett. 1989. "The Advent of Zoning." *Planning Perspectives* 4: 1–13.

Prince William County, Virginia. 2006. "Subdivision Ordinance. Section 800. Buffer Areas, Landscaping, and Tree Cover Requirements." http://www.pwcgov.org/docLibrary/PDF/005016.pdf.

Punter, John. 1999. *Design Guidelines in American Cities: A Review of Design Policies and Guidance in Five West Coast Cities.* Liverpool: Liverpool University Press.

Punter, John. 2000. "Regulation and Control." In *Design Professionals and the Built Environment: An Introduction,* edited by Paul Knox and Peter Ozolins, 295–306. London: Wiley.

Punter, John, and Matthew Carmona. 1997. *The Design Dimension of Planning: Theory, Content and Best Practice for Design Policies.* London: E & FN Spon.

Purdy, Lawson, Harland Bartholomew, Edward M. Bassett, Andrew Wright Crawford, and

Herbert S. Swan. 1920. *Zoning as an Element in City Planning, and for Protection of Property Values, Public Safety, and Public Health*. Washington, DC:American Civic Association.

Rabin, Yale. 1989. "Expulsive Zoning: The Inequitable Legacy of Euclid." In *Zoning and the American Dream*, edited by Charles M. Haar and Jerold S. Kayden, 101–21. Chicago: Planners Press.

Relph, E. 1987. *The Modern Urban Landscape*. Baltimore: Johns Hopkins University Press.

Reps, J. W. 1964. "Requiem for Zoning." In *Planning 1964*. Chicago: American Society of Planning Officials.

Reps, John. 1965. *The Making of Urban America: A History of City Planning in the United States*. Princeton, NJ: Princeton University Press.

Reps, John. 2002. "Bastides: New Urbanism in 13th Century France." Transcript of presentation to Council IV, Santa Fe, NM, October 18. http://www.charrettecenter.com/nucouncil/go.asp?a=spf&pfk=3&gk=59.

Reynard, Pierre Claude. 2002. "Public Order and Privilege: Eighteenth Century French Roots of Environmental Regulation." *Technology and Culture* 43 (1): 1–28.

Robinson, Charles Mulford. 1901. *The Improvement of Towns and Cities or The Practical Basis of Civic Aesthetics*. New York: G.P. Putnam's Sons.

Robinson, Charles Mulford. 1916. *City Planning*. New York: G.P. Putnam's Sons.

Rochester, New York, City of. 1931. Building Code of the City of Rochester, New York.

Rosenthal, Gilbert A. 2009. *The High Costs of Low Income Housing*. Philadelphia: Wallace, Roberts & Todd.

Saalman, Howard. 1968. *Medieval Cities*. New York: George Braziller.

Saginaw, City of. 1956. *Zoning in Saginaw*. Planning Bulletin, no. 1.

Salins, Peter D. 1993. "Zoning for Growth and Change." In *Planning and Zoning New York City: Yesterday, Today and Tomorrow*, edited by Todd W. Bressi, 165–84. New Brunswick, NJ: Center for Urban Policy Research.

Samuels, Ivor. 2008. "Typomorphology and Urban Design Practice." *Urban Morphology* 12 (1): 58–62.

Scheer, Brenda, and David Scheer. 1998. "Typology and Urban Design Guidelines: Preserving the City without Dictating Design." In *Nineteenth Century Urban Morphology*, edited by Attilio Petrucciolli. Aga Khan Series. Cambridge, MA: MIT Department of Architecture.

Scheer, Brenda Case. 2008. "Urban Morphology and Urban Design." *Urban Morphology* 12 (2): 140–42.

Scheer, Brenda. 2001. "The Anatomy of Sprawl." *Places: A Forum of Environmental Design* 14 (2): 25–37.

Scheer, Brenda Case. 2011. *The Evolution of Urban Form: Typology for Planners and Architects*. Chicago: American Planning Association.

Schevill, Ferdinand. 1909. *Siena: The History of a Medieval Commune*. New York: Harper & Row.

Schill, Michael H. and Susan Wachter. 1995. The Spatial Bias of Federal Housing Law and Policy: Concentrated Poverty in Urban America. *University of Pennsylvania Law Review* Vol. 143, No. 5.

Schwieterman, Joseph P., and Dana M. Caspall. 2006. *The Politics of Place: A History of Zoning in Chicago*. Chicago: Lake Claremont Press.

Scott, Mel. 1969. *American City Planning since 1890*. Berkeley: University of California Press.

Shoup, Donald. 2005. *The High Cost of Free Parking*. Chicago: American Planning Association.

Shoup, Donald. 2008. "Graduated Density Zoning." *Journal of Planning Education and Research* 28 (2): 161–79.

Shutkin, William. 2004. "From Pollution Control to Place Making: The Role of Environmental Regulation in Creating Communities of Place." In *Regulating Place: Standards and the Shaping of Urban America*, edited by Eran Ben-Joseph and Terry S. Szold, 253–70. New York: Routledge.

Siegan, B. H. 1972. *Land Use without Zoning*. Lexington, MA: Lexington Books.

Sies, Mary Corbin, and Christopher Silver, eds. 1996. *Planning the Twentieth Century American City*. Baltimore: Johns Hopkins University Press.

Silver, Christopher. 1991. "The Racial Origins of Zoning: Southern Cities from 1910–1940." *Planning Perspectives* 6 (2): 189–205.

Simpson, Michael. 1985. *Thomas Adams and the Modern Planning Movement: Britain, Canada and the United States, 1900–1940*. London: Alexandrine Press.

Slone, Daniel K., and Doris S. Goldstein. 2008. *A Legal Guide to Urban and Sustainable Development*. Hoboken, NJ: Wiley.

Smardon, Richard C., and James P. Karp. 1992. *The Legal Landscape*. Hoboken, NJ: John Wiley & Sons.

Smith, Adam. (1776) 1904. *Wealth of Nations*. 5th ed. Edited by Edwin Cannan. London: Methuen & Co.

Southworth, Michael, and Eran Ben-Joseph. 2003. *Streets and the Shaping of Towns and Cities*. Washington, DC: Island Press.

Staley, Samuel R., and Eric R. Claeys. 2005. "Is the Future of Development Regulation Based in the Past? Toward a Market-Oriented, Innovation Friendly Framework." *Journal of Urban Planning and Development* 131 (4): 202–13.

Stanislawski, Dan. 1946. "The Origin and Spread of the Grid-Pattern Town." *Geographical Review* 36 (1): 105–20.

Stanislawski, Dan. 1947. "Early Spanish Town Planning in the New World." *Geographical Review* 37 (1): 94–105.

Steuteville, Robert. 2010. "Form-Based Codes: Progress, but a Long Way to Go." New Urban News blog post, September 13, 2010. http://newurbannetwork.com/.

Stilgoe, John R. 1983. *Common Landscapes of America, 1580 to 1845*. New Haven, CT: Yale University Press.

Stockman, Paul K. 1992. "Note, Anti-Snob Zoning in Massachusetts: Assessing One Attempt at Opening the Suburbs to Affordable Housing." *Virginia Law Review* 78: 535.

Stone, Brian Jr. 2004. "Paving over Paradise: How Land Use Regulations Promote Residential Imperviousness." *Landscape and Urban Planning* 69 (1): 101–13.

Swan, Herbert S. 1920. "What Zoning Does." American Civic Association. Series vol. 13, no. 15, June 30, 46–47.

Talen, Emily. 2008. *Design for Diversity: Exploring Socially Mixed Neighborhoods*. London: Elsevier.

Talen, Emily. 2011. "Sustainability in Planning." In *Oxford Handbook of Urban Planning*, edited by R. Weber and R. Crane. Oxford: Oxford University Press.

Talen, Emily, and Gerrit Knaap. 2003. "Legalizing Smart Growth: An Empirical Study of Land Use Regulation in Illinois." *Journal of Planning Education and Research* 22 (3): 345–59.

Taubert, C. A. 1926. "Zoning for Iowa Municipalities." *American Municipalities* 51 (1): 24, 30.

Tindall, William. 1914. *Standard History of the City of Washington from a Study of the Original Sources*. Knoxville, TN: H. W. Crew & Co.

Toll, Seymour. 1969. *Zoned American*. New York: Grossman.

Tracy, Seve. 2004. *Smart Growth Zoning Codes: A Resource Guide*. Sacramento, CA: Local Government Commission.

Triggs, H. Inigo. 1909. *Town Planning: Past, Present and Possible*. London: Methuen & Co.

Unwin, Raymond. 1909. *Town Planning in Practice: An Introduction to the Art of Designing Cities and Suburbs*. London: T. Fisher Unwin.

Urban Land Institute. 1941. *The Denver Plan, Volume 7: The Problem of Decentralization and Disintegration in Cities*. Washington, DC: Urban Land Institute.

Van Buren, Maud. 1915. "Why Women Should Study Town Ordinances and Town Budgets." *American City* 12 (5): 411.

Van Nest Black, Russell, assisted by Mary Hedges Black. 1935. *Building Lines and Reservations for Future Streets*. Harvard City Planning Studies, vol. 8. Cambridge, MA: Harvard University Press.

Veiller, Lawrence. 1910. *The National Housing Association: A New Organization "to Improve Housing Conditions Both Urban and Su, in Every Practicable Way."* New York: National Housing Association.

Veiller, Lawrence. 1914. *Protecting Residential Districts*. National Housing Association Publications, no. 26. September. New York: National Housing Association.

Veiller, Lawrence. 1917. *Industrial Housing*. New York: National Housing Association, 1–29.

Village of Oak Park, Illinois. 1947. Revised Zoning Ordinance, Passed by the President and Board of Trustees of the Village of Oak Park, June 23, 1947.

Von Hoffman, Alexander. 1996. *Local Attachments: The Making of an American Urban Neighborhood, 1850 to 1920*. Baltimore: Johns Hopkins University Press.

Ward, David, and Olivier Zunz, eds. 1992. *The Landscape of Modernity*. New York: Russell Sage Foundation.

Warner, Sam B., Jr. 1969. *Streetcar Suburbs: The Process of Growth in Boston, 1870–1900*. New York: Atheneum.

Weaver, Clifford L., and Richard F. Babcock. 1980. *City Zoning: The Once and Future Frontier*. Chicago: Planners Press.

Weiss, Marc. 1987. *The Rise of the Community Builders: The American Real Estate Industry and Urban Land Planning*. New York: Columbia University Press.

Weiss, Marc A. 1992a. "Density and Intervention: New York's Planning Traditions." In *The Landscape of Modernity: New York City, 1900–1940*, edited by David Ward and Olivier Zunz, 46–75. Baltimore: Johns Hopkins University Press.

Weiss, Marc A. 1992b. "Skyscraper Zoning: New York's Pioneering Role." *Journal of the American Planning Association* 58 (2): 201–12.

Wells, Amy Stuart, Jennifer Jellison Holme, Anita Tijerina Revilla, and Awo Korantemaa Atanda. 2004. "How Desegregation Changed Us: The Effects of Racially Mixed Schools

on Students and Society." http://www.teacherscollege.edu/newsbureau/features/
wells033004.htm.

Wermiel, Sara E. 2000. *The Fireproof Building: Technology and Public Safety in the Nineteenth-Century American City*. Baltimore: Johns Hopkins University Press.

Wheelock, Arthur K. 2000. *The Public and Private in Dutch Culture of the Golden Age*. Newark: University of Delaware Press.

Whitnall, Gordon. 1931. "History of Zoning." *Annals of the American Academy of Political and Social Science* 155 (2): 1–14.

Whitten, Robert H., and Frank R. Walker. 1921. *The Cleveland Zone Plan—Report to the City Plan Commission*. Cleveland: City of Cleveland, City Plan Commission.

Whitten, Robert H. 1922. "The Atlanta Zoning Plan." Atlanta: City of Atlanta, April 22, 114–15.

Whyte, William. 1958. "Are Cities Un-American?" In *The Exploding Metropolis*, edited by William Hollingsworth Whyte, 23–52. Berkeley: University of California Press.

Wickersham, Jay. 2001. "Jane Jacob's Critique of Zoning: From Euclid to Portland and Beyond." *Boston College Environmental Affairs Law Review* 28 (4): 547–64.

Williams, Frank B. 1913. "Zone System Advocated to End City Congestion; How Berlin Partially Solved Problems That Are Vexing New York: Agitation There for Taller Buildings in the Business District." *New York Times*, December 12, SM14.

Williams, Frank B. 1914. *Building Regulation by Districts: The Lesson of Berlin*. New York: National Housing Association.

Williams, Frank B. 1922. *The Law of City Planning and Zoning*. New York: MacMillan.

Williams, Frank B. 1951. "Striking Innovations in New York City's Proposed Rezoning." *American City*, June, 99.

Williams, Frank Backus. 1919. *Akron and Its Planning Law*. Akron, OH: Akron Chamber of Commerce.

Williams, Norman. 1956. "The Evolution of Zoning." *American Journal of Economics and Sociology* 15 (3): 253–64.

Williamson, C. C. 1916. "Shall New York City Untax Buildings?" *Survey*, June 24, 332–34.

Willis, Carol. 1993. "A 3-D CBD: How the 1916 Zoning Law Shaped Manhattan's Central Business Districts." In *Planning and Zoning New York City: Yesterday, Today and Tomorrow*, edited by Todd W. Bressi, 30–53. Rutgers, NJ: Center for Urban Policy Research.

Wolf, Michael Allan. 2008. *The Zoning of America: Euclid v. Ambler*. Lawrence: University of Kansas Press.

Woodbury, Coleman. 1929. "Some Suggested Changes in the Control of Urban Development." *Journal of Land and Public Utility Economics* 5 (3): 249–59.

Young, Hugh E. 1937. "Need for Some Practical Method of Rezoning Urban Areas." Paper presented at the Meeting of the City Planning Division, American Society of Civil Engineers, New York, 21 January.

Youngson, A. J. 2002. *The Making of Classical Edinburgh*. Edinburgh: Edinburgh University Press.

Zoning Study Group, Los Angeles, CA. 1928. "The Standardization of Zoning Symbols." *City Planning*, January, 34–43.

Zunz, Olivier. 1982. *The Changing Face of Inequality: Urbanization, Industrial Development, and Immigrants in Detroit, 1880–1920*. Chicago: University of Chicago Press.

Index

Page numbers with "f" refer to photos and illustrations, those with "t" refer to tables.

145t; side, 32–33t, 48, 78, 83, 92, 142–43, 145t, 180; *See also* Setbacks

Z

Zoning: bulk, 22, 23; circumvention strategies, 4, 93; contextual *vs.* non-contextual, 187, 193; disconnect with spatial logic, 10, 53, 57–58, 83, 104, 119–20 (*See also* Phoenix, AZ; Pima County, AZ); disconnect with urban form, 119–20, 121f, 127; as dominant rule in American experience, 3; down-zoning, 122, 153–54, 155, 157f; effects of lack (*See* Towns with unguided zon-ing); exceptions (*See* Review process; Variances); floating, 177, 181; focus on costs and process rather than ef-fect, 10–12; function, 21, 24, 27, 101–11; holistic approach, 104; hybrid, 7, 187; increasing complexity, 11, 53, 57, 120; as a legal process, 10; nega-tive perception of, 4, 10, 203–4; over-lay, 61, 120, 177, 181, 187; overview, 21–36, 201–2; spot, 105, 115; step down, 114, 114f; stepped back (*See* Building height, height-to-area ratio); total elimination, 180–81; *vs.* building codes, 21